Hiking Glacier and Waterton Lakes National Parks

Help Us Keep This Guide Up to Date

Every effort has been made by the authors and editors to make this guide as accurate and use-
ful as possible. However, many things can change after a guide is published—trails are rerouted,
regulations change, techniques evolve, facilities come under new management, etc.

We would love to hear from you concerning your experiences with this guide and how you
feel it could be improved and kept up to date. While we may not be able to respond to all
comments and suggestions, we'll take them to heart, and we'll also make certain to share them
with the authors. Please send your comments and suggestions to the following address:

> The Globe Pequot Press
> Reader Response/Editorial Department
> P.O. Box 480
> Guilford, CT 06437

Or you may e-mail us at:

> editorial@GlobePequot.com

Thanks for your input, and happy trails!

A FALCON GUIDE®

Hiking Glacier and Waterton Lakes National Parks

A Guide to More Than 60 of the Area's
Greatest Hiking Adventures

Third Edition

Erik Molvar

FALCON GUIDE®

GUILFORD, CONNECTICUT
HELENA, MONTANA
AN IMPRINT OF THE GLOBE PEQUOT PRESS

A FALCON GUIDE ®

Text design by Nancy Freeborn
Maps created by XNR Productions Inc. © Morris Book Publishing, LLC
Photographs are by Erik Molvar, unless otherwise credited.

Libary of Congress Cataloging-in-Publication Data
Molvar, Erik.
  Hiking Glacier and Waterton Lakes National Parks : a guide to more than sixty of the area's greatest hiking adventures / Erik Molvar.– 3rd ed.
     p. cm. – (A Falcon guide)
  Includes bibliographical references and index.
  ISBN-13: 978-0-7627-3632-4
  ISBN-10: 0-7627-3632-1
  1. Hiking–Montana–Glacier National Park–Guidebooks. 2. Trails–Montana–Glacier National Park–Guidebooks. 3. Hiking–Alberta–Waterton Lakes National Park–Guidebooks. 4. Trails–Alberta–Waterton Lakes National Park–Guidebooks. 5. Glacier National Park (Mont.)–Guidebooks. 6. Waterton Lakes National Park (Alta.)–Guidebooks. I. Title. II. Series.
  GV199.42.M92G5647 2006
  96.5'10978652–dc22
                            2006004805

Manufactured in the United States of America
Third Edition/First Printing

This book is dedicated to Sandy Staskus and Hope Brayton.
No one could ask for finer hiking partners.

Contents

Acknowledgments xiii
Introduction 1
    Natural History 1
    Using This Guide 4
    Planning Your Trip 4
    A Few Words of Caution 7
Short Strolls and Nature Walks 11
    Glacier National Park 11
    Waterton Lakes National Park 19
Trail Finder Table 22
Map Legend 24

The Hikes

The North Fork 25
  1 Boulder Pass 27
  2 Bowman Lake–Brown Pass 33
  3 Akokala Lake 34
  4 Numa Ridge Lookout 36
  5 Quartz Lakes Loop 37
  6 Logging Lake 38
    Connecting Hikes 41

The Lake McDonald Area 43
  7 Trout Lake 45
  8 Huckleberry Mountain Lookout 49
  9 Apgar Lookout 50
 10 Lake McDonald 52
 11 Lincoln Lake 53
 12 Fish Lake 55
 13 Mount Brown Lookout 57
 14 Snyder Lakes 58
 15 Avalanche Lake 59
    Additional Hikes 61

The Highline and Waterton Lake Vicinity 63
 16 Hidden Lake 65
 17 The Garden Wall 67
 18 The Northern Highline 70
 19 Waterton Valley 72
    Connecting Hikes 76

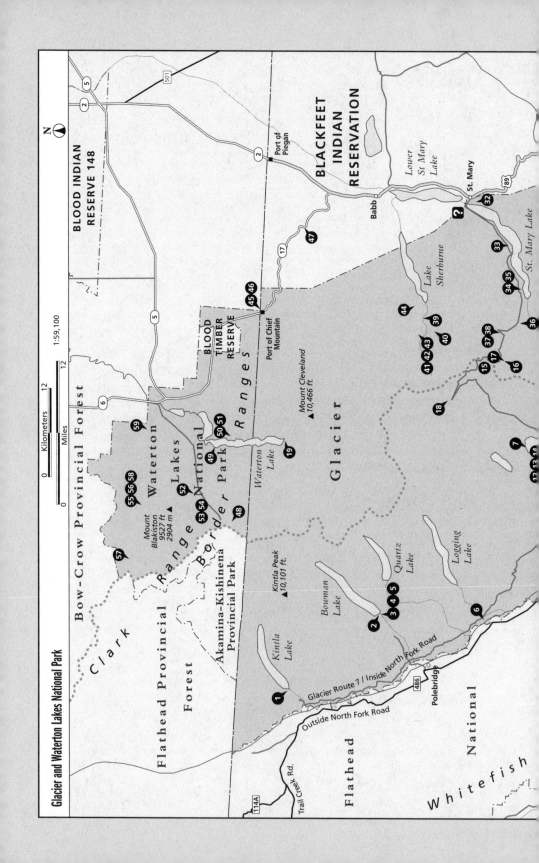

Glacier and Waterton Lakes National Park

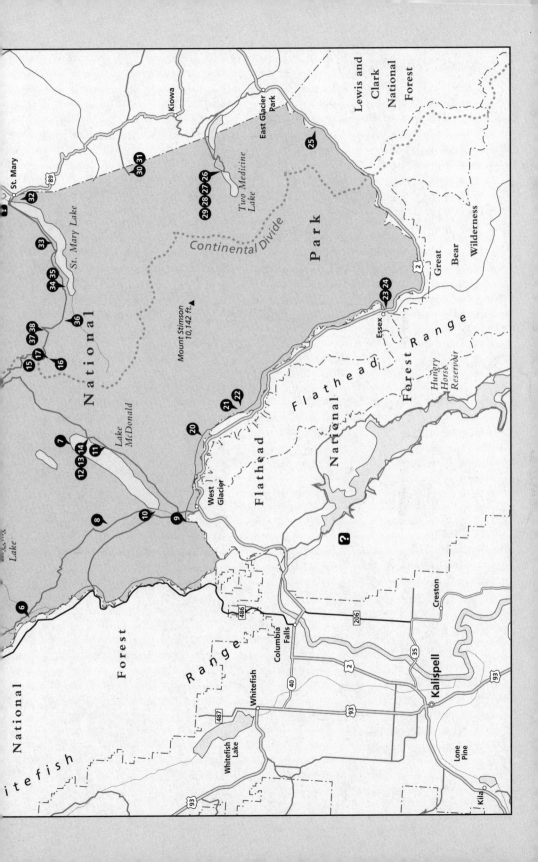

The Southern Sector 79
20 Harrison Lake 81
21 Loneman Lookout 83
22 The Nyack–Coal Creek Loop 84
23 Lake Isabel 88
24 Scalplock Lookout 92
25 Firebrand Pass–Ole Lake 94
    Additional Hikes 96

Two Medicine 99
26 Scenic Point 101
27 Cobalt Lake–Two Medicine Pass 103
28 Upper Two Medicine Lake 105
29 Dawson-Pitamakan 106
30 Cut Bank Creek 109
31 Medicine Grizzly Lake–Triple Divide Pass 113
    Connecting Hikes 117

The St. Mary Valley 119
32 Red Eagle Lake 121
33 Otokomi Lake 126
34 St. Mary and Virginia Falls 127
35 St. Mary Lake 128
36 Gunsight Pass 130
37 Piegan Pass 134
38 Siyeh Pass 136
    Connecting Hikes 138

Many Glacier 139
39 Cracker Lake 141
40 The Grinnell Complex 143
41 Swiftcurrent Pass 147
42 Iceberg Lake 149
43 Ptarmigan Tunnel 151
44 Poia Lake–Redgap Pass 153
    Additional Hikes 156

The Belly River Country 157
45 The Belly River Trail 159
46 Mokowanis River–Stoney Indian Pass 162
47 Slide Lake–Gable Pass 165
    Connecting Hikes 168

Waterton Lakes National Park 169
48 The Carthew-Alderson Trail 171
49 Bertha Lake 175
50 Crypt Lake 177
51 Vimy Peak 180
52 Lineham Falls 182
53 Rowe Lakes 184
54 The Tamarack Trail 186
55 Blakiston Valley 189
56 The Snowshoe Trail–Twin Lakes 192
57 Lost Lake–Avion Ridge 195
58 Goat Lake 198
59 The Oil Basin Loop 200
    Additional Hikes 204

Extended Trips 205
    The Continental Divide National Scenic Trail 206
    The Great Northern Traverse 207
    The Highline Trail 208
    The North Circle 208

Appendix A: Further Reading 210
Appendix B: For More Information 211
Appendix C: Fishing Opportunities 212
Appendix D: Backcountry Campground Table 214
Index 217
About the Authors 219

Acknowledgments

This guide would not have been possible without the years of excellent service put in by the rangers with whom I had the pleasure of dealing. I would like to thank Mr. Jack Potter, GNP Chief of Science and Resource Management, for his editorial input throughout the writing of this book. Thanks to Dennis Divoky of Glacier National Park for providing the map of recent fires. I also thank Nancy Hoffman and Tom Habecker, former Glacier rangers, for their helpful comments and suggestions concerning the guide. Clyde Lockwood of the Glacier Natural History Association provided the initial assistance in dealing with publishing firms, and I am grateful for his continued support of my efforts. Randall Schwanke, Locke Marshall, Bill Thorpe, and Chrisy Gustavison of Waterton Lakes National Park provided editorial assistance for the Canadian hikes. Thanks to Renelle Jacobsen for her hospitality and friendship. And thanks to Little Joe Manley just for being himself.

Introduction

Glacier National Park was established in 1910 to preserve over one million acres of unspoiled wilderness. More than 730 miles of trail in the park provide access to soaring peaks and verdant forests, mountain meadows and fish-filled lakes—truly a backpacker's paradise. Here hikers have the opportunity to leave the hectic pace of "civilization" far behind and seek a form of refuge in the silent grandeur of the mountains. Tragically, most of the visitors to Glacier National Park never stray far from their automobiles, but those adventurous souls who do plunge into the wilderness discover a wealth of natural beauty around every turn of the trail.

Where the prairie meets the sky, jagged peaks rim the deep, cold lakes that form the nucleus of Waterton Lakes National Park. The park is crisscrossed with well-maintained trails that visit a broad spectrum of habitats, from alpine meadows to lowland forests and high plains grasslands. The scale of Waterton Park's trail system is diminutive when compared to Glacier's multitude of long treks; most hikes in the Canadian park can be completed in a single day. This quick and easy access to the high country makes Waterton an ideal destination for hikers with limited time to burn, as well as beginners who are just learning to appreciate the wonders of the mountains.

Natural History

Geology

The rock strata of Glacier National Park were laid down more than a billion years ago as sediment on the bottom of an inland sea. The oldest layer is of buff-colored Altyn limestone, with subsequent layers of greenish Appekuny argillite and reddish Grinnell argillite being deposited on top as mudstone and sandstone. Tectonic forces brought enormous pressure on the strata in this area, causing them to fold upward and eventually break. After the break, the forces continued, forcing a huge slab of rock to slide eastward a distance of 42 miles over neighboring strata. This geologic feature is known as the Lewis Overthrust, and it is responsible for creating the original mountain masses of the park.

During the last great ice age, continual heavy snowfall collected in pockets and valleys and compressed under its own weight to form glaciers. These glaciers began to move downhill, pulled by the forces of gravity. As they moved, they carved the rock of the valley walls and floors, scouring deep U-shaped trenches with natural amphitheaters, or cirques, at their heads. When the glaciers retreated, they left behind piles of debris called lateral moraines (along the sides of valleys) and terminal moraines (where the foot of the glacier had been). Terminal moraines formed natural dams in many cases, creating some of the many lakes that dot the park. The action of glaciers on the mountains has resulted in horn peaks and arêtes. The action of later, smaller glaciers has carved smaller indentations, or hanging cirques, high on the

Looking up the Canyon Creek Valley (Cracker Lake hike)

walls of the original valleys. The remnants of these later glaciers remain active in many parts of the park but are shrinking today due to global warming.

Biological Communities

Glacier National Park is a healthy, functioning system of communities that supports a wide variety of interdependent plant and animal species. At the end of the last ice age, temperatures at lower elevations began to rise. This encouraged faster-growing plants and pushed cold-weather-loving flora like relict tundra communities to higher elevations. As a result, an increase in elevation brings the hiker into communities that are very similar to those that dominate the subarctic and arctic regions. The lowlands reflect the convergence of a wide variety of plant communities—cedar-hemlock assemblages from the Pacific Northwest, grassland communities from the Great Plains, bunchgrass communities from the Great Basin, and fire-dependent lodgepole pine forests from the Rockies. The widely divergent plant communities that coexist in the park showcase a great diversity of animal species in a relatively small area.

The Role of Forest Fires

Wildfires are a natural and healthy part of Glacier's forest ecosystem. The forests have evolved with fire over the course of thousands of years, and the passage of blazes creates a mosaic of different habitat types, which in turn supports Glacier's outstanding diversity of wildlife and wildflowers. Some forest types, such as lodgepole pine, are

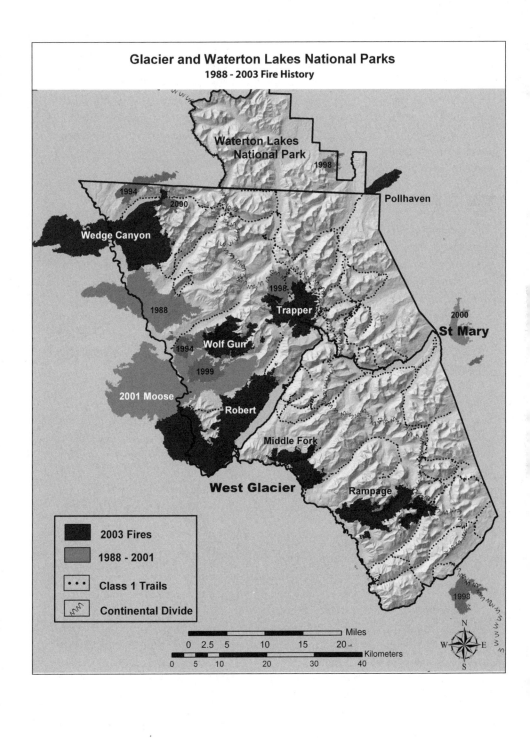

Glacier and Waterton Lakes National Parks
1988 - 2003 Fire History

Waterton Lakes
National Park

1998

Pollhaven

1994

2000

Wedge Canyon

1988

1998

Trapper

2000

St Mary

1994

Wolf Gun

1999

2001 Moose

Robert

Middle Fork

West Glacier

Rampage

1998

Legend:

2003 Fires

1988 - 2001

Class 1 Trails

Continental Divide

Miles

0 2.5 5   10   15   20

Kilometers

0   5   10   20   30   40

N
W · · E
S

completely fire-dependent. Before the value of fires was well known, or in response to threats to structures or adjacent lands, federal agencies spent billions of taxpayer dollars trying to snuff them out. This misguided effort actually increased the likelihood of large, severe fires in an ecosystem better adapted to smaller, frequent burns. The map on the previous page shows the extent of Glacier's recent forest fires, which typically have occurred during unusually hot, dry summers that may be linked to global warming. Far from being a disaster, these fires have resulted in important benefits for most wildlife, and there is now a trend to allow fires to burn unimpeded in order to reap the ecological benefits for the land.

Using This Guide

This guide provides information that will help hikers choose backpacking trips according to their available time and abilities. It also gives a detailed description of the trail system and interprets natural features found along the trails. Use this guide in conjunction with topographic maps, which can be purchased at the St. Mary or Apgar visitor centers, local gift and sporting goods stores, or through the U.S. Geological Survey, Denver Federal Center, Denver, CO 80225. The 1:100,000 scale topo map of the entire park gives a general impression of the landforms that will be encountered, and 1:24,000 scale quadrangle maps are available for those desiring greater detail. The appropriate quadrangle maps are listed for each major hike in the guide.

Each trail description begins with a quick and easy reference section outlining the physical characteristics of the trail. The outline includes distances (in miles and kilometers), the hike type (day hike or backpack, which is usually longer and includes an overnight stay), altitude gain and loss, maximum elevation, appropriate topo maps, and degree of difficulty. The difficulty rating can be interpreted as follows: **Easy** trails can be completed without difficulty by hikers of all abilities; **moderate** hikes will challenge novices; **moderately strenuous** hikes will tax even experienced hikers; and **strenuous** trails will push the physical limits of the most Herculean hiker.

Next you'll find directions to the trailhead followed by a detailed interpretive description of the trail, including geologic and ecological features, fishing opportunities, campsites, and other important information. Photographs have been included to give the reader a visual preview of some of the prominent features along the trail.

The key points at the end of each hike provide a mile-by-mile breakdown of the trail using landmarks, trail junctions, and gradient changes. Note that most trail signs in the park have distances posted in kilometers; an easy rule of thumb is that 5 kilometers is roughly equal to 3 miles.

Planning Your Trip

Only backpackers with backcountry permits may camp and build fires in designated areas on the Glacier trail system. These permits cost $4.00 per person (over the age of seventeen) per night and are available at all visitor centers and some ranger stations. An annual backcountry pass can be purchased for $50. If you would like to reserve a backcountry permit more than twenty-four hours in advance, you can apply by mail during the preceding spring for an additional charge of $20. The permit is good only for the campgrounds and dates that are specified; deviation from your camping itinerary is strictly prohibited. For backpacks in popular areas, it is wise to get your permits a day in advance of the start of your trip. Permits are not required for day trips. Hikers planning to do off-trail climbing or mountaineering are advised to register at any ranger station or visitor center before setting off. Anglers should be aware of special regulations concerning catch limits and closed water in the park. No formal license or permit is required. For more information on park regulations, call the parks at the addresses listed in Appendix B.

How to Use the Maps

The maps in this book that depict a detailed close-up of an area use elevation tints, called hypsometry, to portray relief. Each gray tone represents a range of equal elevation, as shown in the map's scale key. These maps will give you a good idea of elevation gain and loss. The darker tones are lower elevations, and the lighter grays are higher elevations. The lighter the tone, the higher the elevation. Narrow bands of different gray tones spaced closely together indicate steep terrain, whereas wider bands indicate areas of more gradual slope.

Maps that show larger geographic areas use shaded, or shadow, relief. Shadow relief does not represent elevation; it demonstrates slope or relative steepness. This gives an almost 3-D perspective of the physiography of a region and will help you see where ranges and valleys are.

Both day hikes and backpacks in Glacier are typically out-and-back propositions; in most cases, you will need to retrace your steps, while in others, you can link up with another trail that will take you back to civilization via a different route. The

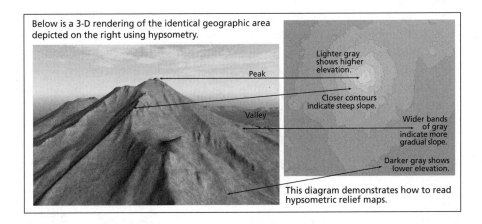

Below is a 3-D rendering of the identical geographic area depicted on the right using hypsometry.

Peak

Valley

Lighter gray shows higher elevation.

Closer contours indicate steep slope.

Wider bands of gray indicate more gradual slope.

Darker gray shows lower elevation.

This diagram demonstrates how to read hypsometric relief maps.

Logan Pass mountain goat PHOTO BY MONICA BAER

key to a quality hiking experience is good planning. Hikers who underestimate the distance or time required in completing a hike may find themselves hiking in the dark, a dangerous proposition at best. An experienced hiker traveling at a fast clip without rest stops can generally make 3 miles per hour on any terrain, and perhaps more if the distance is all downhill. Novices and out-of-shape hikers generally have a maximum speed of 2.5 miles per hour. Note that these rates do not include stops for rest and refreshment, which add tremendously to the hiker's enjoyment and appreciation of the surroundings. Eight miles a day is a good goal for travelers new to backpacking, while old hands can generally cover at least 12 miles comfortably. To fully enjoy your hike, travel below top speed, focusing more attention on the surrounding natural beauty and less on the exercise of hiking itself.

Crossing the International Border

Glacier and Waterton Lakes National Parks have been formally joined together as an international peace park, and visitors to one park commonly also visit the other. Border crossings have become more regulated in recent years, and visitors planning an international visit should prepare accordingly. Plan to bring passports as a means of positive identification for all members of your party. The Canadian government also requires visitors to carry sufficient cash or travelers checks to cover all potential expenses. Several hundred dollars is a recommended minimum, and credit cards cannot be counted toward this total. A ferry links Waterton townsite with the Goat Haunt Ranger Station on the U.S. side of the border. Hikers and backpackers entering the United States at Goat Haunt must possess an American or Canadian passport.

Park Shuttle

Starting in 2007, the National Park Service will begin a free shuttle service along the Going-to-the-Sun Road. The shuttle will drop off and pick up hikers every 30 minutes at trailheads along the road.

A Few Words of Caution

Weather

Weather patterns in the mountains of Glacier National Park may change frequently and without warning. Cold temperatures can occur even during the height of summer, and nighttime temperatures routinely dip into the 40s and even 30s (Fahrenheit) on clear nights. Thunderstorms may change cloudless days into a drenching misery, so appropriate rain gear should be carried by all hikers. Ponchos are generally sufficient for day hikes, but backpackers should carry full rain suits, as water from wet vegetation will quickly soak travelers who rely solely on ponchos for protection. Through June and starting again in late August, snowfall is a distinct possibility in the high country, and overnight backpackers should carry clothing and gear with this possibility in mind. Detailed short-range forecasts are available at visitor centers and are usually reliable.

Grizzly Bears

Grizzly bears are natural residents of the parks, and you will be passing through their territory during the course of day hikes and backpacks. By exercising precautions and treating the bears with respect, the hiker can minimize the chances of confrontation or harmful encounters with these wild and beautiful creatures. First of all, give bears a wide berth, as the bear will perceive a direct approach as a threat. Many a photographer has met his end while trying to get just a little closer for that perfect shot. Females with cubs and bears in the vicinity of a kill are particularly sensitive to intrusions by humans.

In camp, cook all food in designated cooking sites at least 100 yards from your tent site, as the odors produced by cooking may attract scavenging bears. Always hang all food on cache poles and wires provided at each campground. Bring a rope at least 30 feet long for this purpose. Hanging your pack not only prevents bear encounters, it also protects your pack from rodents that chew at pack straps for their

Vimy Peak from Bears Hump

salt. In areas of dense brush along trails, it may be necessary to announce your presence to bears. Bear bells may be worn for this purpose; clapping and shouting at appropriate times works just as well.

Remember that a bear will try to avoid contact with humans, so if you meet a bear along the trail, the odds are good that it will turn and flee. In the event of a human-bear confrontation, the best course of action is to talk in a firm, unexcited voice to the bear while waving your arms slowly and backing away. Do not attempt to run away from the bear, as this action may cause the bear to identify you as prey and give chase. With a top speed of 40 miles per hour, a grizzly can certainly catch a running person if it has the inclination. Climbing a tree is a means of escape if an appropriate tree is nearby and one has sufficient time to do so (which is usually not the case). Playing dead—curling into a ball face-down and covering the neck and stomach—should only be used as a last resort after the bear has decided to attack. This action may save the victim from mortal wounds. But it is easier by far to avoid a bear encounter than to get out of one.

Water Supplies

The pristine streams and lakes of Glacier and Waterton National Parks are quite refreshing, but they may contain a microorganism called *Giardia lamblia,* which causes severe diarrhea and dehydration in humans. The microorganism is spread through the feces of mammals, especially beavers, which inhabit many low-elevation stream systems. The water can be rendered safe by boiling it for at least one minute or by passing it through a filter system with a mesh no larger than two microns. Iodine tablets and other purification additives are not considered completely effective against *Giardia.* Any surface water supply is a potential source of this organism, and hikers that drink from lakes and streams assume the risk of contracting the painful symptoms.

Short Strolls and Nature Walks

Glacier National Park

These trails are for visitors who don't have much time to enjoy the backcountry of the Waterton-Glacier area, or who simply want a nice little stroll that won't exhaust the kids. Many of these trails are self-guiding nature trails, with pamphlets or displays that shed light on the landscape of the Northern Rockies. Most of these trails are considered easy and would be appropriate for small children and persons who have reason to doubt their physical fitness. Each hike description includes the level of difficulty and total miles.

Johns Lake Loop   Easy, 2.4 miles (3.9 km)
This popular loop begins at the Johns Lake Trailhead, 1.5 miles east of Lake McDonald Lodge on the Going-to-the-Sun Road. It runs through the forest above the head of Lake McDonald, visiting a woodland lake as well as Sacred Dancing Cascade and McDonald Falls along McDonald Creek. Parts of the trail receive heavy horse use from trail rides that originate at Lake McDonald Lodge.

The hike begins with a moderate climb into the cedar-hemlock forest south of Going-to-the-Sun Road. Turn left at the first junction as the trail rises into an old burn populated by Douglas fir and lodgepole pine. Beargrass (a member of the lily family) and huckleberry thrive in the sunny understory found here. Follow the signs for Johns Lake as the path returns to the closed-canopy forest. The path reaches Johns Lake 0.2 mile later. This shallow pool in the woodlands reflects the summits of Mounts Stanton and Vaught.

A connecting trail runs northward from the lakeshore toward Avalanche Lake; avoid it in favor of the wider path bound for Going-to-the-Sun Road. This trail descends through the deep shade of western hemlocks, and a carpet of moss covers the forest floor. Upon reaching the road, cross the crosswalk and turn right (north) to reach the paved pathway that descends to Sacred Dancing Cascade. Cross the bridge that leads across McDonald Creek just below a stairstep waterfall.

On the far bank, turn left (south) and choose the primitive path with the "no horses" sign. This path follows the rims of low cliffs that guard McDonald Creek, with fine views of the riffled whitewater and turquoise pools. The path soon reaches McDonald Falls, and a spur track runs to the lip where the water plunges over a thundering cataract. The trail then wanders through a bottomland forest of hemlock to reach the North Shore Road. Shuttle hikers will turn right on this road to reach the McDonald Creek Trailhead; loop hikers should turn left, crossing the road bridge and then following a horse trail back to the Johns Lake Trailhead.

McDonald Creek   Easy, 6.8 miles (10.9 km)

This hike begins from a marked trailhead on the Lake McDonald North Shore Road, 0.3 mile beyond the bridge over McDonald Creek. It follows a fragment of the old packers' trail that ran up the McDonald Creek Valley before the Going-to-the-Sun Road was built. This reach of McDonald Creek is guarded by the low walls of a distinctive little gorge, and through it the aquamarine waters flow down rushing waterfalls and through quiet runs. Part of the trail is used for trail rides originating at Lake McDonald Lodge; be prepared to meet horses along the way. The hike is particularly striking in the silence of early winter, when massive icicles hang from the walls of the gorge.

The trail begins by wandering northwest through a mixed woodland of hemlock, larch, and Douglas fir that occupies the bottomlands along McDonald Creek. After a short journey, the path approaches the stream, with its turquoise waters swirling down between slanted slabs of stone. To view the roaring cataract of McDonald Falls, take a short side trip down the stream bank on an unofficial trail marked with a "no horses" sign. The main path now runs northeast along the rim of a small gorge. The crenellated facade of Mount Brown looms across the valley, a constant presence along this portion of the route. The path soon reaches the sturdy bridge over Sacred Dancing Cascade, and just upstream the water descends gracefully across a lengthy series of tiny stairsteps.

The wider path leads across the stream to a parking area and beyond to Johns Lake, while the McDonald Creek Trail is the narrow gravel pathway that continues upstream along the north bank of the creek. After passing a small waterfall, the trail turns inland to enter the silent hallways of the climax coniferous forest. When it next emerges at the streamside, the waters glide placidly through cedar bottoms. The lofty edifice of Mount Cannon rises ahead, and soon Mount Vaught and Heavens Peak appear on the north side of the valley. Watch for moose as well as beaver, which have dammed some of the slow-moving backwaters in this area.

The path next wanders inland, passing through a deep forest of hemlock. The trail becomes more primitive as you proceed, due in large part to the prohibition of horses starting in 2006. The track soon crosses a gravelly wash where floodwaters from the slopes of Mount Vaught have buried the tree trunks in rocky debris. On the far side, the path improves for a long sojourn through the hemlocks. At the end of it, travelers are rewarded as the trail emerges beside the rocky upper gorge of McDonald Creek. Here, the waters churn through violent waterfalls, and the imposing summit of Mount Cannon rises regally above the stream. Watch your step: There are no guardrails here to prevent a tumble into the churning whitewater. The path ends suddenly atop the bedrock with views of a particularly impressive falls.

Trail of the Cedars   Easy, 0.7 mile (1.1 km)

This self-guiding nature trail is located directly across Going-to-the-Sun Road from the Avalanche Creek Campground. It forms a semi-loop through the old-growth

Columbian ground squirrel PHOTO BY MONICA BAER

forest in the bottoms of Avalanche Creek. Avalanche Gorge lies at the apex of the loop, with swirling turquoise waters and sculpted argillite walls. The northern leg is boardwalk while the southern leg is paved, with benches along the way so you can stop and enjoy the grandeur of the forest. The entire loop is accessible to wheelchairs. The trailhead is about 0.3 mile from the parking lot.

From the trailhead, follow the boardwalk that runs through the forest to the north of Avalanche Creek. The old-growth forest that rises from these damp and fertile bottoms has remained undisturbed for centuries, and the trees have grown tall and stout in the absence of fire and avalanche. The oldest trees are red cedar and black cottonwood, species that are more commonly found along coastal rivers of the Pacific Northwest. Ferns and devil's club occupy the understory. Most of the younger trees are western hemlock, which can be identified by its drooping treetop leader. It is the most shade-tolerant of Glacier's conifers, and its seedlings can thrive beneath a closed-canopy forest where those of other species cannot.

Note the diversity of tree sizes and ages; as the oldest trees succumb to disease and fall to the forest floor, they create sunny gaps in the canopy so that light can reach the ground and allow new seedlings to take root. Over the span of centuries, this gradual replacement of the stand results in a broad diversity of tree heights, forming a multi-layered canopy that offers a multitude of ecological niches for forest creatures that have specialized diets and food-gathering techniques. This results in a diversity of such forest dwellers as birds, voles, and squirrels. It is this diversity of plant and animal life that makes the old-growth forest so valuable from an ecological standpoint.

As it makes its way through the forest, the boardwalk passes a mossy outcrop of stone. Water seeps constantly from the fissures in the rock, and in the winter great stalactites of ice form here. The path then crosses a bridge at the mouth of Avalanche Gorge, where the water has carved a deep and whorled channel into the argillite. Moss grows thick at the edges of the gorge, thriving in the constant mist provided by a waterfall just upstream. Watch for a small gray bird known as the water ouzel, which nests behind waterfalls and makes frequent dives into the current in a quest for aquatic insects. On the far bank of the creek, a paved path leads westward, following Avalanche Creek as it passes through an abandoned loop of the Avalanche Creek Campground. Note the differences in the forest understory compared to the far bank; it will take centuries for the forest to recover from the clearing of underbrush and the compacting of soil that once took place here. Follow the paved path back to Going-to-the-Sun Road, then turn right (north) to return to your vehicle.

Sun Point Nature Trail   Easy, 1.3 miles (2.1 km)
This short trek begins from the Sun Point parking area, 11 miles east of Logan Pass on Going-to-the-Sun Road. It offers excellent views of St. Mary Lake, with a stunning waterfall at the end of the hike. It is a self-guiding nature trail with pamphlets available at the beginning of the trail.

The hike begins by dipping down to a fork in the trail. Bear left on a spur path to make the short climb to Sun Point, which overlooks St. Mary Lake. A sign points out the names of the massive summits that ring the lake. These summits have a reddish cast: They are composed of Grinnell argillite, a mudstone that is rich in iron and turns red as the iron oxidizes. During the uplift that created the Rocky Mountains some 65 million years ago, these old seafloor sediments were tilted skyward, and the direction of the tilt can be seen today in the slant of the rock strata.

After returning to the trail junction, hike westward as the trail runs level above the shores of St. Mary Lake. A sparse growth of wind-torn lodgepole pines allows fine views of the water and the peaks that surround it. The turquoise glacier-fed lake is almost 300 feet deep, occupying a basin that was carved out by a massive valley glacier during the Pleistocene epoch. The ice was so deep that it reached the tops of the highest summits. The U-shaped cross-section of the valley is the telltale footprint of the long-vanished glacier. As the path crosses the sliderock beneath a low cliff, note the green coloration of the bedrock. This is Appekuny argillite, older than the Grinnell formation but made of a similar mudstone.

Beargrass field PHOTO BY MONICA BEAR

The path enters a woodland of spruce and Douglas fir as it approaches Baring Creek. Bear left at the junction as the main trail crosses a footlog to reach the base of Baring Falls. This impressive cascade drops across a sheer cliff of argillite into a natural amphitheater in the rock. Turn around here and retrace your steps to complete the hike.

Beaver Pond Trail   Easy, 3.4 miles (5.5 km)
This hike begins at the Red Eagle Trailhead. Take the Going-to-the-Sun Road 0.25 mile west from St. Mary township to a paved road that enters on the south before the entrance station. Take this paved road, bearing right, about 0.5 mile to a parking lot with a trailhead sign. Though lacking in spectacular scenery, the loop runs through a pleasant landscape of coniferous forests, grassy meadows, and aspen groves. It receives few visitors and thus is a good place to find solitude.

The trail begins by climbing the hill to the original St. Mary Ranger Station, built in 1910 of native timber. Behind the old buildings, the path ascends to a low ridgetop that bears the scars of periodic lightning fires. This ridge is a terminal moraine of the glacier that carved the St. Mary Valley, bulldozed into place by the slow but inexorable surge of the glacial ice and deposited at the toe of the glacier. The path follows the ridgetop through shady stands of Douglas fir and grassy meadows that provide views of Red Eagle Mountain to the southwest and East Flattop Mountain to the north. Eventually the woodland opens out into rank grasslands bordered by aspen groves, and Split Mountain appears up the valley of Red Eagle Creek.

The trail soon reaches an old, stagnant beaver pond. The beavers are long gone, but the pond is a good spot to look for birdlife. The trail then turns west and descends to the abandoned Red Eagle Road, now a hiking trail. Turn right as the old road parallels the shore of St. Mary Lake, yielding occasional views of the water. The roadbed bears the traveler back to the parking lot to complete the loop.

Running Eagle Falls   Easy, 0.6 mile (1 km)

This short stroll begins at the Red Eagle Falls parking area on the north side of Two Medicine Road about 2 miles past the park entrance station. It leads to an odd waterfall that emerges from an underground cave during late summer but pours over a higher sill during spring runoff. A wheelchair-accessible loop leads to a view point of the falls and returns a different route along the Two Medicine River, while a hikers' spur leads to a closer view of the falls crossing Dry Fork Creek.

The walk begins in an open woodland of spruce and fir that is underlain by a vigorous undergrowth of shrubs. A few old cottonwoods date from past floods: Cottonwood seedlings require bare soil and plenty of groundwater to get established, a combination that is unique to rivers that scour their banks with periodic floods. The two major peaks visible along the way are Rising Wolf Mountain to the northwest and Spot Mountain to the northeast. The path soon reaches a broad stretch of bare gravel where the Dry Fork joins the Two Medicine River. The Dry Fork floods each spring during the snowmelt season, and the force of these periodic deluges is sufficient to sweep the banks bare of vegetation.

After crossing a footbridge over the river, the path climbs to reach an overlook below Running Eagle Falls. This unique cataract pours over a sill of stone 40 feet high during early summer. But when the river level drops, the upper channel dries up and the falls emerges from a hidden grotto some 20 feet below the lip of the falls. A rough and uneven path leads the remaining distance to the foot of the falls, which thunders into a placid pool of deep turquoise water.

Appistoki Falls   Moderate, 1.2 miles (1.9 km)

This trail departs from the marked Scenic Point Trailhead on the Two Medicine Road, approximately 4 miles beyond the entrance station, and climbs to a small waterfall in the barren gorge of Appistoki Creek. It begins in a pleasant woodland of subalpine fir, lit by the blossoms of beargrass in early summer of favorable years. The beargrass is not a grass at all but a member of the lily family, with great bulb-shaped clusters of tiny white flowers. It blooms on a three-year cycle, with most plants in a given locale coming into bloom during the same year. The path rises gently through

Waterton Lakes trail flora PHOTO BY MONICA BAER

the forest, which thins out with increasing elevation. The barren face of Appistoki Peak looms to the west, while the similar summit of Scenic Point rises to the east.

The trail strikes Appistoki Creek at the base of the mountains as it emerges from a desolate vale between the peaks. Turn right at the junction to reach an overlook on the rim of a rocky ravine. From here, the main waterfall can be seen as it slides down across an inclined face of stone, with pools and lesser cascades below it.

Aster Park   Moderate, 3.8 miles (6.1 km)

This route begins at the South Shore Trailhead, located at the west end of the Two Medicine boat dock parking lot. It combines the early reaches of the Two Medicine Loop with a spur trail that visits a pretty waterfall and then climbs to a high overlook above Two Medicine Lake.

The hike begins by climbing gently into the subalpine forest to the south of Two Medicine Lake. At the top of the rise is a trail junction; a spur path descends to Paradise Point on the lakeshore, while the main trail wanders inland. It passes stagnant pools, beaver ponds, and wetlands, and open meadows beside the marshes offer outstanding views of the peaks: Appistoki Peak and Never Laughs Mountain to the south, Sinopah Mountain above the head of the lake, and Rising Wolf beyond the far shore. A footbridge leads across Aster Creek, and on the far bank is the junction with the Aster Park Trail.

Turn left as this spur trail rises gently through the pines and firs. Soon a side path splits away toward the base of Aster Falls, where Aster Creek sluices down through a cleft in the bedrock, arcing downward in ribbonlike streams. The main trail makes several upward switchbacks, then settles into a steady westward grade through the trees. At the top of a low headwall, there are fine aerial views of Two Medicine Lake and the crags that surround it. The trail then turns south into the hanging valley of Aster Creek before climbing to its end on a rocky overlook at the edge of the Two Medicine Valley.

Apikuni Falls   Moderately strenuous, 2.0 miles (3.2 km)

This short, steep trail begins at the Apikuni Falls Trailhead, 3.3 miles west of the Many Glacier Entrance Station. It leads up to the desolate cliffs of Apikuni Mountain to visit a long and slender waterfall. There are excellent mountain views throughout the hike.

The trek begins on Apikuni Flats, where grassy meadows offer views of the major peaks up the valley: Mount Gould, with its chiseled countenance; the symmetrical pyramid of Grinnell Point to the north of it; and between them the Garden Wall, graced with the Salamander and Grinnell Glaciers. At the far edge of the flats, the path undertakes a relentless and calf-burning climb, passing through aspen groves and lodgepole pine stands as it ascends to the base of the limestone cliffs. Altyn Peak rises to the west of Apikuni Creek, while to the east are the outer bulwarks of Apikuni Mountain (the reddish summit of this peak can be seen through the mouth of the hanging valley above).

The path ultimately climbs onto rocky and barren slopes where only a few firs survive, and the bleached and gnarled skeletons of long-dead whitebark pines rise mournfully to the sky. Swiftcurrent Lake and Lake Josephine can now be glimpsed in the valley to the west, while to the south the broad panorama of Wynn and Allen Mountains rises beyond Sherburne Reservoir. Apikuni Falls can be seen ahead, dropping through a cleft in the limestone walls. The path becomes primitive with steep, uneven footing as it navigates a rocky ravine to reach the base of the falls.

Swiftcurrent Nature Trail (Loop)   Easy, 2.5 miles (4 km)

This self-guided nature walk begins at the Swiftcurrent Picnic Area on the west shore of Swiftcurrent Lake and circles the lakeshore. The scenery is spectacular, but hikers will also walk past the Many Glacier Hotel and along several roadways, so this is not a wilderness hike. Pamphlets interpreting the landscape are available at the trailhead.

From the picnic area, hike southward as the trail crosses the braided channels of Swiftcurrent Creek. The stream is bordered by a low growth of willows, which thrive in saturated soils. The trail soon enters a lakeshore woodland of subalpine fir and lodgepole pine. Allen Mountain is the prominent peak to the south, with Mount Wynn to the left of it. After passing the boat dock, the trail crosses Cataract Creek and winds onto the south shore of the lake. The massive summit of Altyn Peak now rises to the north. The forest soon thins, and the trail breaks out of it entirely as it reaches Many Glacier Hotel. Enjoy the spectacular views that encompass Mount Gould to the west, Grinnell Point above the head of the lake, and Mount Wilbur to the northwest. As you follow the lakeshore promenade, scan the lower slopes of Altyn Peak for grizzly bears and bighorn sheep. The trail now runs beside the road, following the lakeshore as it bends westward to return to the picnic area.

Bullhead Lake   Easy, 6.6 miles (10.6 km)
This hike begins at the west end of the Swiftcurrent Motor Inn coffee shop parking lot and follows the Swiftcurrent Valley past a chain of pretty lakes, visiting Redrock Falls along the way.

The trail winds westward along the valley floor, among groves of tall aspen interspersed with lodgepole pine. The cliffs of Grinnell Point rise to the south, and as the trail runs westward, the summit of Grinnell Peak comes into view along the same ridge. The trail passes to the north of Fishercap Lake, which can only be glimpsed briefly through a few holes in the vegetation. It then climbs gently, crossing a small stream on its way to Redrock Lake. Notice that harsh growing conditions have stunted the pines and aspens around the lake. The trail continues west, passing Redrock Falls above the head of the lake. Two miles beyond Redrock Lake, the trail reaches Bullhead Lake. A northward glance reveals Mount Wilbur, Iceberg Peak, and the North Swiftcurrent Glacier on the east face of Swiftcurrent Mountain.

Rainbow Falls   Easy, 1.4 miles (2.3 km)
This well-maintained trail is a popular stroll for visitors who take the boat tour to the head of Waterton Lake. The hike begins on the Waterton Lake Trail, which runs westward from the ranger station. Barren summits of sedimentary rock flank both sides of Waterton Lake. As the trail nears the Waterton River, bear left on the hiker trail and then turn left at a marked junction with the Rainbow Falls Spur Trail. This path wanders up the east bank of the river, which is bordered by dense thickets of willow, a favorite winter forage of moose. After half a mile, the trail reaches Rainbow Falls. Here, the translucent waters of the river foam over a series of low waterfalls.

Waterton Lakes National Park

Bears Hump   Moderately strenuous, 0.9 mile (1.5 km)
This trail begins at the Waterton Ranger Station and climbs the mountain slopes to visit a spectacular overlook of Waterton Lake. The hike begins with a steady climb through sparse woodlands of aspen and Douglas fir. Looking uphill, the twisted strata of Mount Crandall can be viewed through the trees. This mountain was originally

known as Bear Medicine Mountain by the Pikuni (Blackfoot) tribe, after the bear's hump appearance of the spur that the trail ascends. After reaching the first bench, the climb levels off a bit, then steepens to a veritable staircase up the mountainside. The climb increases further after the second rest bench, and aerial views of the Prince of Wales Hotel with its solitary spire can be seen to the south.

The climb ends atop the rocky dome of the Bears Hump. Spectacular views stretch in all directions, highlighted by the sapphire waters of Waterton Lake stretching southward into the United States. From north to south, the rugged crags rising above its far shore are Vimy Peak, Mount Boswell, and Mount Cleveland, which is the tallest summit in either national park at 10,466 feet. Mount Richard is the most prominent peak on the eastern shore of the lake, and in the distance is the jagged jawbone of the Citadel Peaks, known as *Ataniauxis,* or "The Needles," to the Pikuni people. Looking west, views up Carthew Creek feature the rocky summit of Buchanan Peak. And to the east, the Waterton River wanders out onto the verdant grasslands of the high plains.

Lower Bertha Falls   Easy, 3.8 miles (6.1 km)
This trail begins at the Bertha Lake Trailhead in the southwestern corner of Waterton townsite, across from the automobile campground. This popular day hike along Waterton Lake offers interpretive signs along the route, explaining the ecology of the ever-changing forest. At the end of the trek is the graceful veil of Lower Bertha Falls.

The trail begins in a stand of aspens, climbing gradually as it follows the western shore of Waterton Lake. As the trail rises above the lakeshore, there is a mixed forest of lodgepole pine, fir, and mountain maple. Rocky outcrops are home to the limber pine, which thrives in extreme environments. An overlook about a mile down the trail offers sweeping views of the ranges to the east of the lake, as far south as Mount Cleveland across the international border.

Just beyond this overlook, the Bertha Lake Trail splits off from the trail running along the shores of Waterton Lake. A left turn here yields a steep half-mile descent to the Bertha Bay Campground; turn right on the Bertha Lake Trail. It bends to the west, entering the beargrass–studded Bertha Creek Valley. After a distance of a mile, the trail reaches the foot of Lower Bertha Falls. Here, Bertha Creek cascades across layers of resistant rock, tumbling into a rushing flume created by a joint in the bedrock. This spot is a nice place for a picnic and marks the end of the easy day hike. Ambitious travelers can continue up the trail to Bertha Lake (see Hike 49).

Cameron Lake   Easy, 2.2 miles (3.5 km)
This trail begins on the north side of the Cameron Lake Picnic Area. It runs along the western shore of Cameron Lake, one of the prettiest lakes in the Waterton-Glacier area. A self-guiding pamphlet is available at the trailhead, and it interprets the ecology of the subalpine forest found along the lake. From the picnic area, the trail runs through the spruce and fir woodland beside the lake, climbing and falling moder-

ately. As it nears the head of the lake, the trail seeks out a small point, and avalanches from Forum Peak have cleared away the trees for outstanding views of the spectacular Mount Custer headwall and the deep turquoise waters of the lake.

Blakiston Falls   Easy, 1.6 miles (2.6 km)

This trail begins from the Red Rock Canyon parking lot. From the trailhead, cross Red Rock Creek and turn left, following its northwest bank to reach a stout bridge above Bauerman Creek. Mount Blakiston rises to the south, while Anderson Peak is to the west. Once across this bridge, take the rightmost trail, which is for hikers. The trail climbs gently through coniferous forestland, with views of Mount Blakiston through numerous openings. At Blakiston Falls, the trail passes a wooden observation platform that leans out over the water to provide excellent views of the thundering cascade.

Trail Finder Table

Number	Hike	Waterfalls Easy	Waterfalls Moderate	Waterfalls Difficult	Lowland Lakes Easy	Lowland Lakes Moderate	Lowland Lakes Difficult	Glacier Views Easy	Glacier Views Moderate	Glacier Views Difficult	Long Back-packing Trips Easy	Long Back-packing Trips Moderate	Long Back-packing Trips Difficult	Alpine Meadows Easy	Alpine Meadows Moderate	Alpine Meadows Difficult	Alpine Lakes Easy	Alpine Lakes Moderate	Alpine Lakes Difficult	Lookouts and Mountaintops Easy	Lookouts and Mountaintops Moderate	Lookouts and Mountaintops Difficult
1	Boulder Pass									●			●									
2	Bowman Lake–Brown Pass									●												
3	Akokala Lake					●															●	
4	Numa Ridge Lake					●																
5	Quartz Lakes Loop					●																
6	Logging Lake				●																	
7	Trout Lake						●															
8	Huckleberry Mountain Lookout																					●
9	Apgar Lookout				●																●	
10	Lake McDonald						●															
11	Lincoln Lake			●																		
12	Fish Lake					●																
13	Mount Brown Lookout																					●
14	Snyder Lakes																	●				
15	Avalanche Lake	●															●					
16	Hidden Lake		●												●			●				
17	The Garden Wall														●							
18	The Northern Highline											●			●							
19	Waterton Valley				●											●						
20	Harrison Lake				●																	
21	Loneman Lookout																					●
22	The Nyack–Coal Creek Loop											●									●	
23	Lake Isabel																	●				
24	Scalplock Lookout																		●			●
25	Firebrand Pass–Ole Lake																	●				
26	Scenic Point																					
27	Cobalt Lake–Two Medicine Pass																●					
28	Upper Two Medicine Lake																	●				
29	Dawson–Pitamakan									●									●			

Trail Finder Table

Number	Hike	Waterfalls			Lowland Lakes			Glacier Views			Long Back-packing Trips			Alpine Meadows			Alpine Lakes			Lookouts and Mountaintops		
		Easy	Moderate	Difficult	Easy	Moderate	Difficult	Easy	Moderate	Difficult	Easy	Moderate	Difficult	Easy	Moderate	Difficult	Easy	Moderate	Difficult	Easy	Moderate	Difficult
30	Cut Bank Creek																		●			
31	Medicine Grizzly Lake–Triple Divide Pass																●					
32	Red Eagle Lake				●																	
33	Otokomi Lake																	●				
34	St. Mary and Virginia Falls	●																				
35	St. Mary Lake		●																		●	
36	Gunsight Pass			●						●									●			
37	Piegan Pass		●												●							
38	Siyeh Pass									●					●							
39	Cracker Lake									●								●				
40	The Grinnell Complex																●					
41	Swiftcurrent Pass															●						●
42	Iceberg Lake																	●				
43	Ptarmigan Tunnel									●						●						
44	Poia Lake–Redgap Pass					●									●							
45	The Belly River Trail		●															●				
46	Mokowanis River–Stoney Indian Pass		●															●				
47	Slide Lake–Gable Pass					●										●						
48	The Carthew–Alderson Trail								●									●				
49	Bertha Lake		●																●			
50	Crypt Lake		●																●			
51	Vimy Peak																					●
52	Lineham Falls		●																			
53	Rowe Lakes																		●			
54	The Tamarack Trail												●		●				●			
55	Blakiston Valley		●																●			
56	The Snowshoe Trail–Twin Lakes															●			●			
57	Lost Lake–Avion Ridge												●						●			
58	Goat Lake																		●			
59	The Oil Basin Loop												●						●			

Map Legend

Boundaries

National wilderness/preserve boundary

National park boundary

State park boundary

Reservation boundary

International boundary

State boundary

Transportation

2 U.S. highway

49 State highway

486 Primary road

Other road

Featured trail

Optional trail

Other trail

Railroad

Hydrology

Intermittent stream

Falls

Lake

Glacier

Physiography

Continental Divide

Pass

▲ Spot elevation

Symbols

24 Trail start

Trail marker

Interpretive Trail

Wheelchair-accessible trail

Developed campground

Undeveloped campground

Backcountry campground

Ranger station

Port of entry

Visitor center

Picnic area

Food and lodging

Riding stable

Boat dock

Lookout

Overlook

Point of interest

Town

Falls

The North Fork

The North Fork of the Flathead River runs through a broad, forested valley bounded to the west by the Whitefish Range and on the east by the craggy Livingston Range. Trails generally begin among low ridges and wind into the high country through deep, forested valleys. The climate here reflects the maritime influence of storm fronts from the Pacific, and as a result the North Fork country gets quite a bit of precipitation over the course of a year, most of which falls in the wintertime as snow. The vegetation of the valley floor is dominated by lodgepole pines, which are dependent on periodic fires to maintain a competitive edge over more shade-tolerant species. The serotinous cones of lodgepoles are covered with resin that melts and allows the cone to release seeds only in the presence of heat provided by forest fires. The seeds then fall on fertile soil in openings created by the fire, where they germinate and thrive in the direct sunlight. This valley was occasionally used by the Kootenai tribe of the inland Northwest for hunting and gathering purposes on their way to the plains buffalo hunting grounds.

Wildlife in this part of the park reflects the boreal nature of the region, with plentiful elk and white-tailed deer. Signs of taiga species such as the lynx and the fisher are occasionally seen among the thick stands of lodgepole pine at lower elevations. The first wolf pack to repopulate the West since the 1930s was established here in 1986, and hikers that see tracks or hear the howl of this endangered animal can consider themselves truly fortunate. Bird-watchers will find the large glacial lakes of this area good places to see ospreys, bald eagles, and common loons.

The North Fork Valley has burned extensively since 1988, with a number of different fires resculpting the forest vegetation. The burns are most extensive between Columbia Falls and Polebridge, but about half of the roadside forest north of Polebridge is also a recovering postfire landscape.

The North Fork Valley can be accessed via the Inside North Fork Road (Glacier Route 7), which runs along the river, inside the park boundary. There are auto campgrounds at Quartz and Logging Creeks along this improved gravel road, as well as campgrounds at the foot of Bowman and Kintla Lakes. A riverside campground near Round Prairie serves boaters traveling down the North Fork or hikers who take the short stroll in from the access road. An alternate route into the North Fork area is the Polebridge Road, which can be accessed from the terminus of the Camas Road or from the town of Columbia Falls and which runs 16 miles north to the settlement of Polebridge. This road is heavily traveled by logging trucks and is frequently in rough condition. Just north of this quaint community, a new two-lane

Porcupine Ridge (Boulder Pass hike)

bridge crosses the river to link up with Glacier Route 7. Polebridge is an authentic frontier community, serving a handful of former homesteads and one ranch on the west bank of the river. This "town" boasts a mercantile store that sells gas and groceries, a hostel, rental cabins, and the Northern Lights Saloon, which serves meals and libations to the weary traveler in an atmosphere of down-home hospitality.

Most of the hikes in the North Fork stick to the lower elevations, and the closed canopy of the forest makes for limited views along the trail. Burns and lakes provide vistas, while the forest abounds with wild berries in the late summer. Lakes and streams typically harbor native westslope cutthroat trout; rainbow trout were introduced in some areas. In general, the lakes provide much better fishing than the streams because the streams are very pure and contain few nutrients to sustain a productive food web. Check the park fishing regulations for closures and catch limits before you set out.

1 Boulder Pass

A backpack from Kintla Lake to Upper Kintla Campground, 12.0 miles (19.2 km) one way; from Kintla Lake to Boulder Pass, 18.1 miles (29.2 km) one way; or from Kintla Lake to Goat Haunt Ranger Station, 31.8 miles (51.2 km) one way.

Elevation gain: 3,470 feet
Elevation loss: 2,510 feet
Maximum elevation: 7,478 feet

Difficulty: Moderately strenuous (east to west); strenuous (west to east)
Topo maps: Kintla Lake, Kintla Peak, Mount Carter, Porcupine Ridge

Finding the trailhead: Drive north on Glacier Route 7 to its northern terminus at Kintla Campground. The trail begins at the northeast corner of the campground, near the lakeshore.

The Hike

The Boulder Pass Trail provides access to some of the most rugged and beautiful high country areas in Glacier Park. High elevations between Boulder and Brown Passes lead to high snow accumulations and late snowmelt, making this trail impassable early in the season. This trail may be entered and exited via three trailheads: Kintla Lake, Goat Haunt Ranger Station, and Bowman Lake. Any combination of hiking experiences, from day hikes to extended expeditions, are available to hikers on this trail.

The hike begins at Kintla Lake, which is set in a forested valley between tree-clad hills. As the trail winds around the north lakeshore, watch for signs of the mule deer and mountain lions that inhabit the dense forest. Approximately 3.5 miles from the campground, a primitive connecting trail from Starvation Creek joins the Boulder Pass Trail from the north. The Boulder Pass Trail continues to follow the lakeshore for another 3 miles to Kintla Lake (head) Campground, a heavily used area on the lakeshore. Along the way, watch for signs of the 2003 Wedge Canyon Fire on the opposite shore.

Shortly after the campground, at the head of the lake, the trail passes the Kintla Lake patrol cabin, where the trail leaves the lakeshore to begin a gentle ascent to Upper Kintla Lake. The trail passes open benches bearing the marks of the 2003 fire; the cascades of Kintla Creek are now visible. Across the valley and high into the basin you can see the area burned in the 2000 Parke Peak Fire. Occasional avalanche chutes from Long Knife Peak provide vistas of Parke Peak and the Harris Glacier across the valley. The trail reaches the foot of Upper Kintla Lake some 2.5 miles beyond the patrol cabin. The cockscomb peak at the head of the lake is Gardner Point. The trail follows the north shore of the lake, providing views of Kinnerly Peak across the valley. After 2.5 miles, the trail reaches a spur trail to the campground at the head of the lake, which is beautifully situated among stands of fir and spruce.

Thunderbird Mountain from Boulder Pass overlook

Leaving the lakeshore and campground behind, the trail crosses Kintla Creek and begins a steep ascent along the west slope of Gardner Point. There are many switchbacks through scattered stands of spruce and open jungles of cow parsnip, a favorite springtime food for grizzlies, before the trail emerges into alpine parkland at the head of the small valley. All along this section of the trail are views of Kintla and Kinnerly Peaks to the west and the Agassiz Glacier at their feet. Looking back toward Upper Kintla Lake, Long Knife Peak can be seen, marking the boundary between Canada and the United States. The trail then reverses its direction, climbing northward to the Boulder Pass Campground. Just below the pass, the trail passes through stands of young alpine larch, an uncommon tree that exists here near the southern extreme of its range.

From the west end of Boulder Pass, the trail winds for several miles through a high, glacier-carved valley, across moraines left by the retreating ice. Pyramid-shaped piles of rock called cairns mark the location of the trail so that it can be found in times of deep snow. At the east end of the pass, the trail branches into two parts. The more northerly path, the original trail when the Boulder Glacier stretched across the pass, is now a goat path, which ascends the terminal moraine of Boulder Glacier and winds upward for a mile to a lookout point, high above the Bowman Valley. This lookout affords the most spectacular views of Thunderbird Mountain and many of the high peaks of the Livingston and Lewis Ranges.

The more southerly path descends onto a rocky shelf occupied by several tarns and continues its decent around the curve of the Hole in the Wall, a perfectly formed hanging cirque that sits some 1,800 feet above the floor of the Bowman Valley. There are steep snowdrifts along this upper section, usually until August. When the trail reaches the eastern edge of the Hole in the Wall, a spur trail descends to the floor of the cirque, where a beautiful alpine campground is located among meadows of wild-flowers and subalpine firs. This campground is frequented by mountain goats and several pestiferous mule deer, which you should not feed for any reason.

After passing Hole in the Wall, the trail continues its gentle descent to Brown Pass, a low saddle at the base of Thunderbird Mountain. Huckleberries grow in great profusion along this section of trail and provide a free food source for hikers and ani-mals alike when they ripen in early August. At the pass is the junction with the Bow-man Lake Trail. A short jaunt of 0.3 mile down this trail brings the hiker to the Brown Pass Campground, a pleasant area set among windblown firs. Looking east-ward from Brown Pass, the jagged spur ridge shaped like a wolf's lower jaw are Citadel Peaks, and the massive peak behind it is Mount Cleveland, at 10,466 feet the highest point in the park. Beyond Brown Pass, the Boulder Pass Trail descends steeply beneath the Thunderbird Glacier to a tarn at the head of Olson Creek Val-ley. A steep snowdrift extends down to the edge of the water in spring, and several early-season hikers have slid down the drift to receive an icy and unplanned bath. The pond itself is set among dense willows and may harbor an occasional moose.

Once the trail reaches the valley floor, it begins a long, slow descent to the Water-ton Valley. The trail passes through a fairly open section to Hawksbill Campground, a small area situated below a clifflike spur ridge scraped sheer on both sides by gla-ciers. The trail continues eastward through open forest to the junction with a spur trail to Lake Francis Campground, which lies on the shore of a beautiful lake beneath rocky cliffs. The lake is noted for its mosquitoes and fine fishing for rain-bow trout. The trail continues to the Lake Janet Campground, which is located on the bank of Olson Creek, some distance from its namesake lake. Grizzly bears are frequently spotted in the avalanche paths on the ridge above this campground.

The trail continues down the Olson Creek Valley, past shallow, and sometimes mucky, Lake Janet, and into a forest of Douglas firs. An occasional opening in the canopy provides a backward look at glacier-clad Porcupine Ridge, as well as views of Citadel Peaks and Mount Cleveland ahead. Finally, the trail makes a brief descent to the floor of the Waterton Valley and meets the Waterton Lake Trail. To reach Goat Haunt, the trail turns south and east, crossing the Waterton River via a suspension bridge and then turning north to the ranger station complex.

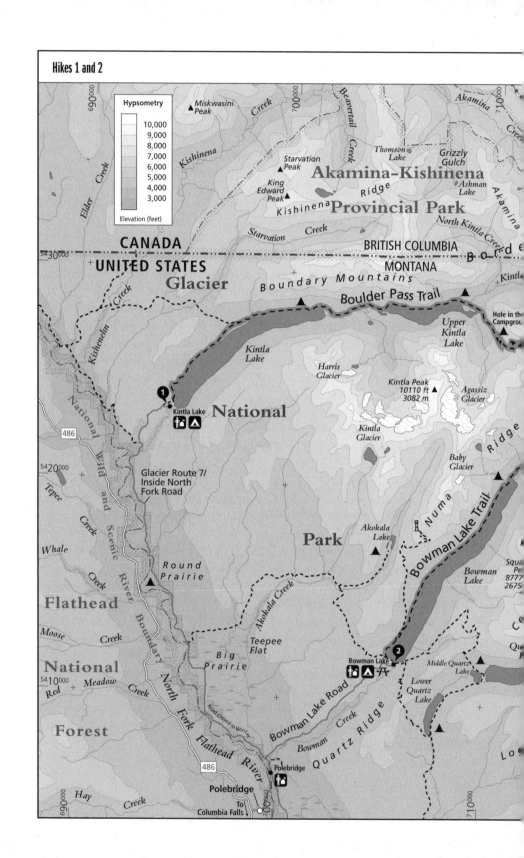

Hikes 1 and 2

Hypsometry

Elevation (feet)

10,000
9,000
8,000
7,000
6,000
5,000
4,000
3,000

Miskwasini Peak

Creek

Kishinena

Starvation Peak

King Edward Peak

Akamina-Kishinena

Thomson Lake

Grizzly Gulch

Ashman Lake

Kishinena Ridge

Provincial Park

North Kintla Creek

Akamina

Creek

Akamina

Beavertrail Creek

Starvation Creek

CANADA

UNITED STATES

Glacier

BRITISH COLUMBIA

MONTANA

Border

Kintl

Boundary Mountains

Boulder Pass Trail

Upper Kintla Lake

Hole in the Campgrou

Kintla Lake

Harris Glacier

Kintla Peak 10110 ft 3082 m

Agassiz Glacier

1

Kintla Lake

National

Kintla Glacier

Baby Glacier

Ridge

Numa

Bowman Lake Trail

Glacier Route 7/ Inside North Fork Road

Akokala Lake

Park

Squa Pe 8777 2675

Bowman Lake

National Wild and Scenic River

Tepee Creek

Whale Creek

Round Prairie

Akokala Creek

Flathead

Moose Creek

Teepee Flat

Bowman Lake

2

Middle Quartz Lake

Qu

Ce

National

Red Meadow Creek

Big Prairie

Bowman Lake Road

Lower Quartz Lake

Forest

Road Closed in Winter

Bowman Creek

Quartz Ridge

Lo

North Fork Flathead River

Polebridge

Polebridge

To Columbia Falls

Hay Creek

Elder Creek

Kishenehn Creek

Boundary Creek

486

486

Kishenehn Creek

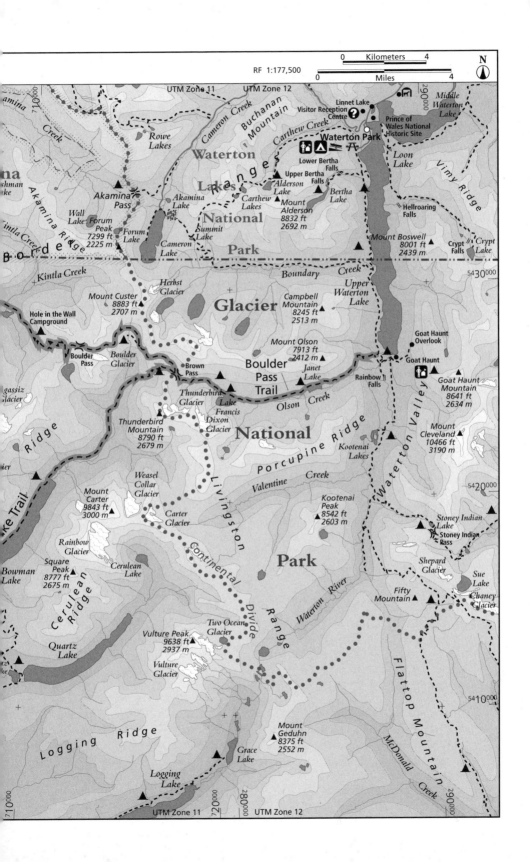

Key Points

0.0 Trail sign. Trail follows shore of Kintla Lake.

4.0 Junction with connecting trail to Kishenehn Ranger Station. Keep right for Boulder Pass Trail.

6.7 Kintla Lake Campground. Trail leaves Kintla Lake; moderate uphill to Upper Kintla Lake.

9.4 Foot of Upper Kintla Lake. Trail follows shore of Upper Kintla Lake.

12.0 Upper Kintla Campground. Trail crosses Kintla Creek and ascends steeply to Boulder Pass Campground.

17.6 Boulder Pass Campground.

18.1 Boulder Pass. Junction campground is 0.1 mile to the left; stay to right for Boulder Pass Trail, which descends moderately steeply into Hole in the Wall.

21.6 Junction with trail into Hole in the Wall Campground (0.5 mile); stay left for Brown Pass.

23.2 Brown Pass. Junction with trail to Bowman Lake. Stay left for trail to Goat Haunt Ranger Station, which descends moderately steeply to Olson Creek.

25.3 Hawksbill Campground. Trail gradually descends through Olson Creek Valley.

25.5 Junction with spur trail to Lake Francis Campground.

28.3 Lake Janet Campground.

31.3 Junction with Waterton Lake Trail. Stay right for Goat Haunt Ranger Station; turn left to Waterton township (8.7 miles).

31.5 Suspension bridge over Waterton River.

31.6 Junction with Rainbow Falls Trail. Stay left for Goat Haunt.

31.8 Goat Haunt Ranger Station.

2 Bowman Lake–Brown Pass

A backpack from Bowman Lake to Brown Pass, 13.8 miles (22 km) one way.

See map on pages 30 and 31.
Elevation gain: 2,200 feet
Maximum elevation: 6,255 feet

Difficulty: Moderately strenuous
Topo maps: Quartz Ridge, Kintla Peak, Mount Carter

Finding the trailhead: Follow Glacier Route 7 north to junction with Bowman Lake Road, just north of Polebridge. Take Bowman Lake Road (a narrow but graded gravel road) to terminus at Bowman Campground. Trail departs from northeast corner of campground, near the lakeshore.

The Hike

The Bowman Lake Trail may be used as a backpack in itself or in conjunction with the Boulder Pass Trail for extended trips. The trail winds past Bowman Lake before ascending a U-shaped valley carved by a glacier between rugged peaks. Ultimately, the trail climbs to Brown Pass, where views of peaks and glaciers can be seen in all directions.

The trail follows the northwestern shore of Bowman Lake for 7 miles of gentle up and down hiking to a backcountry campsite near the head of the lake, popular with hikers and boaters alike. The lake is prime osprey and bald eagle habitat and is frequently closed to boating, fishing, and hiking above the upper campground to protect the nest sites of eagles. Views across the lake include Square Peak, Rainbow Peak, and Mount Carter.

The trail leaves the lakeshore after the upper campground, climbing gently through forest and marsh. The valley is populated with wary herds of elk. The bugling vocalizations of bull elk announcing their presence to females can sometimes be heard echoing off of the cliff walls in late August and early September. About 3 miles beyond the campground, the trail crosses Pocket Creek and Bowman Creek in short order and then continues for another half mile to the base of Brown Pass.

At this point, the trail begins a steep ascent around the north slope of Thunderbird Mountain. Clearings in the forest provide views of Hole in the Wall Falls across the valley and Boulder Peak high above. Halfway to the pass, the forest opens into open brushy meadows with babbling brooks and small waterfalls. Shortly before reaching the pass, the trail passes through the Brown Pass Campground, set among dense stands of subalpine fir. When the trail reaches the pass, you can see the serrated ridge of the Citadel Peaks and the massive bulk of Mount Cleveland by looking east, down the Olson Creek Valley.

Key Points

0.0 Trail sign. Trail follows northwest shore of Bowman Lake.

0.7 Junction with Numa Ridge Lookout Trail. Stay right for Brown Pass.

7.1 Bowman Lake (head) Campground. Trail ascends gently, crossing Pocket and Bowman Creeks, then ascends steeply to Brown Pass.

13.6 Brown Pass Campground.

13.8 Brown Pass. Junction with Boulder Pass Trail.

3 Akokala Lake

A day hike or short backpack from Bowman Campground to Akokala Lake, 5.8 miles (9.5 km) one way.

Elevation gain: 1,105 feet
Elevation loss: 400 feet
Maximum elevation: 5,135 feet

Difficulty: Moderate
Topo maps: Quartz Ridge, Kintla Peak

Finding the trailhead: Take Glacier Route 7 north to Bowman Lake Road turnoff, just north of Polebridge. Take Bowman Lake Road east to terminus at Bowman Campground. Trail departs from north side of campground, away from the lakeshore.

The Hike

Following this trail you'll find a pleasant hike across wooded ridges and valleys to a low-elevation lake surrounded by precipitous peaks. The trail leaves Bowman Campground, climbing through dense forest and swamplands to the ridgeline of Numa Ridge. Along the crest of the ridge, openings were created by recent fires which allowed enough sunlight to reach the forest floor for beargrass and other wildflowers to proliferate.

The trail descends steeply, once again entering dense "doghair" lodgepole stands, until it reaches Akokala Creek. The trail then turns eastward, following the rushing course of the stream upward through more burned areas. The trail rises gently and then levels out shortly before reaching the marshy shores of Akokala Lake and its campsite at the outlet.

A short trip through dense underbrush lands the hiker on the south shore of the lake, with its magnificent view of the peaks beyond. Reuter Peak and the south ridge of Kintla Peak form the northern rim of the valley, while the pointed summit of Mount Peabody can be seen at the valley's head. Numa Ridge rises steeply to the east, overshadowing the southeast shore of the lake. Akokala Lake is frequently murky and is not known for its fishing.

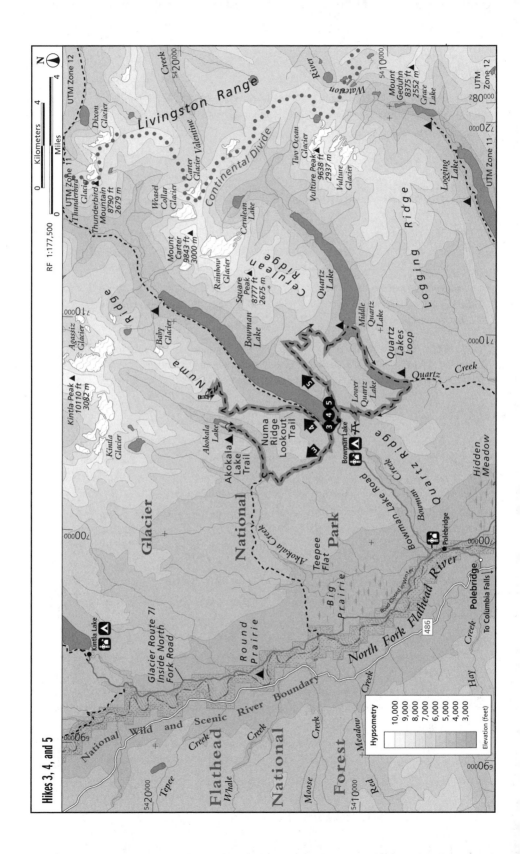

Hikes 3, 4, and 5

Key Points

0.0 Trail sign. Trail ascends Numa Ridge, then descends steeply to Akokala Creek.

3.6 Junction with Akokala Creek Trail. Stay right for Akokala Lake.

5.8 Akokala Lake Campground.

4 Numa Ridge Lookout

A day hike from Bowman Campground to Numa Ridge Lookout, 5.6 miles (9 km) one way.

See map on page 35.
Elevation gain: 2,930 feet
Maximum elevation: 6,960 feet

Difficulty: Moderate
Topo maps: Quartz Ridge, Kintla Peak

Finding the trailhead: Take Glacier Route 7 north to Bowman Lake Road turnoff, just north of Polebridge. Take Bowman Lake Road east to terminus at Bowman Campground. Trail departs from north side of campground, away from the lakeshore.

The Hike

Numa Ridge Lookout is one of the easiest lookouts to reach in the park. The trail climbs 3,000 feet over the course of 5 miles, passing up the forested flanks of Numa Ridge to a swampy saddle, which is good habitat for northern bog lemmings. The trail climbs out of the trees onto an open grassy swale for the last 0.25 mile. Upon reaching the manned lookout, which lies on the west face of Numa Ridge, the hiker will find spectacular views of Square Peak, Rainbow Peak, and Mount Carter across Bowman Lake, plus sweeping vistas of the Whitefish Range across the forested North Fork Flathead River. Akokala Lake and Reuter Peak lie to the north of the lookout. Looking toward the north, you will have excellent views of the 2003 Wedge Canyon burn as well as the older Red Bench Fire, which burned 37,000 acres in 1988. Bring water.

Key Points

0.0 Trail sign. Trail follows shore of Bowman Lake.

0.7 Junction with Numa Ridge Lookout Trail. Stay left for Numa Ridge Lookout. Trail ascends south face of Numa Ridge, then follows ridgeline to lookout.

5.6 Numa Ridge Lookout.

5 Quartz Lakes Loop

A long day hike or short backpack from Bowman Campground to the Quartz Lakes, 6.2 miles (10 km) one way or a 12.8-mile (20.5 km) loop.

See map on page 35.

Elevation gain: 1,470 feet

Elevation loss: 1,100 feet

Maximum elevation: 5,500 feet

Difficulty: Moderate

Topo map: Quartz Ridge

Finding the trailhead: Take Glacier Route 7 north to Bowman Lake Road turnoff, just north of Polebridge. Take Bowman Lake Road east to terminus at Bowman Campground. Trail departs from the southeast corner of the campground, at the backcountry parking area.

The Hike

The Quartz Lakes Loop begins and ends at the Bowman Lake auto campground. It passes over the crest of Cerulean Ridge to drop into the Quartz Creek Valley at Quartz Lake, then turns southwest for 3 miles along the valley floor before climbing back over Quartz Ridge to its starting point. The loop makes for a pleasant day hike, and there are several backcountry camping areas for hikers looking for an overnight experience. The loop can also be accessed via a 7-mile trail that runs up Quartz Creek from the Inside North Fork Road.

After leaving the Bowman Lake Campground, the loop begins as a trunk trail that crosses Bowman Creek at the foot of the lake and winds around the south shore where it rises for 0.4 mile to a fork. The easier route is the left fork, which allows the hiker to hike the loop in a clockwise direction. This fork rises gently for about 2.5 miles to the crest of Cerulean Ridge and then crosses the ridge crest into the Quartz Creek drainage. The trail dips into an area burned in the 1988 Red Bench Fire, where fireweed and grasses are giving way to conifers as the area continues the succession back to forest. The opening of the forest canopy allows views of the rugged outlying mountains of the Livingston Range, including Logging Mountain in the foreground and the taller, more jagged Vulture Peak behind it. The trail descends to a campground at the foot of Quartz Lake, which supports a good population of rainbow and cutthroat trout.

The trail exits this campground from its west side and runs southwest, passing the south shore of shallow Middle Quartz Lake. The trail continues through open forest to the southwest for about a mile before reaching the head of Lower Quartz Lake, which it follows to its foot. At the campground set on both sides of the outlet, the trail forks. The Quartz Creek Trail continues to follow the south bank of the creek to the Inside North Fork Road, while the loop trail crosses the outlet via a trail bridge and turns northward. From this point, the trail climbs through the burn to crest Quartz Ridge, at which point it reenters the forest for a rather steep descent back to the trunk trail, 0.4 mile from the trailhead.

Key Points

0.0 Trail sign. Trail crosses Bowman Creek and ascends gradually along the shore of Bowman Lake.

0.4 Junction with Quartz Lakes Trail. Stay left for Quartz Lake; turn right for Lower Quartz Lake. Trail to the left ascends gradually to ridgeline, then descends moderately steeply to Quartz Lake.

6.2 Quartz Lake Campground. Trail to Lower Quartz Lake departs from the southwest corner of the campground. Trail follows the south shore of Middle Quartz Lake, then descends to Lower Quartz and follows the lakeshore to the outlet stream.

9.3 Lower Quartz Campground. Loop trail crosses the outlet stream to the north. Trail to the southwest follows Quartz Creek to Glacier Route 7 (6.8 miles). Trail crosses Quartz Ridge.

12.4 Trail junction with trunk trail to Bowman Campground. Turn left to return to starting point.

12.8 Return to trailhead.

6 Logging Lake

A day hike or backpack from Glacier Route 7 (Inside North Fork Road) to Logging Lake, 4.4 miles (7 km) one way; or Glacier Route 7 to Grace Lake, 12.8 miles (20.5 km) one way.

Elevation gain: 477 feet
Maximum elevation: 3,930 feet

Difficulty: Easy
Topo maps: Demers Ridge, Vulture Peak

Finding the trailhead: The trailhead is located at the Logging Creek Campground, 20 miles north of the Camas Road junction on the Inside North Fork Road.

The Hike

The Logging Lake Trail follows the course of Logging Creek from the North Fork Flathead River lowlands to its headwaters in the Livingston Range. The trail starts off with a short climb to the top of a densely wooded plateau and then proceeds along the rim of a shallow canyon. Here you enter the area burned in the 2001 Moose Fire and several other smaller fires in the 1990s. As is typical of North Fork trails, this trail provides an easy hike through gentle terrain. Occasionally, the trail ventures near the rim of a small canyon, offering a brief glimpse of Logging Creek below. In accordance with its gentle terrain and mature forests, the trail offers no views of the glacier-carved peaks until it reaches Logging Lake.

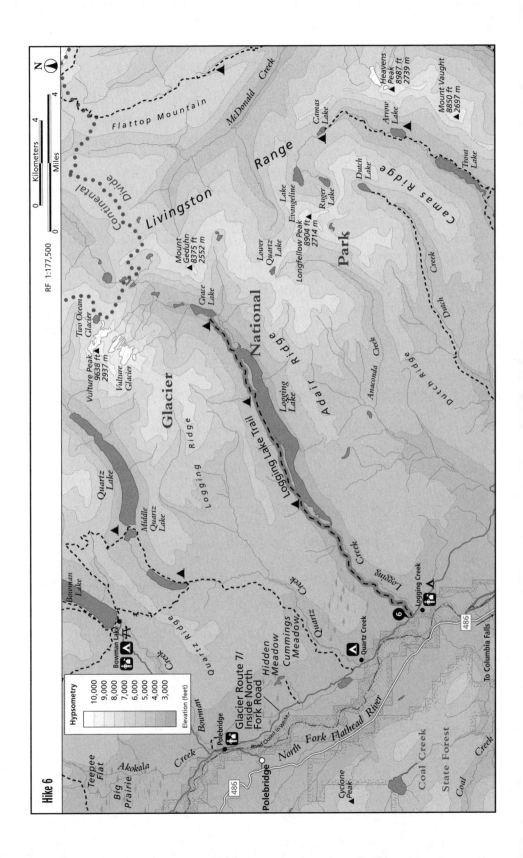

Hike 6

RF 1:177,500

N

Kilometers 0 4

Miles 0 4

Hypsometry

10,000
9,000
8,000
7,000
6,000
5,000
4,000
3,000

Elevation (feet)

Teepee Flat

Big Prairie

Akokala Creek

Bowman Lake

Quartz Lake

Middle Quartz Lake

Bowman Creek

Quartz Ridge

Polebridge

Glacier Route 7/ Inside North Fork Road

Hidden Meadow

Cummings Meadow

Quartz Creek

Quartz Creek

Polebridge

Road Closed in Winter

North Fork Flathead River

Cyclone Peak

486

To Columbia Falls

Coal Creek

Coal Creek

State Forest

Quartz Creek

Logging Creek

486

Logging Creek

6

Anaconda Creek

Dutch Ridge

Dutch Creek

Glacier

Logging Ridge

Logging Lake Trail

Logging Lake

Adair Ridge

Logging Creek

Grace Lake

National

Park

Vulture Peak 9638 ft 2937 m

Two Ocean Glacier

Vulture Glacier

Mount Geduhn 8375 ft 2552 m

Continental Divide

Livingston

Range

Flattop Mountain

McDonald Creek

Lower Quartz Lake

Evangeline Lake

Longfellow Peak 8904 ft 2714 m

Ruger Lake

Camas Lake

Dutch Lake

Arrow Lake

Trout Lake

Camas Ridge

Heavens Peak 9987 ft 2739 m

Mount Vaught 8850 ft 2697 m

The first campground along the trail is about half a mile east of the lake's outlet, on the north shore. This campground, situated on a beautiful little bay, affords the first view of the lake and the peaks that rise at its eastern end. Mount Geduhn and Anaconda Mountain rise at the head of the valley. There is no free-flowing water source near this campground.

Four miles farther along the trail is the next campsite at Adair Creek. The view here is less spectacular, but the creek provides a supply of running water to the campsite. From this point, it is approximately 1.5 miles to the head of the lake. The head of Logging Lake is currently closed to fishing and most other human activity because it is a nesting area for bald eagles. A few fortunate hikers may be treated to the sights and sounds of adult eagles teaching their young to fly, fish, and hunt for food. If you are one of the lucky ones, take care to remain hidden, as eagles are easily disturbed by the presence of humans.

Wildlife is abundant along the entire length of the trail. Deer, squirrels, and even mountain lions inhabit the forested valley, and the call of the loon is frequently heard on Logging Lake.

Grace Lake Option: Grace Lake is about 1.5 miles farther up the trail from the head of Logging Lake, a total of 12.8 miles from the trailhead. Grace Lake is reported to provide the finest fishing in the park, as it supports a large population of healthy west-slope cutthroat trout. This lake is nestled among the peaks of the Livingston Range. Because thick timber surrounds most of the lake, fly casting is a difficult proposition. However, a short bushwhack to the head of the lake provides access to a talus slope with ample casting room for the fisherman. The campsite at Grace Lake is seldom visited and provides solitude for the hardy souls who reach it.—*Matt Cutler*

Key Points

0.0 Trail sign.

4.4 Logging Lake. Trail follows the north shore of the lake.

4.9 Junction with Logging Patrol Cabin Trail (0.2 mile). Stay left.

5.0 Junction with Lower Logging Campground Trail (0.2 mile). Stay left.

9.8 Adair Campground.

11.4 Head of Logging Lake.

12.8 Grace Lake Campground.

Connecting Hikes

Kishenehn Creek trails. A network of primitive trails runs north from the Inside North Fork Road to the Kishenehn patrol cabin and beyond to the Canadian border along the North Fork of the Flathead River. An access trail runs from the Kishenehn Creek Trail across Starvation Creek and Ridge to Kintla Lake. The Kishenehn complex is used primarily for administrative and fire-suppression purposes. The trail from the foot of Kintla Lake to Kishenehn Creek has been abandoned, as has the trail up Starvation Creek. Similarly, the trail from Round Prairie to the foot of Kintla Lake has been abandoned.

An administrative trail up **Akokala Creek** exists between the North Fork Road and the West Lakes Trail (running from Bowman to Akokala Lake). This trail receives a low level of maintenance and is difficult to find in places.

A secondary trail runs along **Quartz Creek** some 7 miles from the Quartz Creek Campground to Lower Quartz Lake. This trail is moderately popular with horse parties.

Dutch Creek complex. The complex of trails between Logging Creek and Dutch Creek has been abandoned. The Dutch Lake Trail was burned over extensively by the Moose Fire in 2001 and the Anaconda Fire in 1999. The fallen trees are generally cut out each year in the fall.

The Lake McDonald Area

L ake McDonald, near the west entrance of Glacier, is the largest body of water in the park. It is 10 miles long and has a maximum depth of 472 feet. The lake's bed was carved out by a huge glacier that filled the entire valley, leaving a characteristic U-shaped basin. Lake McDonald once offered pretty fair fishing for native cutthroat and bull trout, but the movement of lake trout up McDonald Creek from Flathead Lake has decimated the native fish population, and the lake now provides very poor fishing (though not bad for the lake trout!). At the foot of the lake lie the low foothills of the Apgar Range, which burned in the 2003 Robert Fire, and Belton Hills, while the snowcapped peaks of the Continental Divide loom to the east of the lake's head. The country is characterized by low, east–west ridges rising in the east to rugged peaks. Most of the forest on the west side of Lake McDonald was burned in the intense Robert Fire of 2003—the towns of West Glacier and Apgar and the lakeshore residents had to be evacuated as the fire moved eastward.

West Glacier is the western gateway to the park and serves as the rafting hub for that side of the park. Many and varied tourist services are offered at West Glacier, Apgar Village, and Lake McDonald Lodge, including guided horse trips, gas, restaurants, and lodging. Belton Chalets Inc. runs the Sperry Chalet, which can only be reached via foot or horseback along the Gunsight Pass Trail (see the "St. Mary Valley" section). Reservations should be made far in advance for all lodging accommodations. Major car campgrounds are located at Apgar and Avalanche Creek, and these tend to be crowded and noisy. A quieter tents-only campground is located on Sprague Creek near Lake McDonald Lodge. The Going-to-the-Sun

Goats at Gunsight Pass

Road is closed to bicyclists from 11:00 A.M. to 4:00 P.M. over most of its length due to the heavy car traffic on this narrow road during midday.

Hikes in the Lake McDonald area tend to pass through heavy forest, with little opportunity for sweeping views until treeline is reached. Wildlife viewing opportunities are somewhat limited due to the dense vegetation, but mountain lions, deer, and elk all inhabit the forested foothills around Lake McDonald. The high country is home to mountain goats as well as smaller denizens of the talus slopes, including marmots and ground squirrels. Loons and bald eagles are occasionally seen on the glacial lakes that dot the area.

7 Trout Lake

A day hike or backpack from North McDonald Road Trailhead to Trout Lake, 3.5 miles (5.5 km); North McDonald Road to Arrow Lake Campground, 7.0 miles (11 km); North McDonald Road to Camas Lake, 10.6 miles (17 km); or Glacier Route 7 to Camas Lake, 13.9 miles (22.5 km). All distances are one way.

Elevation gain to Camas Lake: 3,150 feet
Elevation loss to Camas Lake: 1,240 feet
Maximum elevation: 5,353 feet

Difficulty: Moderately strenuous
Topo maps: Camas Ridge East, Mount Cannon

Finding the trailhead: Take the Going-to-the-Sun Road 0.5 mile east of Lake McDonald Lodge to the North Lake McDonald Road, which enters from the north. Turn north, and drive across McDonald Creek and around the east side of Lake McDonald. The pavement will end shortly after the McDonald Creek Bridge; continue past the Lake McDonald Ranger Station approximately 0.5 mile to a marked trailhead sign with a wide spot for parking. The Trout Lake Trail begins at this wide spot in the road.

The Hike

The lakes of Camas Creek can be reached by a low-maintenance, often boggy trail up the creek from the Inside North Fork Road (which was heavily burned in the 2001 Moose Fire) or by using a well-maintained cutoff trail that climbs over Howe Ridge to Trout Lake, a route that is 3.4 miles shorter. Horse parties favor the former route because of its low gradient, while hikers generally prefer the latter. Trout Lake and even Arrow Lake are reasonable day hike destinations from the North McDonald Road, and overnighters can camp at backcountry campsites at Arrow and Camas Lakes. Because the trail from Arrow Lake to Camas Lake is quite hard to follow and crosses five major fords, it is recommended only for determined hikers. All waters in the Camas Creek drainage are flyfishing only; use of spinning tackle is strictly prohibited.

The trail begins on the northeast shore of Lake McDonald, from a dirt road that winds part of the way around the north end of the lake. The first 2.5 miles pass through an area heavily burned by the 2003 Robert Fire. It climbs quickly to cross a rushing stream and then ascends the west bank of the stream toward the crest of Howe Ridge. About halfway to the top, the trail passes through an opening dominated by bear grass and serviceberry bushes. From here a backward glance reveals Lake McDonald and the peaks to the south. The trail resumes the climb, passing into the woods en route to the wooded saddle where it meets the Howe Ridge Trail.

After cresting the ridgeline, the trail descends steeply, switching back across the wooded north slope of Howe Ridge. Shortly before reaching the valley floor, the trail intersects with the Camas Creek Trail and turns eastward to the foot of Trout Lake. There is a hitching rail and picnic area at the foot of Trout Lake, and across the

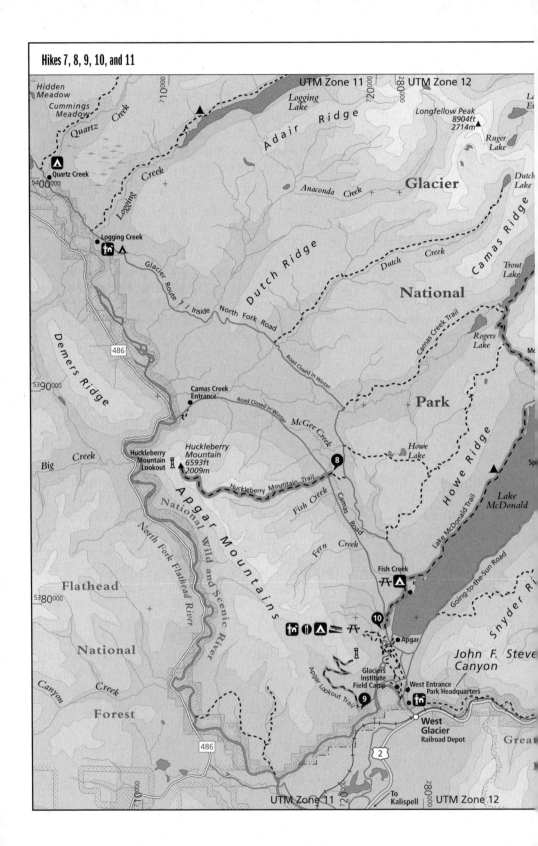

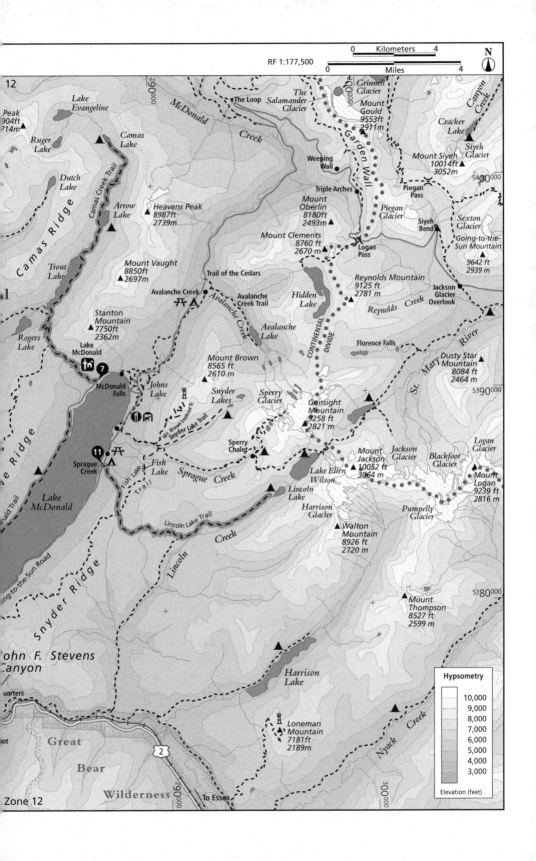

RF 1:177,500

0   Kilometers   4

0   Miles   4

N

Hypsometry

10,000
9,000
8,000
7,000
6,000
5,000
4,000
3,000

Elevation (feet)

Peak
904ft
714m

Lake
Evangeline

Camas
Lake

Ruger
Lake

Dutch
Lake

Arrow
Lake

Heavens Peak
8987ft
2739m

Trout
Lake

Mount Vaught
8850ft
2697m

Rogers
Lake

Lake
McDonald

Stanton
Mountain
7750ft
2362m

Avalanche Creek

Trail of the Cedars

Avalanche
Creek Trail

Avalanche
Lake

Mount Brown
8565 ft
2610 m

Johns
Lake

McDonald
Falls

Snyder
Lakes

Sperry
Glacier

Sprague
Creek

Fish Lake

Lake
McDonald

Sprague Creek

Lincoln
Lake

Lincoln Lake Trail

Lincoln   Creek

Harrison
Glacier

John F. Stevens
Canyon

Snyder Ridge

uarters

Great

Bear

Wilderness

To Essex

Zone 12

McDonald

Creek

Camas Creek Trail

Camas Ridge

The Loop

The
Salamander
Glacier

Grinnell
Glacier

Mount
Gould
9553ft
2911m

Weeping
Wall

Garden Wall

Triple Arches

Mount
Oberlin
8180ft
2493m

Piegan
Glacier

Mount Clements
8760 ft
2670 m

Logan
Pass

Piegan
Pass

Reynolds Mountain
9125 ft
2781 m

Hidden
Lake

CONTINENTAL DIVIDE

Reynolds   Creek

Gunsight
Mountain
9258 ft
2821 m

Mt. Brown Lookout Tr.
Snyder Lake Trail

Sperry
Chalet

Mount
Jackson
10052 ft
3064 m

Jackson
Glacier

Lake Ellen
Wilson

Harrison
Lake

Loneman
Mountain
7181ft
2189m

Cracker
Lake

Siyeh
Glacier

Mount Siyeh
10014ft
3052m

Sexton
Glacier

Siyeh
Bend

Going-to-the-
Sun Mountain
9642 ft
2939 m

Jackson
Glacier
Overlook

St. Mary   River

Florence Falls

Dusty Star
Mountain
8084 ft
2464 m

Blackfoot
Glacier

Logan
Glacier

Mount
Logan
9239 ft
2816 m

Pumpelly
Glacier

Walton
Mountain
8926 ft
2720 m

Mount
Thompson
8527 ft
2599 m

Nyack   Creek

Canyon
Creek

7

11

2

5400 000

5390 000

5380 000

Trout Lake and Heavens Peak

lake the arc of Camas Ridge culminates in Rogers Peak. The trail winds along the forested east shore of Trout Lake—occasional avalanche chutes open views to Stanton Mountain and Mount Vaught—and ascends briefly through Douglas fir forest, with a huckleberry understory, to Arrow Lake. From this lake, McPartland Mountain and Heavens Peak rise to the east.

Camas Lake Option: The trail to Camas Lake can be quite overgrown with head-high cow parsnip by the end of the summer and crosses no less than five major fords along its 3.6-mile length. The trail begins at the campground at the foot of Arrow Lake and immediately fords the outlet to the far bank of Camas Creek. The trail follows the west shore of the lake to its head, where it crosses the inlet stream before continuing across an overgrown meadow. Here, it may be necessary to look for the blaze-orange disks nailed to tree trunks to mark the trail. After leaving the meadow, the trail enters forested bottomland, where it fords Camas Creek again and climbs up its rocky north bank. After surmounting several small hills, the trail emerges into open brush fields, where it descends to the creek and crosses again. These open slopes, overgrown with mountain ash and cow parsnip, dominate the valley as the trail winds around to the northwest toward Camas Lake.

Upon reaching the foot of the lake, the trail crosses its outlet among wet meadows and willow groves before arriving at the forested campground. The entire Camas Valley is prime grizzly bear habitat, so the appropriate precautions should be taken.

The view from Camas Lake is somewhat less than spectacular, consisting of the low, brushy ridges immediately surrounding the lake. From this lake, it is possible to bush-whack (in every sense of the word) westward to the lakes at the head of the valley. Lake Evangeline is said to have outstanding fishing, while Ruger Lake sits at the base of stunning Longfellow Peak. A rock formation on an overlooking spur ridge, locally known as Paul Bunyan's Cabin, overshadows Ruger Lake's western shore.

Key Points

0.0 Trail sign. Trail ascends rather steeply to ridgeline.

2.3 Junction with Howe Ridge Trail. Stay right for Trout Lake. Trail descends to Trout Lake.

3.5 Junction with Camas Creek Trail. Stay right for Trout Lake.

3.6 Trout Lake (foot). Trail follows eastern lakeshore, then ascends gradually to Arrow Lake.

7.0 Arrow Lake Campground. Trail fords Camas Creek to the west shore. Trail follows shore to inlet stream, fords stream, and continues north, up moderate uphill sections and three additional fords, to Camas Lake.

10.6 Camas Lake Campground.

8 Huckleberry Mountain Lookout

A day hike from Camas Creek Road to Huckleberry Lookout, 6.0 miles (9.5 km) one way.

See map on pages 46 and 47.
Elevation gain: 3,403 feet
Maximum elevation: 6,593 feet

Difficulty: Moderately strenuous
Topo maps: McGee Meadow, Huckleberry Mountain

Finding the trailhead: Follow Camas Road northwest out of Apgar. Trailhead is marked on road, about 6 miles northwest of Apgar, on the left.

The Hike

This trail begins near McGee Meadows and climbs steeply up the north bank of McGee Creek through forest before emerging above the trees. The trail continues to climb until it reaches the ridgeline and then turns north, following the crest of the Apgar Mountains for 1.5 miles to the manned lookout.

The slopes below the lookout were burned by a raging wildfire in 1967. The burn site has been colonized by dense stands of lodgepole pines locally known as "doghair." The cones of lodgepoles are serotinous, which means that they remain sealed until the high temperatures of fires melt the seal around the cone, allowing them to open and release the seeds. A few huge larch trees survived the fire by virtue of their thick bark, which peels away from the trunk as it burns, thus protecting the living cambium under the bark from fire damage. The seedlings of both larch and lodgepoles require the open sunlight provided by burned areas to germinate and are known as "fire-adapted" species. From the lookout, the uninterrupted forests of the North Fork Valley stretch away to the foot of the snowcapped Livingston Range, which dominates the eastern skyline.—*Matt Cutler*

Key Points

0.0 Trail sign.

4.5 Turn north following the crest of the Apgar Mountains.

6.0 Huckleberry Mountain Lookout.

9 Apgar Lookout

A half-day hike from Rubideau Road to Apgar Lookout, 2.8 miles (4.5 km) one way.

See map on pages 46 and 47.
Elevation gain: 1,835 feet
Maximum elevation: 5,236 feet

Difficulty: Moderate
Topo map: McGee Meadow

Finding the trailhead: Take the Apgar horse corral road, halfway between West Glacier and Apgar. Follow this road to a Y intersection. Keep left, following the sign to Quarter-Circle Bridge. Cross the bridge and follow the easily passable (road signs to the contrary) road for approximately 1 mile. Turn right at the first opportunity, following the trailhead sign, and follow this road 0.5 mile to the Apgar Lookout Trailhead.

The Hike

This trail provides a short, yet challenging hike that ends with an unusual view of Lake McDonald and the Livingston Range beyond. There are no permanent streams on Apgar Mountain, so water bottles are highly recommended for this trail. The trail starts out as a primitive road, winding across the benchland below Apgar Mountain. Initially, the route runs through forest burned by a ground fire during the Howling Fire of 1994. The blaze burned patchily here; larches in particular were able to survive the fire thanks to their thick, corky bark. Eventually, the road ends, and the trail begins a moderately steep ascent and enters lands that burned with a hot crown fire that consumed the forest almost completely. The path switchbacks across the south face of the hill and affords glimpses through scorched tree trunks of the mountain ranges south of the park. The Flathead Range rises to the southeast, dominated by the snowcapped peak of Great Northern Mountain, the highest peak in the Great

Peaks of the Livingston Range above Lake McDonald

Bear Wilderness. Looking farther west, the Swan Range trails away to the south. In berry season, thimbleberries along the trail provide snacks for hungry hikers, and there are small patches of huckleberry bushes near the lookout.

Once the lookout is reached, the view stretching away to the east reveals the entire length of the Livingston Range, with Lake McDonald prominently nestled among its foothills. The Belton Hills rise steeply at the foot of the lake. Mounts Vaught and Brown are the prominent peaks flanking the upper end of Lake McDonald, and the Garden Wall can be seen at the head of the valley.

Key Points

- **0.0** Trail sign. Trail follows old dirt road.
- **0.8** Trail leaves dirt road, begins ascent of Apgar Mountain.
- **2.8** Apgar Lookout.

10 Lake McDonald

A day hike along the northwest shore of Lake McDonald from the Fish Creek Campground to the head of the lake, 6.6 miles (10.6 km) one way.

See map on pages 46 and 47.
Elevation gain: 160 feet
Elevation loss: 160 feet

Difficulty: Easy
Topo map: Lake McDonald West

Finding the trailhead: From Apgar, follow Camas Road north for 0.8 mile and turn right at the sign for Fish Creek Campground. Follow the Inside North Fork Road past the campground ranger station. As the road turns to gravel, there is a road information sign with a parking area beyond it on the left-hand side. Park here; the hike begins on the opposite side of the road.

The Hike

This relatively obscure and lightly traveled trail follows the roadless northwestern shore of Lake McDonald. Most of the trail is within forest that burned in a hot fire in 2003, with frequent views through the charred snags of the surrounding mountain scenery. Hikers seeking a shorter trip can start at the south end and visit Rocky Point (1.6 miles round-trip), or start from the north end of the trail and hike to the Lake McDonald backcountry camp (4.4 miles round-trip).

After crossing a bridge over Fern Creek, the trail runs through a young forest of lodgepole pine underlain by bear grass. This forest community is typical of postfire coniferous forests in northwestern Montana. The path soon meets a broad trail that begins in the Fish Creek Campground. Follow this wide avenue northeast along the lakeshore to reach a junction with the side trail that runs to a headland known as Rocky Point. This side trip is well worth the effort and ends on an outcrop with superb views up Lake McDonald. The sharp crags above the lake's head are, from left to right, Mount Brown, the Little Matterhorn, Edwards Peak, Gunsight Mountain, and Mount Jackson.

The Lake McDonald Trail makes a stiff climb inland, entering country that burned in 1929 and again during the dry summer of 2003. Young trees grow densely here, competing to become the next dominant members of the forest overstory. The path next emerges from the forest at a pebble beach at mile 1.8; here, Mount Cannon can be seen along with the summits mentioned above. The trail runs close to the shoreline now, revealing glimpses of the turquoise water through the charred snags.

At mile 4.6, a spur trail descends to the Lake McDonald backcountry camp, abandoned after the 2003 Robert Fire. You can look both up and down Lake McDonald from the beach gravels of this point, with views all the way up the McDonald Creek Valley to the Garden Wall. Mounts Stanton and Vaught can now be seen above the north side of the lake.

The main trail continues through the burned forest, swinging inland shortly before joining an old dirt road. The hike follows this route to reach the northern trailhead at the end of the North Shore Road.

Key Points

0.0 Trailhead on Inside North Fork Road.

0.1 Trail crosses Fern Creek.

0.4 Junction with trail from Fish Creek Campground. Bear left.

0.5 Junction with Rocky Point Spur Trail (0.3 mile).

4.6 Spur trail descends to now-abandoned Lake McDonald camp (0.2 mile).

6.6 Trail reaches end of North Shore Road.

11 Lincoln Lake

A long day hike or backpack from Lincoln Lake Trailhead to Lincoln Lake, 8.0 miles (13 km) one way.

See map on pages 46 and 47.
Elevation gain: 2,250 feet
Elevation loss: 800 feet
Maximum elevation: 4,900 feet

Difficulty: Moderately strenuous
Topo maps: Lake McDonald West, Lake McDonald East

Finding the trailhead: Lincoln Lake Trailhead, marked as such by a trail sign on the Going-to-the-Sun Road, approximately 1.5 miles southwest of Lake McDonald Lodge.

The Hike

Lincoln Lake is a low-elevation cirque lake that sits at the foot of 1,344-foot Beaver Chief Falls. It can be reached by an arduous hike over Snyder Ridge from the shores of Lake McDonald or by taking a longer, poorly maintained route up Lincoln Creek from the South Boundary Trail. Views along both routes are minimal until the lake is reached.

The trail begins at a marked trailhead on the Going-to-the-Sun Road and wastes no time in climbing steeply and steadily up forested slopes to the crest of Snyder Ridge. The mossy understory of this forest is home to the pale purple lady's slipper orchid, which can be seen in bloom in early summer. At the crest of the ridge, the trail crosses the Snyder Ridge fire trail and continues to rise gently on wooded benchland. Winding around the south face of a hillside, openings in the trees provide glimpses of the snowcapped Flathead Range to the south of the park. Beargrass, a member of the lily family, dominates the understory of the pine forest on

Lincoln Lake and Beaver Chief Falls

dry sites. This plant blooms on a three- to five-year cycle, and local populations of the plant tend to be synchronized, so that in favorable years, the profusion of bear-grass inflorescences brightens the entire forest. The trail continues to dip and rise as it passes through tiny dales before descending steadily to Lincoln Creek.

Upon reaching the valley floor, the trail enters a series of wet meadows in the forest, on which deer and other animals may be seen in early morning and late evening. The trail running up the creek valley is boggy after snowmelt and becomes quite overgrown with cow parsnip and thimbleberry late in the summer. Brief glimpses of the sheer walls of the valley can be had through the trees along the route to the lake, which is prime black bear habitat.

Upon reaching the lakeshore, the forest opens up to reveal spectacular cliffs on three sides of the lake, with Beaver Chief Falls coursing down the valley's headwall. Above this cirque is a higher cirque containing Lake Ellen Wilson, which was carved out by glaciers after the lower cirque had already been formed. When two or more cirques are superimposed on each other, the resulting geologic feature is called a compound cirque. The campground sits at the foot of the lake, near its shallow outlet. The lake has fair fishing for pan-size cutthroats and larger brook trout.

Key Points

0.0   Trail sign. Trail climbs steeply to ridgeline.

1.7 Junction with Snyder Ridge Trail. Stay straight for Lincoln Lake. Trail descends moderately to Lincoln Creek.

4.4 Junction with Lincoln Creek Trail. Turn left for Lincoln Lake. Trail ascends gently to Lincoln Lake.

8.0 Lincoln Lake Campground.

12 Fish Lake

A half-day hike from Snyder Creek Trailhead to Fish Lake, 2.3 miles (3.9 km) one way.

Elevation gain: 1,000 feet
Maximum elevation: 4,150 feet

Difficulty: Moderate
Topo map: Lake McDonald East

Finding the trailhead: Snyder Creek Trailhead, across the Going-to-the-Sun Road from Lake McDonald Lodge.

The Hike

Fish Lake provides a pleasant hike across wooded ridges to a quiet, reedy lake nestled among tall conifers. The trail follows Snyder Creek for 2 miles, climbing steadily through dense forests, with cedars, hemlocks, and larches of the lower elevations giving way to white pines and Douglas firs. The trail crosses Snyder Creek at mile 2, and the Fish Creek Trail branches off to the west immediately on the west bank of the creek. From this point, the trail ascends slightly to crest wooded benches, winding through a mossy forest to Fish Lake. The lake itself is set in a small forested pocket in Snyder Ridge, from which only the surrounding forest can be seen. Loons are commonly sighted on this small lake, which makes an ideal picnic spot. The Snyder Ridge Trail (poorly maintained) continues west from Fish Lake for 8 miles, eventually returning to the Going-to-the-Sun Road shortly above the foot of Lake McDonald.

Key Points

0.0 Snyder Creek Trailhead.

0.1 Trail sign beyond stables. Stay right for Fish Lake. Trail ascends moderately, following Snyder Creek.

1.7 Junction with Mount Brown Lookout Trail. Stay right for Fish Lake.

1.8 Trail junction with Snyder Lakes Trail. Stay right for Fish Lake. Trail crosses Snyder Creek.

1.9 Junction with Snyder Ridge Trail. Turn right for Fish Lake. Trail turns west along benches of Snyder Ridge.

2.3 Fish Lake.

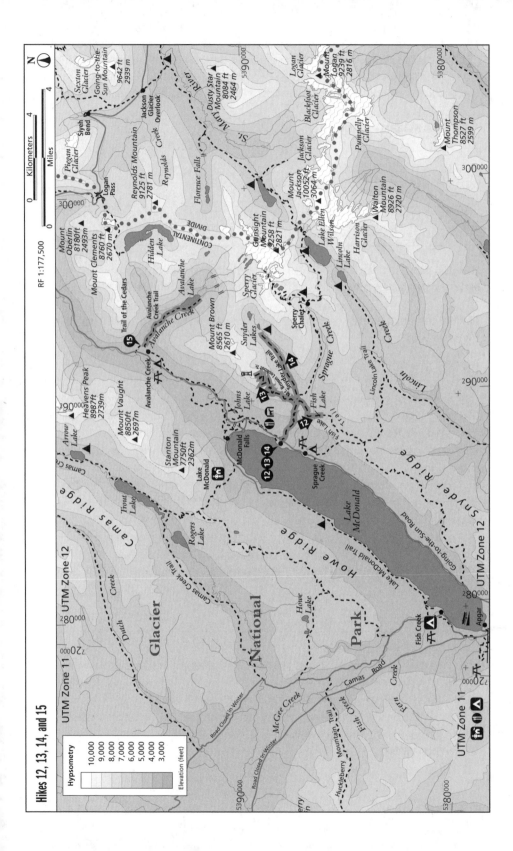

Hikes 12, 13, 14, and 15

RF 1:177,500

Hypsometry

10,000
9,000
8,000
7,000
6,000
5,000
4,000
3,000

Elevation (feet)

13 Mount Brown Lookout

A day hike from Snyder Creek Trailhead to Mount Brown Lookout, 5.4 miles (8.5 km) one way.

See map on page 56.
Elevation gain: 4,305 feet
Maximum elevation: 7,487 feet

Difficulty: Strenuous
Topo maps: Lake McDonald East, Mount Cannon

Finding the trailhead: Snyder Creek Trailhead, marked with a trailhead sign on the Going-to-the-Sun Road, immediately across from the Lake McDonald Lodge coffee shop.

The Hike

The trail to the Mount Brown Lookout is one of the steepest and most grueling trails in the park. It climbs to a fire lookout on a false summit of the peak, affording an unusual view of Lake McDonald and the mountains in the vicinity of Sperry Glacier. The trail begins in the cedar and larch lowlands near Lake McDonald and climbs

Unnamed spire guarding the eastern side of Snyder Creek Valley

up Snyder Creek into a forest dominated by Douglas fir. At mile 1.7, the lookout trail climbs steeply to the north, beginning a steady, leg-burning ascent up switchbacks toward the summit. As the trail climbs upward, it passes through subalpine firs and huckleberry patches higher up before emerging onto an open ridgeline shortly before the lookout. The Park Service has placed a booklet on the history of the fire lookout on the catwalk outside, as well as a log book for hikers to record their own impressions. To the northeast along the ridgeline lies the Little Matterhorn, while the large mountain farther south is Edwards Mountain. The summit of Mount Brown lies 1 mile to the north and can only be reached by a technical ascent.

Key Points

0.0 Snyder Creek Trailhead.

0.1 Trail sign beyond stables. Stay right for Mount Brown Lookout. Trail climbs moderately, following Snyder Creek.

1.7 Junction with Mount Brown Lookout Trail. Turn left for Mount Brown Lookout. Trail switchbacks steeply up the flanks of Mount Brown.

5.4 Mount Brown Lookout.

14 Snyder Lakes

A day hike or short backpack from Snyder Creek Trailhead to Snyder Lake, 4.4 miles (7 km) one way.

See map on page 56.
Elevation gain: 2,047 feet
Maximum elevation: 5,230 feet

Difficulty: Moderate
Topo maps: Lake McDonald West, Lake McDonald East, Mount Cannon

Finding the trailhead: Snyder Creek Trailhead, a marked trailhead on the Going-to-the-Sun Road, immediately across from the Lake McDonald Lodge coffee shop.

The Hike

This trail provides a nice medium-distance day hike or short backpack from Lake McDonald Lodge. From the trailhead, the hiker moves through tall cedars into a higher forest of Douglas fir and larch. The trail follows Snyder Creek eastward. At mile 1.8, the Snyder Lake Trail turns northeast, following Snyder Creek, while the main trail crosses the creek and continues southeastward to Sprague Creek.

The Snyder Lake Trail winds upward gently, through boggy openings, mountain ash thickets, and stands of Douglas fir and subalpine fir. Early in the year, this section of the trail can be quite muddy; waterproof boots are a must. After 2.5 miles, the trail reaches a campground at the outlet of Snyder Lake. This lake is inhabited by cutthroat trout. Upper Snyder Lake is accessible by bushwhacking up the talus slope on the west side of the cliff at the head of the lake and then scrambling up one of the narrow gullies that pierces the cliff at this point. The lakes are set beneath the soaring cliffs of Mount Brown, the Little Matterhorn, and Edwards Mountain. The cliffs are discolored by patches of green and black crustose lichens, fascinating organisms that incorporate separate fungus and algae organisms into one functional unit. On the far side of the Little Matterhorn lies the Avalanche Basin and Sperry Glacier high above it.

Key Points

0.0 Snyder Creek Trailhead.

0.1 Trail sign, beyond stables. Stay right for Snyder Lakes. Trail ascends moderately, following Snyder Creek.

1.7 Junction with Mount Brown Lookout Trail. Stay right for Snyder Lakes.

1.8 Junction with Snyder Lake Trail. Turn left for Snyder Lakes. Trail ascends gently to Snyder Lake.

4.4 Snyder Lake.

15 Avalanche Lake

A half-day hike from Avalanche Creek Trailhead to Avalanche Lake, 3.1 miles (4.4 km) one way.

See map on page 56.
Elevation gain: 505 feet
Maximum elevation: 3,905 feet

Difficulty: Easy
Topo map: Mount Cannon

Finding the trailhead: Trail of the Cedars Trailhead, across the Going-to-the-Sun Road from Avalanche Creek Campground.

The Hike

The Avalanche Lake Trail is one of the most popular hikes in the park, due to its gentle grade and spectacular destination. Hikers seeking solitude should go elsewhere, as throngs of bear bell–bedecked tourists are a given at the height of the season.

The hike begins at the Trail of the Cedars, a wheelchair-accessible boardwalk that winds between the boles of huge cedars and cottonwoods to Avalanche Gorge. The gorge was formed by the force of the stream cutting down through argillite beds, forming fantastic bowls and chutes in the rock. The spray from small waterfalls provides the moisture needed to sustain the profusion of mosses that drape the rocks surrounding the gorge. Water ouzels are commonly seen flying along the water-course and occasionally diving into the churning water, to emerge unharmed and execute "pushups" on the rocks along the stream.

The trail follows the west rim of the gorge, through stands of western hemlock, identified by its drooping topmost leader. This tree is limited to areas of high rainfall, as are the cedars below. The trail winds upward through the forest, following the course of Avalanche Creek. Across the valley to the northeast, the valley of Hidden Creek joins the Avalanche Creek Valley. The trail continues upward through sparse timber and dense underbrush until it reaches the foot of the lake.

Avalanche Lake is rimmed by steep cliffs on three sides. Bearhat Mountain forms the east wall of the valley, while the west wall is formed by Mount Brown. To the south, at the head of the valley, numerous waterfalls cascade downward from the hanging cirque valley formed by Sperry Glacier, which cannot be seen from the lake.

The trail continues around the western shore of the lake to its inlet, where fair fishing for native westslope cutthroats can be had (possession limit is two). Looking north from the head of the lake, Heavens Peak is beautifully framed by the walls of the Avalanche Creek Valley.

Key Points

0.0 Trail of the Cedars boardwalk.

0.3 Trail leaves boardwalk and crosses Avalanche Creek. Junction with Avalanche Creek Trail. Turn left for Avalanche Lake.

2.3 Avalanche Lake (foot).

3.1 Avalanche Lake (head).

Additional Hikes

The **Huckleberry Mountain Trail** is a self-guiding loop that leaves from a parking area on the south side of the Camas Road, just east of the Camas Entrance Station. It originally visited the 1967 burn at the foot of Huckleberry Mountain, but the area was burned over by the Moose Fire of 2001. A pamphlet available at the trailhead sheds light on the ecology of forest regeneration that follows a fire.

The **Camas Creek Trail** is a lightly maintained trail that runs for 7 miles through meadows of tall forbs and grasses and Douglas fir woodlands to Trout Lake. Although the trail is quite brushy in places, it is the favored route for horse parties accessing the Camas Creek Valley.

The **Howe Lake Trail** begins at mile 7.3 of the Inside North Fork Road and winds 2 miles to marshy Howe Lake, where a lucky hiker might encounter both moose and beaver. The trail continues 1.8 miles to connect with the Howe Ridge Trail. The Howe Ridge Trail is a secondary fire-access trail that follows a wooded ridgeline eastward from the Howe Creek bridge to its junction with the Trout Lake Trail, above Kelly Camp Trailhead.

There is an unmaintained trail that runs from mile 3.4 of the Camas Road up the south bank of **Fern Creek** for 3 miles, through a mixed forest of larch and Douglas fir. The trail is difficult to find in places and therefore not recommended for hiking.

McDonald Creek has a gentle trail following its course on each side from the east end of the lake. The west bank trail runs from the automobile bridge over upper McDonald Creek along the creek for 3.4 miles, passing above Sacred Dancing Cascades in its shallow limestone canyon. Another trail runs from the Snyder Creek Trailhead for 5.8 miles to Avalanche Creek Campground. The trail passes diminutive Johns Lake as it winds through the woodland, out of sight of creek and road. Until the trail reaches the McDonald Creek horse bridge, it is frequented by horse parties from the Lake McDonald trail guide operation.

The **Snyder Ridge Trail** runs from mile 4 of the Going-to-the-Sun Road, along the wooded ridge past a junction with the Lincoln Lake Trail, to Fish Lake and beyond to Snyder Creek. The trail is well-maintained only between the Lincoln Lake Trail and Snyder Creek.

A poorly maintained trail runs from the South Boundary Trail up **Lincoln Creek** to a junction with the Lincoln Lake Trail. This trail is very brushy and has no views to recommend it.

The Highline and Waterton Lake Vicinity

The Highline Trail runs along the Continental Divide for almost 20 miles from Logan Pass to Fifty Mountain Campground, where it joins the Waterton Valley Trail in its descent to Goat Haunt Ranger Station on Upper Waterton Lake. For most of its length, the trail runs through alpine meadows, with snowy crags rising on all sides. Wildflower enthusiasts will find the meadows along the trail bursting with a profusion of blossoms throughout the summer. The high, open slopes above the trail provide the finest wildlife-viewing opportunities in the park. Bighorn sheep and mountain goats skirt the bases of towering cliffs, while marmots and pikas scramble around on boulder fields. Colonies of Columbia ground squirrels in the open meadows provide hours of entertainment for travelers who watch the cavorting antics of these social rodents.

Farther north, the Waterton River Valley boasts the best moose habitat in the park. Trails from Waterton Lake connect with short day-hiking opportunities as well as longer hikes in Waterton Lakes National Park in Canada. The North Fork area can be reached via the Boulder Pass Trail, providing options for extended backpacks into the northwestern corner of the park.

The Highline itself is closed to horse traffic from Logan Pass to Granite Park, but a trail along the crest of Flattop Mountain allows horse parties access to the Fifty Mountain area. You can also access Granite Park from the Packer's Roost Trailhead. There are major visitor centers at the north end of the Highline. A number of trails connect the Highline with the North Fork, Belly River, and Many Glacier areas, making the Highline a central component of many extended backcountry expeditions. With this in mind, the campground at Granite Park is

Going-to-the-Sun Road Tunnel near Logan Pass PHOTO BY MONICA BAER

generally reserved during July and August for backpackers with extended itineraries. Granite Park Chalet is equipped with a woodstove and pallets for sleeping and can be reserved at park visitor centers for a small fee.

16 Hidden Lake

A half-day hike from Logan Pass to Hidden Lake Overlook, 1.5 miles (3.5 km) one way; or from Logan Pass to Hidden Lake, 3.0 miles (5 km) one way.

Elevation gain: 550 feet
Elevation loss: 675 feet
Maximum elevation: 7,050 feet

Difficulty: Moderate
Topo maps: Logan Pass, Mount Cannon

Finding the trailhead: Trail begins immediately behind Logan Pass Visitor Center.

The Hike

The trail to Hidden Lake provides one of the quickest access routes to the high country in Glacier Park. It starts as a boardwalk that climbs moderately through

Hidden Lake PHOTO BY MONICA BAER

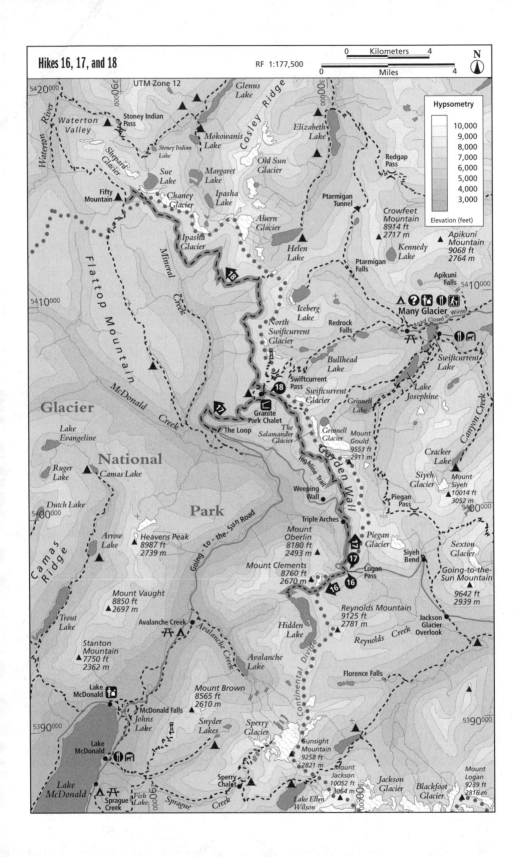

RF 1:177,500

Kilometers

Miles

N

UTM Zone 12

Hypsometry

10,000
9,000
8,000
7,000
6,000
5,000
4,000
3,000

Elevation (feet)

Waterton River

Waterton Valley

Glenns Lake

Stoney Indian Pass

Cosley Ridge

Mokowanis Lake

Elizabeth Lake

Redgap Pass

Stoney Indian Lake

Old Sun Glacier

Shepard Glacier

Sue Lake

Margaret Lake

Ptarmigan Tunnel

Crowfeet Mountain
8914 ft
2717 m

Kennedy Lake

Apikuni Mountain
9068 ft
2764 m

Fifty Mountain

Chaney Glacier

Ipasha Lake

Ipasha Glacier

Aliern Glacier

Helen Lake

Ptarmigan Falls

Apikuni Falls

Mineral Creek

Flattop Mountain

Iceberg Lake

North Swiftcurrent Glacier

Redrock Falls

Many Glacier

Road Closed in Winter

Swiftcurrent Lake

18

Bullhead Lake

Glacier

McDonald Creek

Swiftcurrent Pass

18

Swiftcurrent Glacier

Grinnell Lake

Lake Josephine

Lake Evangeline

National

17

Granite Park Chalet

The Loop

The Salamander Glacier

Grinnell Glacier

Mount Gould
9553 ft
2911 m

Canyon Creek

Cracker Lake

Ruger Lake

Camas Lake

Highline Trail

Garden Wall

Siyeh Glacier

Mount Siyeh
10014 ft
3052 m

Dutch Lake

Park

Weeping Wall

Piegan Pass

Arrow Lake

Camas Ridge

Heavens Peak
8987 ft
2739 m

Going-to-the-Sun Road

Triple Arches

Mount Oberlin
8180 ft
2493 m

Piegan Glacier

Sexton Glacier

Siyeh Bend

Going-to-the-Sun Mountain
9642 ft
2939 m

Mount Vaught
8850 ft
2697 m

Mount Clements
8760 ft
2670 m

17

16

16

Logan Pass

Trout Lake

Avalanche Creek

Hidden Lake

Reynolds Mountain
9125 ft
2781 m

Jackson Glacier Overlook

Stanton Mountain
7750 ft
2362 m

Avalanche Lake

Reynolds Creek

Lake McDonald

Mount Brown
8565 ft
2610 m

Continental Divide

Florence Falls

McDonald Falls

Johns Lake

Snyder Lakes

Sperry Glacier

Lake McDonald

Sperry Chalet

Gunsight Mountain
9258 ft
2821 m

Mount Jackson
10052 ft
3064 m

Jackson Glacier

Blackfoot Glacier

Mount Logan
9289 ft
2816 m

Lake McDonald

Sprague Creek

Fish Lake

Sprague Creek

Lake Ellen Wilson

fields of wildflowers to Hidden Lake Pass, in the shadow of Clements Mountain. From the pass, Reynolds Mountain dominates the southern skyline, while Bearhat Mountain rises on the far side of islet-strewn Hidden Lake. A third of a mile farther is an overlook point, from which the trail descends almost 700 feet to the north shore of the lake, which is reputed to contain large but wary cutthroat trout. A mountaineers' route begins at the south end of the lake, skirting the base of the cliffs along the Continental Divide and then dropping into Floral Park and crossing below the Sperry Glacier to Comeau Pass.

Key Points

0.0 Trail sign.

1.4 Hidden Lake Pass.

1.5 Hidden Lake Overlook. Trail descends fairly steeply to Hidden Lake.

3.0 Hidden Lake.

17 The Garden Wall

A long day hike or extended backpack from Logan Pass to Granite Park Chalet, 7.6 miles (12 km) one way; or from Logan Pass to the Loop on Going-to-the-Sun Road, 11.6 miles (18.5 km) one way.

See map on page 66.
Elevation gain: 830 feet
Elevation loss: 3,026 feet
Maximum elevation: 7,280 feet

Difficulty: Easy
Topo maps: Logan Pass, Many Glacier, Ahern Pass

Finding the trailhead: Trail begins at Logan Pass, across the highway from the visitor center. Exit point is "the Loop," the large hairpin turn on Going-to-the-Sun Road, about 7 road miles west of the pass.

The Hike

The Garden Wall section of the Highline Trail is one of the most popular hikes in the park, owing to its spectacular vistas, excellent wildlife-viewing opportunities, and low level of difficulty. The trail follows the west face of the Continental Divide, maintaining a relatively constant elevation, to Granite Park Chalet, which is currently being offered to hikers as a no-frills shelter. The campground at Granite Park is limited to backpackers on extended trips for most of the season. From Granite Park, the trail leads down to the Going-to-the-Sun Road, terminating at "the Loop," the northernmost hairpin turn on the highway. A spur trail also leads from this trail to "Packer's Roost," farther down the mountainside.

Hoary marmot PHOTO BY MONICA BAER

The Highline Trail crosses excellent habitat for many types of wildlife, and the open subalpine meadows of the Garden Wall allow easy viewing of wild creatures in their natural environments. Columbia ground squirrels abound in the alpine tundra areas, and hoary marmots and pikas are frequently seen among the boulders of talus slopes below cliff faces. Look for mountain goats and bighorn sheep near the bases of the cliffs and among stands of fir. Raptors are commonly seen soaring on thermals high above the alpine meadows, hunting for rodents. The campground at Granite Park is frequented by mule deer, many with impressive racks that remain in velvet throughout the summer. Please do not feed the wildlife in the interest of keeping it wild.

The trail begins at Logan Pass, winding through the twisted forms of subalpine firs and Engelmann spruce. Strong prevailing winds in wintertime blow ice particles that tear the branches from the windward side of the trees, creating a flaglike appearance. In areas of especially high wind, all branches exposed above the snowline may be pruned by windblown ice, creating a low, matlike growth form called *krummholtz* in adult spruce and firs.

After several hundred yards, the trail winds around a sheer cliff face, high above the valley below. The trail continues northward through open stands of fir, following in the shadow of the Garden Wall. This land form was created by the action of glaciers moving down valleys on both sides of a mountain mass. The resulting knife-edge ridge is called an arête. Across the valley, Mounts Oberlin, Clements, and Cannon cradle a high hanging basin formed by glaciers, from which Bird Woman Falls cascades hundreds of feet to the valley floor. The trail emerges into alpine tundra spangled with wildflowers, past gushing rills with their staircase cascades. The trail climbs gently to pass behind Haystack Butte, a rounded promontory jutting into the Logan Creek Valley, which makes an ideal lunch spot. Golden-mantled ground squirrels, identified by the alternating stripes of black and blond on their backs, inhabit the slopes around Haystack Butte.

As the trail winds northward beyond Haystack Butte, it crosses barren, rocky slopes interspersed with mountain meadows. At mile 6.8, the trail to the Grinnell Glacier Overlook enters from the east. This trail is 0.8 mile long and fairly steep, running upward to a high notch in the Garden Wall that overlooks Grinnell Glacier on the east side of the divide. From the terminus of the spur trail, a goat trail winds around to the right, passing along the eastern face of the Garden Wall to a narrow notch that affords a superior view of the glacier.

The Highline Trail continues northward for less than 1 mile, reaching a trail junction at Granite Park Chalet. Views from the chalet include Heavens Peak immediately across the valley, as well as other snowcapped peaks of the Livingston Range trailing away to the north.

From Granite Park Chalet, trails branch off in many directions, offering interesting day trips and backpacking possibilities. To the west, the connecting trail descends past the campground trail junction to switchback down through burned patches of trees from the Trapper Creek Fire of 2003 to reach the Loop, the northern terminus for most hikers. The eastern fork becomes the northern continuation of the Highline Trail, from which routes to Swiftcurrent Pass and Lookout branch after 0.2 mile. Swiftcurrent Lookout provides a sweeping view of the Swiftcurrent drainage, as well as views to the west, after a challenging climb rising 1,000 feet over 2.3 miles. Swiftcurrent Pass is a low saddle with no particularly scenic views until the hiker is descending, which provides trail access to the Many Glacier area.

Key Points

0.0 Trail sign.

3.4 Saddle behind Haystack Butte.

6.8 Junction with Grinnell Glacier Overlook Trail (0.8 mile, maximum elevation 7,600 feet, moderately strenuous). Stay left for Granite Park.

7.6 Granite Park Chalet. Junction with trails leading to Swiftcurrent Pass (0.9 mile, moderate), Swiftcurrent Lookout (2.3 miles, moderately strenuous), and the northern Highline Trail. Turn left for the Loop.

7.8 Junction with Granite Park Campground Trail. Stay left for the Loop.

11.4 Junction with Loop Cutoff Trail. Turn left for the Loop.

11.6 Trail exit at the Loop.

18 The Northern Highline

An extended backpack from Granite Park to Fifty Mountain Campground, 11.9 miles (19 km) one way.

See map on page 66.
Elevation gain: 1,910 feet
Elevation loss: 1,780 feet

Maximum elevation: 7,440 feet
Difficulty: Moderate
Topo map: Ahern Pass

Finding the trailhead: Granite Park Chalet, reached via Logan Pass or "the Loop," the large hairpin turn on Going-to-the-Sun Road, about 7 miles west of the pass; or Fifty Mountain Campground, via Goat Haunt Ranger Station, which is reached by ferry from Waterton townsite or by trail along the western shore of Waterton Lake.

The Hike

The northern section of the Highline Trail is accessible only to hikers on extended trips of more than one night. It runs from Granite Park Chalet to Fifty Mountain Campground, connecting the Garden Wall Trail and the Many Glacier complex with trails out of Goat Haunt on Waterton Lake. The trail stays high in the subalpine country throughout its entire length, and sublime views can be had at any point along the trail. The forests below were burned in 2003 during the Trapper Creek Fire, which cleared the conifers to make way for a profusion of wildflowers.

The trail begins by passing around the east side of the chalet and quickly winds around a meadowy spur ridge and out of sight. Meadows along the trail contain glacier lilies, mountain asters, shooting stars, and Indian paintbrushes at different times of the summer. To the west, the peaks of the Livingston Range are constant companions to the hiker as the trail runs to the north. To the southwest lies Heavens Peak, while Longfellow Peak is the large mountain farther to the north and behind it. Several miles out from the chalet, the trail rounds a rocky knob and turns eastward briefly, hugging the cliff wall. A persistent snowdrift in this area makes early-season travel on this section hazardous, if not impossible. The rocky basin beyond is prime habitat for mountain goats and hoary marmots, who graze together in the meadows below the cliff walls.

As the trail reaches the north end of the basin, another trail cuts off to the east, traveling 0.4 mile to the low saddle of Ahern Pass. From the vicinity of the pass, the Ahern Glacier can be seen clinging to the southeast face of Ipasha Peak, with waterfalls cascading down the cliff face below it into Helen Lake. A mountaineers' route exists to the Iceberg Notch, immediately above the pass; and from the notch seasoned climbers may tempt the fates by passing along a narrow goat trail that hugs the face of Iceberg Peak above several thousand feet of vertical exposure.

Continuing northward from Ahern Pass, the Northern Highline begins a long, gradual descent through open forests of subalpine firs dotted with wildflowers toward Cattle Queen Creek. A hazardous snowslip exists where the trail crosses this creek and may not melt away until late July. Proceed with caution while crossing snowy slopes, as slipping or falling through spells certain injury and may even be fatal. The Cattle Queen Valley is rather brushy, with forbidding walls on both sides. From this creek, the trail begins a long and steady ascent, covering almost 2,000 feet in 4 miles. The trail continues upward beyond the timberline, winding through rocky meadows populated with ground squirrels and songbirds.

A mile before reaching Fifty Mountain Campground, the trail reaches its highest point as it passes over a rocky saddle in a scree slope wasteland. The snowcapped peaks of the Livingston Mountains stretch away as far as the eye can see to the west and south, while Mount Kipp overlooks the trail to the east. The rocky ridge with serpentine snowfields on its face is Trapper Peak, with pyramid-shaped Mount Geduhn behind it to the south. The horn peak to the south of Geduhn is Anaconda Peak. The saddle also offers a fine vantage point for viewing the Flattop Mountain burn of 1998. This fire was started by a series of lightning strikes and burned in a patchy mosaic across the timberline woodland atop Flattop Mountain to the west.

Just north of this saddle, a spur trail ascends steeply to a notch that overlooks Sue Lake and the glacier-clad summits of the Mokowanis River Valley. The main trail descends into the forest fringe that occupies the edge of the high shelf below, where it enters Fifty Mountain Campground. The Flattop Mountain Fire burned into the campground in 1998, clearing the area of subalpine firs. Please do not feed the wildlife, as feeding encourages the animals to scavenge for human refuse instead of foraging for their natural foods. Deer and mountain goats are particularly fond of salt, which is lacking in their high-altitude diets. Secure all sweaty clothing and gear out of their reach, and use the pit toilet provided at the campground when nature calls. Trails from the campground descend to the west to Flattop Mountain and to the north to Goat Haunt Ranger Station.

Key Points

0.0 Trail sign, Granite Park Chalet.

0.2 Junction with Swiftcurrent Pass Trail. Stay left for the Northern Highline.

0.5 Junction with Granite Park Campground Trail. Stay right for the Northern Highline.

4.5 Junction with Ahern Pass Trail (0.4 mile, easy). Stay left for Fifty Mountain.

6.5 Trail reaches its lowest elevation as it crosses Cattle Queen Creek.

10.9 Junction with Sue Lake Overlook Trail (0.4 mile, maximum elevation 7,700 feet, strenuous). Stay left for Fifty Mountain.

11.9 Fifty Mountain Campground.

19 Waterton Valley

A half-day hike or short backpack from Goat Haunt Ranger Station to Kootenai Lakes, 2.8 miles (4.5 km) one way; or a backpack from Goat Haunt to Fifty Mountain Campground, 10.5 miles (17 km) one way.

Elevation gain to mountain: 2,480 feet
Maximum elevation: 7,000 feet
Difficulty: Easy (to Kootenai Lakes); strenuous (to Fifty Mountain)

Topo maps: Porcupine Ridge, Mount Geduhn, Ahern Pass

Finding the trailhead: Goat Haunt Ranger Station, reached by ferry from Waterton townsite, or by trail along the western shore of Upper Waterton Lake. The trailhead is located next to the stables, south of the ranger station.

The Hike

The Waterton Valley Trail links Goat Haunt Ranger Station, at the head of Upper Waterton Lake, to the high alpine country of the Highline Trail. It offers an easy stroll through the forest on the valley floor to the Stoney Indian Pass junction, then begins a steep, seemingly endless climb across an open, brushy slope to the Fifty Mountain Campground. Kootenai Lakes provide a popular day hike destination for anglers and wildlife viewers from Goat Haunt. The lakes also offer backcountry campsites for a short-range, easy backpack. Increased border security has made backcountry entry into Glacier from Canada more challenging; only U.S. or Canadian citizens are allowed to make the border crossing using this trail.

The trailhead for the Waterton Valley Trail is behind the stable area in the Goat Haunt Ranger Station complex. After leaving the paved walkways and buildings behind, the trail passes beneath a canopy of large old-growth conifers interrupted by an occasional wet meadow. At mile 2.5 there is a junction with the Kootenai Lakes Trail, which runs 0.3 mile to a campground at the foot of the lower lake. These shallow lakes provide good fishing for large brook trout, and the willows that crowd the shores provide a favored food source for the moose that are frequently seen here. Forested areas provide prime habitat for black bears. The lakes are overlooked to the west by the Citadel Peaks, the rocky spires at the tail end of Porcupine Ridge.

The main valley trail continues southward, rising imperceptibly at first and then climbing into broken hillsides before reaching the junction with the Stoney Indian Pass Trail. Near this junction, groves of old-growth spruce grow at the fringes of grassy meadows. About 1 mile above this junction, the trail begins to climb in

Moose at Kootenai Lakes ▶

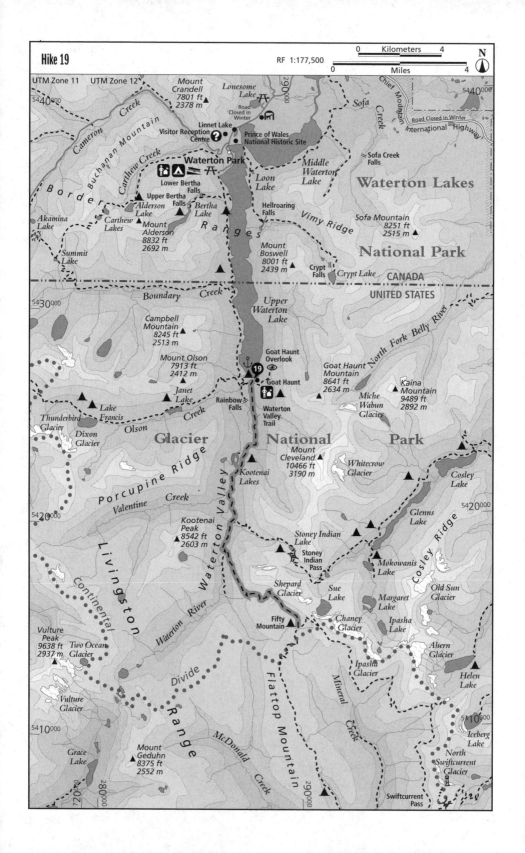

earnest, passing high above the rushing torrent of the Waterton River. The trail switchbacks as it climbs out of the forest and onto a hot, west-facing slope covered with cow parsnip and brushy vegetation. For 3 miles the trail winds upward, testing the endurance of the most seasoned hiker. The trail passes above a lonely stand of conifers and continues climbing into an alpine parkland below Cathedral Peak, where glacier lilies nod their yellow heads just after snowmelt.

The trail finally reaches its highest point as it passes the ruins of a stone shelter hut, which was never completed, high in an alpine meadow. The view from this point is one of the most spectacular in the park, encompassing the entire Livingston Range and parts of the Lewis Range in the Logan Pass vicinity. From this saddle, it is an easy and short descent into the tree-filled bowl below, where the trail enters the Fifty Mountain Campground. This campground is frequented by almost-tame mule deer that will try to steal food and sweat-soaked clothing from unwary hikers. Trails leaving the campground run southwest to Flattop Mountain and southeast along the Highline Trail to Logan Pass.

Key Points

0.0   Trail sign. Trail follows the Waterton Valley floor.

2.5   Junction with Kootenai Lakes Trail (0.3 mile). Stay left for Fifty Mountain.

4.9   Junction with Stoney Indian Pass Trail. Stay right for Fifty Mountain.

5.0   Patrol cabin. Trail begins steep ascent along the west slope of the Continental Divide.

10.1   Fifty Mountain saddle.

10.5   Fifty Mountain Campground.

Connecting Hikes

Flattop Mountain Trail. This trail provides access to the Fifty Mountain area and is frequently used by horse parties. The trail begins at Packer's Roost, a trailhead and old cabin, on a short spur road off the Going-to-the-Sun Road about 23 miles east of West Glacier. The trail follows the floor of the McDonald Creek Valley to a crossing of Mineral Creek, where the trail turns north up Flattop Creek. A trail once followed McDonald Creek to West Flattop Mountain, but it has been abandoned. This entire area was burned by the Trapper Creek Fire of 2003. The trail climbs to the crest of Flattop Mountain, where a mosaic of burns dating from 1998 provides good views of the surrounding peaks. It is 5.7 miles to the Flattop Mountain Campground and 6.3 miles farther from this campground to Fifty Mountain Campground.

Mineral Creek Trail. A low-maintenance status trail runs from the Flattop Mountain Trail on the McDonald Creek Valley floor up Mineral Creek to an old cabin that burned in 2003. The trail is in poor shape and really doesn't access any scenic areas anyway, so there really isn't much reason to venture this way. This was the original trail to Fifty Mountain before the Highline Trail was completed from Granite Park in 1932. It does not receive regular maintenance, so check for the current status.

Kootenai Creek Trail. A low-maintenance trail runs from the Waterton Valley Trail southward, following the river to a patrol cabin on Kootenai Creek. The junction is poorly marked and is likely to be missed by hikers who aren't looking for it.

Waterton Lake. A trail runs from Goat Haunt around the western shore of Waterton Lake to Waterton township on the Canadian side of the border. There are campsites near the Boulder Pass junction and just north of the Canadian border. The total distance of 6.7 miles can be avoided by taking a tour boat that covers the same route several times a day.

The North Boundary Trail. A well-maintained trail runs from the Waterton Lake Trail some 5.8 miles up Boundary Creek to the international boundary, where the trail turns north to Summit Lake. There it connects with the scenic Carthew–Alderson Trail, which runs west to Cameron Lake and east to Waterton townsite.

Rainbow Falls. A short, well-maintained trail starts with the Waterton Lake Trail and runs from Goat Haunt up the east bank of the Waterton River to a series of cascades on the river. The total distance is 0.7 mile from Goat Haunt, making it a popular day hike for hikers taking the boat tour from Waterton township.

Goat Haunt Overlook. Take the Waterton Valley Trail south from Goat Haunt for 0.1 mile to the Goat Haunt Overlook junction. The overlook trail runs eastward, climbing fairly steeply for 1 mile on a secondary trail to an overlook high on a spur ridge of Goat Haunt Mountain. From the overlook, Citadel Peaks and the Brown

Pass area are visible to the west, and looking north over Upper Waterton Lake, bare peaks stretch away to the horizon.

Goat Haunt Shelters. A short, well-maintained trail runs east for 0.2 mile around the head of Waterton Lake to the Goat Haunt Shelters, which are located on the hillside above the boat docks.

Porcupine Lookout. The trail to Porcupine Lookout has been reopened and now offers a challenging day hike ending with spectacular views of the peaks in the Goat Haunt area.

The Southern Sector

The entire southwest portion of Glacier National Park is a wild, seldom-visited country that has changed little since pre-Columbian times. Trails tend to favor long-range trips of several days, as the hiker must travel through about 7 miles of foothills before reaching the scenic peaks of the spine of the Continental Divide. The distances involved in traveling in the southwest make this area ideal for horse parties. Trails connect this area with the Two Medicine drainage via Cut Bank and Two Medicine Passes. This area of the park is the ideal destination for backpackers seeking solitude and a wilderness-oriented experience.

The drainages of Nyack and Coal Creeks have been officially designated as a wilderness camping zone. Trails in the zone tend to be primitive, with relatively low-maintenance status and many creek fords. Camping is allowed outside designated sites anywhere in the zone by permit (available from the Apgar or St. Mary Visitor Centers). Developed campsites are also available in the wilderness zone where stock and fires are permitted.

Year-round access to the southwest corner of the park is available via the South Boundary Trail from West Glacier in the north and Izaak Walton Ranger Station in the south. There are also three major foot fords across the Middle Fork of the Flathead River, which allow more direct access to this area during the low-water months of July and August. Detailed maps of the fords are available at the visitor center at Apgar. The Marias Pass area is accessible via a series of trails that depart from U.S. Highway 2.

Visitor facilities are few and far between on the road between West and East Glacier. Gas and groceries are available near the community of Essex, but you should expect to pay inflated prices here. The historic Izaak Walton Inn in Essex was built as a retreat for Great Northern Railway employees and is a center for cross-country skiing activities in the winter and hiking in the summer.

The valley of the Middle Fork is a major wintering ground for the herds of elk that inhabit this area, and ospreys are frequently seen along the riverbank. The valley bottoms of tributary streams provide ideal summer habitat for black bears, and

Mount Stimson from Upper Nyack Creek

grizzly bears inhabit the more open slopes of the hills above. The southwestern sector receives a fairly high level of winter precipitation, which supports lush forests
interrupted by jungles of cow parsnip and thimbleberry. Fishing is prohibited in the
streams south of Harrison Creek; Beaver Woman and Buffalo Woman Lakes have no
fish in them.

20 Harrison Lake

A day hike (when river levels are low enough to ford) or backpack from U.S. Highway 2 to foot of Harrison Lake, 2.9 miles (4.5 km) one way; from US 2 to Harrison Lake Campground, 4.8 miles (7.5 km) one way; or from West Glacier to Harrison Lake Campground, 11.9 miles (19 km) one way.

Elevation gain: 400 feet
Maximum elevation: 3,693 feet
Difficulty: Easy (without ford)

Topo maps: West Glacier, Nyack, Lake McDonald East

Finding the trailhead: Ford across Middle Fork of the Flathead River accessible from US 2, 6.5 miles east of West Glacier. For a current map of the ford, please ask at the Apgar Visitor Center. The trail can also be accessed via the South Boundary Trail from West Glacier.

The Hike

Harrison Lake is a seldom-visited, fairly large lake that sits among forested foothills near West Glacier. It is accessible via ford from US 2 or by hiking the South Boundary Trail northeast from West Glacier. The hike ascends a gentle valley that burned during 2003 to reach the foot of the lake and then follows its western shore. Occasional avalanche chutes have made clearings from which Loneman Mountain and Mount Thompson can be viewed across the lake. The trail reaches its terminus at the head of the lake, which is not particularly noted for its fishing. A trail once climbed toward the head of the valley but is now abandoned.

Adventurous hikers may bushwhack their way through dense brush approximately 4 miles to the head of the valley, where they will be rewarded with spectacular views of waterfalls cascading down from the glaciers poised high on the sides of the surrounding peaks.

Key Points

0.0 Trail sign, West Glacier. Trail follows Middle Fork of the Flathead eastward.

5.3 Junction with Lincoln Creek Trail. Stay right for Harrison Lake.

7.1 Junction with Harrison Lake Trail. Turn left for Harrison Lake. Hikers using the Harrison Creek ford enter the trail at this point. Trail climbs gently, following Harrison Creek.

10.0 Foot of Harrison Lake.

11.9 Harrison Lake Campground.

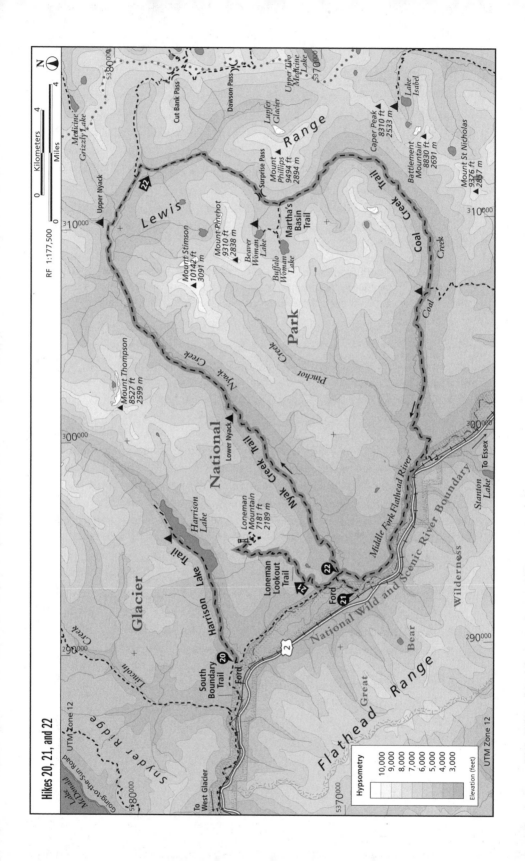

Hikes 20, 21, and 22

RF 1:177,500

Hypsometry

10,000
9,000
8,000
7,000
6,000
5,000
4,000
3,000

Elevation (feet)

21 Loneman Lookout

A long day hike from Nyack Creek ford to Loneman Lookout, 6.5 miles (10.5 km) one way.

See map on page 82.
Elevation gain: 3,900 feet
Maximum elevation: 7,181 feet

Difficulty: Moderately strenuous
Topo map: Nyack

Finding the trailhead: Nyack Creek ford, accessible from a road off U.S. Highway 2, approximately 11 miles east of West Glacier. Please ask at the Apgar Visitor Center for a detailed map of the ford.

The Hike

Loneman Lookout is a seldom-visited, unmanned fire lookout that rises above the old Nyack Ranger Station. After fording the Middle Fork of the Flathead River (ask

Sharp spire of Mount St. Nicholas above Middle Fork of the Flathead

for conditions), the trail follows the Boundary Trail north, across Nyack Creek. At mile 1.2, the Loneman Lookout Trail leaves the South Boundary Trail and climbs onto a bench, which it follows for several miles before climbing steeply up the west face of Loneman Mountain. Almost the entire trail is within the area burned by the Harrison Fire in 2003. Grassy meadows begin to dominate the landscape halfway to the summit, and the trail makes a complete circuit of the mountain in its last mile. The summit overlooks Harrison Lake and Walton Mountain to the north, with the peaks of the Great Bear Wilderness looming to the south, crowned with Great Northern Mountain. To the southeast, the rocky fang beyond Threetops Mountain is Mount St. Nicholas.

Key Points

0.0 Nyack Trailhead on the north bank of the Middle Fork of the Flathead River.

0.1 Trail sign, beyond old Nyack Ranger Station. Turn left for Loneman Lookout. Trail runs westward, following the Middle Fork.

0.8 Junction with Nyack Creek Trail fording Nyack Creek. Stay left for Loneman Lookout.

1.2 Junction with Loneman Lookout Trail. Turn right for lookout. Trail ascends fairly steeply to Loneman Lookout.

6.5 Loneman Lookout.

22 The Nyack-Coal Creek Loop

A backpack from Nyack Creek ford to Coal Creek ford, 37.3 miles (60.0 km) one way; or full loop, 41.5 miles (66.8 km).

See map on page 82.
Elevation gain: 2,260 feet
Elevation loss: 2,260 feet
Maximum elevation: 5,780 feet

Difficulty: Moderate. Trail is often difficult to follow, and river and stream crossings are hazardous during high-water period.
Topo maps: Nyack, Stanton Lake, Mount Jackson, Mount Stimson, Mount St. Nicholas

Finding the trailhead: Nyack Creek ford or Coal Creek ford, both of which are accessible from U.S. Highway 2 east of West Glacier. Ask for a detailed map of fords at Apgar Visitor Center.

The Hike

The Nyack–Coal Creek Loop provides the primary access route into and through the Nyack wilderness camping zone, with a spur trail to Cut Bank Pass linking it to trails in the Two Medicine area. Minimum-impact camping is permitted anywhere within the wilderness zone with a few basic restrictions. Developed campsites are also available in the wilderness zone through the normal permit process. Fishing in the area's streams is not permitted. Trails tend to be brushy and hard to find, and you should expect to encounter obstacles such as knee-deep fords and blowdowns on this trail, especially early in the year. The Nyack wilderness offers the most primitive hiking conditions found anywhere in the park and is not recommended for inexperienced hikers.

The loop begins at the Nyack Creek ford of the Middle Fork of the Flathead (detailed maps of river fords are available at the Apgar Visitor Center) and joins the South Boundary Trail at the old Nyack Ranger Station site. After following the river valley northwest for 0.5 mile, the trail crosses Nyack Creek via a deep but slow-moving ford and reaches the junction with the Nyack Creek Trail. Loop hikers turn eastward here, ascending gentle benches clad with mature forest and a brushy understory above the north bank of the creek. The trail soon crosses an area burned by the 2003 Harrison Fire. The trail passes through many quagmires before reaching the rim of a steep, forested canyon through which the rushing torrent of Nyack Creek makes its way. After 4.5 miles from the junction with the South Boundary Trail, the trail reaches the Lower Nyack Campground, set among towering old-growth larches and cottonwoods.

For the next 7 miles the trail winds up the wooded valley, with occasional clearings that allow the hiker to view the rocky faces of Threesuns Mountain and Mount Stimson. About 1.5 miles beyond the lower patrol cabin, the trail fords a large seasonal tributary and then hugs the sidehill while continuing up the west bank of Nyack Creek. At mile 12.8 of the loop, the trail fords Nyack Creek twice and then doglegs to the east. High winds in the winter of 1988–89 blew down most of the trees in this area, opening up sweeping views of Blackfoot Mountain and the Pumpelly Glacier to the northwest, as well as Mount Stimson to the south and the peaks around Cut Bank Pass to the east. The trail climbs gently through thick brush for another 1.5 miles to the Upper Nyack Campground, with its wooded setting on the fringe of a large gravel wash that provides spectacular views in all directions.

As the trail approaches the Upper Nyack cabin, it passes along the rim of yet another steep canyon. The trail winds through pleasant forest for several miles before reaching the Cut Bank Pass Trail junction, at which it opens up into the brushy swampland of the upper creek bottoms. After several miles of mucky going through the brush, the trail fords Nyack Creek and enters an old-growth spruce stand. The trail reaches a sizeable tributary coming in from the south and turns up the west bank for several hundred yards before crossing it and following up the north bank. After several upward switchbacks lead past cascades and over a modest hill, the main trail levels off and begins the long, gradual ascent to Surprise Pass. As the trail emerges into open avalanche fields, it crosses and recrosses the small creek, finally disappearing into a stand of subalpine fir slightly to the west of the valley's floor. From here, the trail passes through open forest with a copious understory of huckleberries, which make delicious eating when in season. The trail crosses the summit of Surprise Pass and descends almost imperceptibly to the Martha's Basin Trail junction at the head of the Coal Creek Valley (see Martha's Basin Option following).

After reaching the Martha's Basin junction, the loop trail (hereafter officially designated the Coal Creek Trail) descends the steep, brushy Coal Creek Valley to the southeast. Shortly before the valley doglegs to the southwest, the trail crosses Coal Creek at the first of five major fords that exist between Surprise Pass and the Coal Creek Campground. From this ford, it's about 5 miles of hiking through the blackened snags left from the Rampage Fire to Elk Creek, on which the campground is located. The 2003 Rampage Fire burned up to the ridges on both sides of the valley and jumped over the wall below Caper Peak into Lake Isabel and ran all the way to Two Medicine Pass. The trail crosses several talus slopes shortly before reaching the campground, and these openings afford views of precipitous Mount St. Nicholas across the valley. At the campground, the Fielding–Coal Creek Trail enters the loop from the south.

Leaving the campground, the loop trail runs along the north bank of Coal Creek for 2 more miles before crossing one final ford just before reaching the Coal Creek patrol cabin. This area also burned in 2003, and evidence of fires in 1958 and 1984 can additionally be seen. From this point, the valley widens. The trail winds on high benches above the creek for 3.6 miles before reaching a junction with the South Boundary Trail. By bearing to the south, hikers can reach the Coal Creek ford of the Middle Fork after a distance of 0.4 mile, thereby accessing US 2 about 16 miles east of West Glacier. Hikers wishing to complete the loop by trail should turn north onto the South Boundary Trail to return to the Nyack Creek ford. This section of the South Boundary Trail used to be extremely difficult to find, but it has been upgraded and is now much easier to follow.

The South Boundary Trail completing the loop runs down to the mouth of Coal Creek, where it fords the creek just above the site of an old bridge. After crossing the creek, the trail hugs the Middle Fork fairly closely, dipping into a small dale to cross a tiny tributary of the river. The trail then enters unburned forest, where it is fairly obvious, rising and falling as it winds along the river, always to the south (or river) side of the small hillocks on the river's north shore. About half a mile from the Nyack Ranger Station, the trail skirts the south edge of a large meadow, where the only signs of a trail are orange disks nailed to trees at odd intervals. From this point, it is easy to bushwhack to the ranger station, if one gets lost, by skirting the meadow's south edge and bearing due west.

Martha's Basin Option: The Martha's Basin Trail crosses the headwaters of Coal Creek to climb gradually through fields of bear grass into a cirque that lies between Mount Pinchot and Peril Peak. After about a mile, the trail forks. The left fork climbs 0.5 mile to Buffalo Woman Lake, which lies below rugged Peril Peak. The right fork descends gently across an old burn for 0.7 mile to a campground at Beaver Woman Lake. The campground, set among old spruce trees, shows the wear and tear of years of use by horse parties.

Key Points

0.0 Nyack Creek ford. Blazed trail starts from north bank of Middle Fork of the Flathead River.

0.1 Trail sign. Turn left for Nyack Creek. Trail follows the Middle Fork, crossing Nyack Creek just before junction.

0.8 Junction with Nyack Creek Trail. Turn right for Nyack Creek. Trail climbs gently, following the west bank of Nyack Creek.

5.4 Lower Nyack Campground.

7.4 Lower Nyack patrol cabin.

14.4 Upper Nyack Campground.

15.5 Upper Nyack patrol cabin.

17.0 Junction with Cut Bank Pass Trail. Stay right for Coal Creek.

19.2 Trail leaves Nyack Valley and begins moderate ascent to Surprise Pass.

21.7 Surprise Pass.

22.4 Junction with Martha's Basin Trail. (**Option:** Turn right for Buffalo Woman Lake [1.6 miles] or Beaver Woman Lake Campground [2.1 miles].) Keep left for Coal Creek. Trail descends Coal Creek Valley, fording the creek five times.

31.2 Coal Creek Campground. Junction with Fielding–Coal Creek Trail. Stay right for Coal Creek ford. Trail continues gradual descent, fording Coal Creek once.

33.3 Coal Creek patrol cabin.

36.9 Junction with South Boundary Trail. Stay left for Coal Creek ford (0.4 mile). Turn right for Nyack Creek ford.

41.4 Junction with Nyack Creek Ford Connector Trail. Turn left for the ford.

41.5 Nyack Creek ford of the Middle Fork.

23 Lake Isabel

A backpack from Walton Ranger Station to Lake Isabel, 16.9 miles (27 km) one way.

Elevation gain: 1,915 feet
Maximum elevation: 5,835 feet

Difficulty: Moderate
Topo maps: Essex, Blacktail, Mount Rockwell

Finding the trailhead: Trail departs from the north end of the Walton Ranger Station complex, which is located on U.S. Highway 2 at the southernmost extremity of the park.

The Hike

Lake Isabel is a subalpine cirque lake that sits at the base of Vigil Peak. Because the trail to the lake is long and somewhat tedious, the lake receives few visitors and thus is a prime destination for hikers seeking solitude. A trail connects the Park Creek Trail with the Two Medicine country via Two Medicine Pass, providing interesting options for backpackers with extended itineraries. Lake Isabel can also be accessed by a shorter route from Two Medicine via Cobalt Lake.

The trail begins at the Walton Ranger Station and follows the South Boundary Trail for 3.2 miles as it climbs the hillsides above the Middle Fork of the Flathead. The snowy Flathead Range can be seen to the south through openings in the forest. The trail descends gently to the flat top of a high bluff overlooking the river and passes among the huge boles of old-growth larches and Douglas firs before turning east up the Park Creek Valley.

After passing along forested hillsides for several miles, the trail emerges into swampy meadows of tall grass and cow parsnip, from which the low foothills of the Lewis Range can be seen on all sides. Four miles beyond the mouth of the valley lies the Lower Park Creek Campground, set in grassy meadows at the junction with the Fielding–Coal Creek Trail. The trail exits the campground around the north wall of the patrol cabin and continues northeast through jungles of cow parsnip before climbing gently onto hills that crowd the creek as the valley becomes narrower. As you pass through closed-canopy stands of Douglas fir, black bears may be sighted digging for roots along the trail. Avalanche chutes occasionally interrupt the canopy, allowing views of rugged Salvage Mountain and Church Butte to the north. About 2 miles below the campground you can easily see evidence of the 2003 Rampage Fire that jumped the wall above Lake Isabel.

Some 7.4 miles beyond the lower campground, the trail crosses a footbridge before passing beside a patrol cabin into the Upper Park Creek Campground. At this point, the trail forks, with the right fork climbing steeply to Two Medicine Pass

Lake Isabel and Battlement Mountain

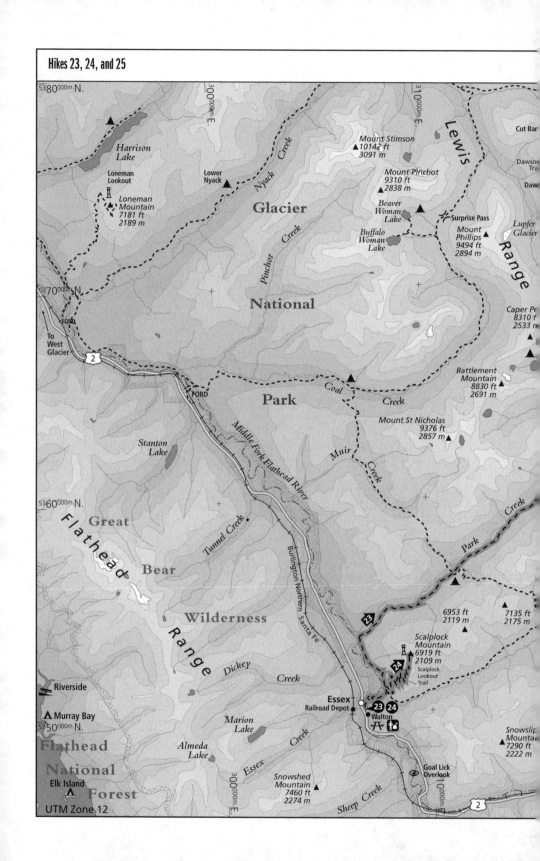

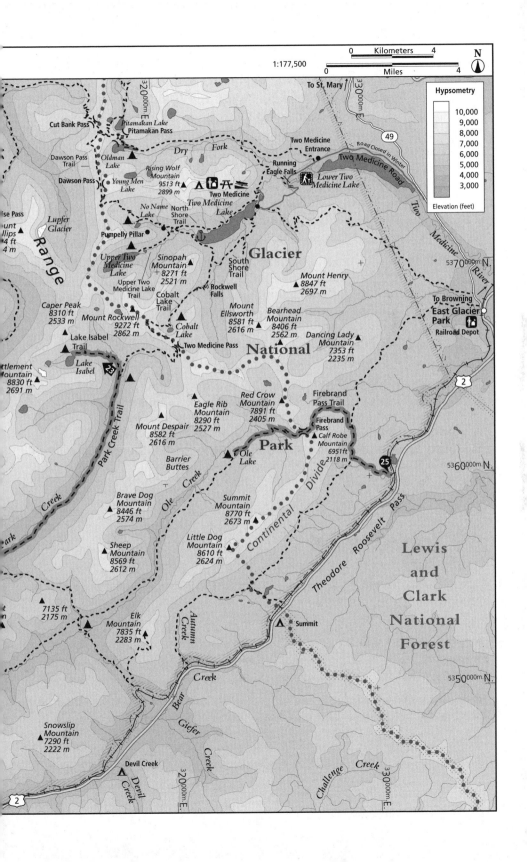

Kilometers

1:177,500

Miles

N

Hypsometry

10,000
9,000
8,000
7,000
6,000
5,000
4,000
3,000

Elevation (feet)

To St. Mary

Cut Bank Pass

Pitamakan Lake
Pitamakan Pass

Dry   Fork

Two Medicine
Entrance

49

Road Closed in Winter

Dawson Pass
Trail

Oldman
Lake

Rising Wolf
Mountain
9513 ft
2899 m

Running
Eagle Falls

Two Medicine
Road

Two Medicine
Lake

Dawson Pass

Young Men
Lake

Lower Two
Medicine Lake

se Pass

Lupfer
Glacier

No Name
Lake

North
Shore
Trail

Two Medicine
Lake

5370000m N.

unt
illips
4 ft
4 m

Range

Pumpelly Pillar

Upper Two
Medicine
Lake

Sinopah
Mountain
8271 ft
2521 m

South
Shore
Trail

Glacier

Mount Henry
8847 ft
2697 m

To Browning

East Glacier
Park

Railroad Depot

Upper Two
Medicine Lake
Trail

Rockwell
Falls

Mount
Ellsworth
8581 ft
2616 m

Bearhead
Mountain
8406 ft
2562 m

Caper Peak
8310 ft
2533 m

Mount Rockwell
9272 ft
2862 m

Cobalt
Lake
Trail

Cobalt
Lake

Dancing Lady
Mountain
7353 ft
2235 m

2

Lake Isabel
Trail

Two Medicine Pass

National

ttlement
ountain
8830 ft
2691 m

Lake
Isabel

23

Red Crow
Mountain
7891 ft
2405 m

Firebrand
Pass Trail

5360000m N.

Park Creek Trail

Eagle Rib
Mountain
8290 ft
2527 m

Firebrand
Pass

Calf Robe
Mountain
6951 ft
2118 m

25

Mount Despair
8582 ft
2616 m

Park

Ole Lake

Continental

Barrier
Buttes

Ole Creek

Theodore Roosevelt Pass

Creek

Brave Dog
Mountain
8446 ft
2574 m

Summit
Mountain
8770 ft
2673 m

Divide

Lewis

and

Sheep
Mountain
8569 ft
2612 m

Little Dog
Mountain
8610 ft
2624 m

Clark

rk

7135 ft
2175 m

Elk
Mountain
7835 ft
2283 m

Autumn Creek

Summit

Summit

National

Forest

5350000m N.

Creek

Snowslip
Mountain
7290 ft
2222 m

Bear

Giefer

Creek

Challenge   Creek

Devil Creek

Devil
Creek

2

and the left fork winding around to the west on its way to Lake Isabel. The trail crosses the west branch of Park Creek over a wooden bridge and ascends moderately for a distance of 1 mile across marshy hillsides covered with mountain ash. Almost immediately you will enter the 2003 Rampage Fire area, which burned virtually the entire basin. The trail then enters the vale of Lake Isabel's outlet stream, which it crosses and follows to the foot of the lake. At the east end of the lake, the trail passes among the twisted wrecks of trees brought down by an avalanche during the winter of 1989–90. The campground lies on the north side of the lake, about one-third mile from its foot. There is good fishing for westslope cutthroat in the 12- to-14-inch class right from the campground. There are also bull trout in the lake, and if caught they must be released. Observant hikers may see evidence of grizzly bear activity around the lake.

Key Points

0.0 Trail sign. Trail climbs moderately, as it runs northwest following the Middle Fork of the Flathead River.

1.1 Junction with Ole Creek Trail. Stay left for Lake Isabel.

1.5 Junction with Scalplock Lookout Trail. Stay left for Lake Isabel.

3.2 Trail leaves the Middle Fork, turning northeast up the Park Creek Valley.

7.2 Lower Park Creek Campground. Junction with Fielding-Coal Creek Trail. The trail to Lake Isabel and Two Medicine Pass exits campground to the north of patrol cabin. Trail ascends gently, following Park Creek. Ford of creek immediately before campground.

14.6 Upper Park Creek Campground. Junction with Two Medicine Pass Trail (3.8 miles to pass). Stay left for Lake Isabel. Trail climbs moderately to the north.

16.9 Lake Isabel Campground.

24 Scalplock Lookout

A day hike from Walton Ranger Station to Scalplock Lookout, 4.7 miles (7.5 km) one way.

See map on pages 90 and 91.
Elevation gain: 3,079 feet
Maximum elevation: 6,919 feet

Difficulty: Moderate
Topo map: Essex

Finding the trailhead: Trail departs from the north end of the Walton Ranger Station complex, which is located on U.S. Highway 2 at the southernmost extremity of the park.

A cloudy day on the Scalplock Lookout Trail ▶

The Hike

Scalplock Lookout sits high above the townsite of Essex, at the far southern tip of Glacier National Park. After leaving the South Boundary Trail, the Scalplock Lookout Trail climbs steeply, switching back frequently across pine forest and grassy meadows to the summit. The lookout overlooks the south end of the Flathead Range to the west, with Marion Lake nestled unseen in its foothills.

To the south, the snowcapped peaks of the Bob Marshall Wilderness stretch away as far as the eye can see. Mount St. Nicholas, Salvage Mountain, and Church Butte rise to the immediate north, with other peaks of the Lewis Range behind them.

Key Points

0.0 Trail sign. Trail ascends gradually, following the Middle Fork of the Flathead.

1.1 Junction with Ole Creek Trail. Stay left for Scalplock Lookout.

1.5 Junction with Scalplock Lookout Trail. Turn right. Trail climbs rather steeply up the flanks of Scalplock Mountain.

4.7 Scalplock Lookout.

25 Firebrand Pass–Ole Lake

A long day hike or backpack from the Lubec Trailhead to Ole Lake, 7.7 miles (11 km) one way; or from the Lubec Trailhead to Firebrand Pass, 4.8 miles (7.5 km) one way.

See map on pages 90 and 91.
Elevation gain: 2,210 feet
Elevation loss: 2,680 feet
Maximum elevation: 6,951 feet

Difficulty: Moderately strenuous
Topo maps: Summit, Squaw Mountain, Mount Rockwell

Finding the trailhead: At mile marker 203 on U.S. Highway 2, follow the dirt road across the railroad tracks to a barricaded dirt road that runs for 0.5 mile to the site of the old Lubec Ranger Station (which was burned in 1980). The Firebrand Pass Trail begins at this site.

The Hike

The Firebrand Pass Trail begins at a false summit near Marias Pass and winds around Calf Robe Mountain to Firebrand Pass before dropping down into the Ole Creek Valley. Ole Lake can also be reached via a longer, less scenic route up the Ole Creek Valley from the Walton Ranger Station or from the Fielding–Coal Creek Trailhead. Firebrand Pass makes a reasonable destination for day hikers, while backpackers will find backcountry campsites at Ole Lake.

Looking toward Calf Robe Mountain from the Autumn Creek Trail

The trail starts out on the north bank of Coonsa Creek, which it follows for 0.5 mile before turning slightly north and climbing gently to the junction with the Autumn Creek Trail. Hikers bound for the pass should turn north at this junction and follow the Autumn Creek Trail for 1 mile as it leaves the forest and enters grassy meadows near the junction with the Firebrand Pass Trail, which takes off to the west. Following the Firebrand Pass Trail as it winds upward around the open slopes of Calf Robe Mountain, hikers will see Squaw Mountain straight ahead and Red Crow Mountain as the trail reaches the north slope of Calf Robe. The forest on both sides of the pass burned in the hot fires of the early 1900s.

Key Points

- **0.0** Trail sign. Trail climbs gently, following Coonsa Creek.
- **1.4** Junction with Autumn Creek Trail. Turn right for Firebrand Pass. Trail sidehills along the flanks of Calf Robe Mountain.
- **2.4** Junction with Firebrand Pass Trail. Turn left for Firebrand Pass. Trail ascends rather steeply around the northeast face of Firebrand Pass.
- **4.8** Firebrand Pass. Trail descends steeply to Ole Lake.
- **7.7** Ole Lake Campground.

Additional Hikes

The **South Boundary Trail** from West Glacier along the Middle Fork of the Flathead to Walton Ranger Station varies in condition in different localities. It is in good condition between West Glacier and the old Nyack Ranger Station but is poorly maintained (bring a compass) between Nyack and Coal Creeks, as it disappears in the large meadow southeast of the old Nyack Ranger Station. At this point, bear toward the river, to the west of the meadow, and pass the low hill on the river side. As the trail enters the woods it becomes more distinct; keep your eyes peeled for round blaze orange markers on tree trunks to find the trail. Between Coal Creek and Park Creek, the trail has been washed out and abandoned entirely, making it impossible to follow. Between Park Creek and Izaak Walton, the trail is well-maintained and easily followed.

The trails to **Pinchot Creek** have been abandoned and can no longer be found.

The **Fielding–Coal Creek Trail** connects the drainages of Bear, Ole, Park, Muir, and Coal Creeks several miles above their confluences with the Middle Fork. This trail is well-maintained from its beginning at the end of a primitive dirt road, #1066 near the Bear Creek Guest House, to the lower Park Creek Campground and is poorly maintained from this point to the Coal Creek Campground. The trail climbs gently over a low saddle, 3 miles long, between Bear and Ole Creeks, jogs east with the Ole Creek Trail for 0.2 mile, and then resumes its course over a more strenuous saddle below Soldier Mountain 4.5 miles to Park Creek. From this point, the trail crosses Park Creek and climbs steeply to a saddle behind Rampage Mountain, follows Muir Creek for 3 miles, and then climbs over a slightly lower saddle for 1.8 miles before dropping the final 1.5 miles to Coal Creek.

The **Cut Bank Access Trail** begins at Pitamakan Pass and crosses over Cut Bank Pass before descending steeply 5.4 miles to join the Nyack Creek Trail 2.6 miles above the Upper Nyack Campground. The trail is poorly maintained and hard to follow in some places, so is not recommended for inexperienced hikers or horse parties.

The **Ole Creek Trail** is a well-maintained, if somewhat less than scenic, trail that runs for 15.5 miles up a forested valley to Ole Lake and then continues to Firebrand Pass.

The **Autumn Creek Trail** offers day hike possibilities in the Marias Pass area. The trail begins on the west bank of Autumn Creek as it enters Bear Creek west of the Blacktail Hills, on U.S. Highway 2. The trail is well-maintained as it climbs moderately for 1.6 miles to a low, open saddle below Elk Mountain and then descends 2.4 miles to the junction with a connector trail that runs for a mile past

Three Bears Lake to the highway summit of Marias Pass. The trail is poorly maintained for the next 6.2 miles to the junction with the Lubec Connector Trail, which returns to US 2 at the old Lubec Ranger Station. The trail is well maintained for the next mile between the Lubec Trail and the Firebrand Pass junction and 4.9 miles beyond to the park boundary. It then returns to low-maintenance status for the final 1.8 miles between the park boundary and the trail's terminus at the Midvale Creek bridge behind Glacier Park Lodge. This area is very popular with cross-country skiers in wintertime.

Two Medicine

The mountains of the Two Medicine area were known as the "Backbone of the World" to the Blackfeet Indians, who used the area for vision quests as well as hunting and gathering. The towering spires and sheer cliff walls still provide an awe-inspiring atmosphere for travelers in search of a haven from the hurried pace of the modern world. A well-worn network of trails provides access to peaceful lakes and dizzying heights, through a landscape of unequaled beauty.

In this part of the park, sheer mountains rise abruptly from the rolling prairies of the Great Plains, providing a mixture of flora and fauna from widely different biotic

Mount Sinopah above Two Medicine Lake

communities. Alpine communities of the higher elevations grade into grasslands adapted to the more arid plains. The mountains of the divide form a barrier to moisture-laden maritime air masses, and thus this area is said to be in a rain shadow. Precipitation on the plains falls mostly in the summer in the form of brief thunderstorms, following the rainfall regime of the high plains. This pattern of precipitation favors shallow-rooted grasses over larger trees and shrubs, thus accounting for the lack of lush forests on this side of the divide.

Dry winds roar through the high mountain passes and are a dominant force in shaping the patterns of vegetation in the front ranges. These same winds reach speeds upwards of 80 miles per hour and cause incredibly high wind-chill factors in the winter.

Wildlife in this area reflects the drier nature of the vegetation. Bighorn sheep, favoring grasses as forage, are seen more commonly in this drier area than are mountain goats. Golden eagles are not uncommon, soaring on updrafts created by the warmth of the sun on open grasslands. Waterfalls block the immigration of native fish into most of the lakes—fish found in most lakes were introduced at some time during the past. These planted fish have successfully occupied a vacant niche in the lake ecosystems and now sustain their populations naturally, without the aid of supplementary plantings by the National Park Service.

26 Scenic Point

A half-day hike from Two Medicine Road to Scenic Point, 3.1 miles (5 km) one way; or a backpack from Two Medicine Road to East Glacier, 10.0 miles (16 km) one way.

Elevation gain: 2,242 feet
Maximum elevation: 7,522 feet

Difficulty: Moderately strenuous
Topo map: Squaw Mountain

Finding the trailhead: Trail departs from a marked trailhead on the Two Medicine Road, approximately 11.5 miles west from its junction with Montana Highway 49.

The Hike

This trail is most commonly taken as a short hike from the Two Medicine Road to Scenic Point and back. Through-hikers bound for East Glacier must purchase a Blackfoot conservation permit at a local ranger station, as the route crosses reservation lands. The trail begins immediately off the Two Medicine Road just before an old water tank on the east bank of Appistoki Creek, climbs along the creek past Appistoki Falls, and then ascends high on the arid valley wall above the creek. Looking up the desolate creek valley from this hillside, Mount Henry raises its forbidding head to the south. The trail climbs to the summit of the windblown dome known as Scenic Point. On a clear day, you can see out across the high plains all the way to the Sweetgrass Hills, some 100 miles distant. Looking to the west, Dawson Pass is clearly visible, with jagged peaks surrounding it. Only the most hardy plants grow in the arid, windswept environment on top of Scenic Point, and the poor growing conditions cause a stunted growth form in these plants.

For hikers continuing to East Glacier, the trail drops into a bowl filled with twisted trees before descending onto open slopes and crossing Fortymile Creek. The trail continues across the open east slope of the Front Range, finally descending into the trees and crossing another creek before leaving the park. The trail continues eastward, having a lower maintenance status as it leaves the park, as it crosses a low hillock on its way to a primitive dirt road. After reaching the road, keep a sharp eye out for trail markers, as the trail crosses several jeep roads in this area. The trail emerges from the woods onto a gravel road, which reaches its terminus just north of the Glacier Park Lodge in East Glacier.

Key Points

0.0 Mount Henry Trailhead sign, near water tank.

0.5 Junction with Appistoki Falls Trail (200 yards). Stay left for Scenic Point. Trail ascends the Appistoki Valley, then climbs to Scenic Point.

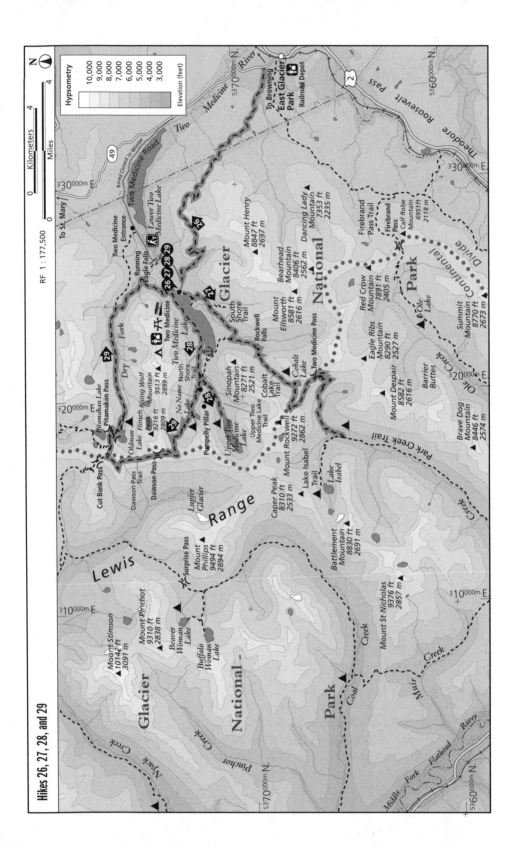

Hikes 26, 27, 28, and 29

3.1 Scenic Point.

10.0 Trail reaches gravel road behind the golf course in East Glacier.

27 Cobalt Lake-Two Medicine Pass

A day hike or backpack from Two Medicine lower boat dock to Cobalt Lake, 5.7 miles (9 km) one way; from Two Medicine lower boat dock to junction with Park Creek Trail, 12.7 miles (20 km) one way; or from Two Medicine upper boat dock to Cobalt Lake, 4.4 miles (7 km) one way.

See map on page 102.
Elevation gain: 1,400 feet
Maximum elevation: 6,620 feet

Difficulty: Moderate
Topo maps: Squaw Mountain, Mount Rockwell

Finding the trailhead: South Shore Trailhead is located at the west end of the Two Medicine boat dock parking lot. Boat users may enter trail system at upper boat dock.

The Hike

The trail to Cobalt Lake winds around the south shore of Two Medicine Lake, ascends the valley between Sinopah Mountain and Painted Teepee Peak to Cobalt Lake, and then continues its ascent to Two Medicine Pass and drops into the Park Creek Valley beyond. Rockwell Falls and Cobalt Lake are popular day hike destinations, and backcountry campsites at Cobalt Lake make more extended sojourns possible. This trail is also popular with anglers bound for Lake Isabel in the Park Creek drainage.

The trail quits the Two Medicine lakeshore shortly after leaving the trailhead and ascends gently some 100 feet through open forest. At mile 0.2, a spur trail takes off to the north 0.4 mile to Paradise Point, a rounded promontory that offers a panoramic vista of Two Medicine Lake and the surrounding peaks. The main trail climbs through stands of subalpine fir interrupted by an occasional beaver pond for another mile to Aster Creek. After crossing Aster Creek, the South Shore Trail reaches the junction with the Aster Falls Trail, which climbs fairly steeply 0.7 mile past a falls to an overlook in a narrow argillite canyon, with pleasant grassy meadows in the valley above it.

The trail continues west, crossing Paradise Creek via a suspension bridge and winding around the base of Sinopah Mountain, through brushy fields of cow parsnip and false huckleberry. At mile 3.4, the trail reaches the base of Rockwell Falls, a series of 20-foot cascades that extends for almost half a mile up the stream's valley. After crossing the creek, the trail ascends rocky, huckleberry-clad benches beside the falls before emerging into a parkland of dwarfed firs and rock gardens. The trail ascends gently for 1 mile before climbing several fir-clad swales to reach a junction that leads to deep blue Cobalt Lake, at the base of Two Medicine Pass. The

Lone Walker Mountain reflected in Upper Two Medicine Lake

campground is located across the outlet of the lake, while the trail to the pass continues to the right around the north shore of the lake.

Two Medicine Pass Option: The trail ascends fairly steeply from Cobalt Lake, across open slopes beneath Mount Rockwell, to the rounded saddle above. The trail then follows the ridgeline southward, crossing the small summit of Chief Lodgepole Peak and offering a view into Paradise Park below to the east. To the west lies the Park Creek Valley, with Eagle Ribs, Mount Despair, and Brave Dog Mountain trailing away to the south. To the west lies Vigil Peak, with Lake Isabel below it and the Cloudcroft Peaks in the background. From the pass, the trail descends steeply for 3.8 miles to an intersection with Park Creek Trail at the Upper Park Creek patrol cabin. The extent of the Rampage Fire is clearly visible as you look toward Lake Isabel. Even the krummholz burned right up to the pass, but the blaze never crossed the Continental Divide.

Key Points

0.0 Trail sign.

0.2 Junction with Paradise Point Trail (0.4 mile). Stay left for Cobalt Lake.

1.2 Junction with Aster Falls Trail (0.7 mile). Stay right for Cobalt Lake. Trail follows lakeshore loosely, crossing Paradise Creek suspension bridge.

2.3 Junction with Two Medicine Pass Trail. Turn left for Cobalt Lake. Boat users enter trail here.

3.4 Rockwell Falls spur junction. Trail ascends steeply, then assumes a gradual grade to Cobalt Lake.

5.7 Cobalt Lake. Trail passes west from lakeshore, ascending to pass.

7.9 Two Medicine Pass.

12.7 Junction with Park Creek Trail.

28 Upper Two Medicine Lake

A day hike or short backpack from the upper boat dock to Upper Two Medicine Lake, 2.2 miles (3.7 km) one way; or from North Shore Trailhead to Upper Two Medicine Lake, 4.8 miles (7.7 km) one way.

See map on page 102.　　　　　　　　　**Difficulty:** Easy
Elevation gain: 300 feet　　　　　　　**Topo maps:** Squaw Mountain, Mount Rockwell
Maximum elevation: 5,464 feet

Finding the trailhead: Two Medicine North Shore Trailhead, on the northern edge of Two Medicine Campground. The trail leaves the campground over a bridge at the outlet of Pray Lake, a small pond just below Two Medicine Lake.

The Hike

The Upper Two Medicine Lake Trail can be reached from the North or South Shore Trails that ring Two Medicine Lake, or by launch to the upper boat dock. The lake is a popular destination for tourists taking motor launch tours.

The Launch and South Shore Trails run in tandem from the head of the lake up the south bank of Two Medicine Creek. Half a mile beyond the lake's head, the trail forks. The right fork connects to the North Shore–Dawson Pass Trail, while the left fork turns northwest to Twin Falls and Upper Two Medicine Lake. Twin Falls is a paired cascade separated by an island in midstream and is well worth the short side trip. The main trail continues westward, through sparse forests to the foot of the lake, where it reaches a backcountry campground. Upper Two Medicine Lake is nestled among sheer peaks of red argillite, from north to south: Pumpelly Pillar, Mount Helen, Lone Walker Mountain, and Rising Bull Ridge. This lake has good fishing for brook and rainbow trout, and mountain goats are often seen capering about on rocky ledges around the lake.

Key Points

0.0 Trail sign. Trail follows the north shore of Two Medicine Lake.

3.3 Junction with Dawson Pass Trail. Turn left for Upper Two Medicine.

3.5 Spur trail to upper boat dock. Boat users enter the trail here. Trail runs southwest, ascending almost imperceptibly.

4.8 Upper Two Medicine Lake and Campground.

29 Dawson-Pitamakan

A day hike or backpack from Two Medicine Campground to Dawson Pass, 6.7 miles (10.8 km) one way; from upper boat dock to Dawson Pass, 3.2 miles (5 km) one way; loop from Two Medicine Campground, 18.8 miles (30 km); or loop from upper boat dock, 16.3 miles (26 km).

See map on page 102.
Elevation gain: 2,935 feet
Elevation loss: 2,935 feet
Maximum elevation: 8,099 feet

Difficulty: Moderately strenuous
Topo maps: Squaw Mountain, Mount Rockwell, Cut Bank Pass

Finding the trailhead: Two Medicine North Shore Trailhead, on the north side of Two Medicine Campground, at the outlet of Pray Lake. Boat travelers will begin from the upper boat dock, meeting the trail after Twin Falls.

The Hike

The Dawson-Pitamakan (pronounced pit-AH-muh-kun) Trail runs from Two Medicine Lake to the Continental Divide and around into the Dry Fork drainage to form a long loop. It offers spectacular views of the spires of the southern Lewis Range, as well as good wildlife-viewing opportunities along its entire length. The trail may be hiked in its entirety in a single day, but it takes several days to fully explore the wonders of this region.

The trail begins at the Two Medicine Campground and winds around the north shore of the lake, beneath the hulking mass of Rising Wolf Mountain. Openings provided by avalanches from the mountain above allow excellent views of the peaks across the lake. The trail winds through a mixed forest that grades into spruce stands before finally emerging to an opening below Sinopah Mountain at the head of the lake. At this point, a connecting trail from the South Shore Trail and the upper boat dock joins the Dawson Pass Trail. Travelers using the tour boat enter the trail here,

Looking into the Upper Nyack Valley ▶

having cut off the first 2 miles of the hike. A short side trip of 0.3 mile down this connecting trail brings you to the South Shore Trail to Twin Falls.

From this point, the trail ascends gently into the Bighorn Basin, a glacier-carved bowl filled with scattered stands of subalpine fir and lush meadows. At mile 4.8, a spur trail descends to No Name Lake, with its attendant campground. The Dawson Pass Trail continues to climb the south slope of Flinsch Peak, offering views of Mount Helen and the knife-edge wall of the Pumpelly Pillar. After 2 miles and 1,200 feet of steady climbing, the trail reaches the windy saddle of Dawson Pass. From this spot, vistas open to the glacier-carved valley of Nyack Creek to the south and the Lupfer Glacier, nestled high on the east slope of Mount Phillips across the valley. From Dawson Pass, mountaineers will find a fairly easy ascent up the south face of Flinsch Peak to its summit. Looking carefully, you can see where the 2003 Rampage Fire burned into the upper basin of Nyack Creek.

From Dawson Pass, the trail turns north, following the Continental Divide along its west face around Flinsch Peak to an unnamed saddle at the head of the Dry Fork Valley. The trail crosses dry, barren rockscapes all along the divide, and backward glances reveal outstanding views of Lone Walker Mountain, Caper Peak, Battlement Mountain, and the spiny summit of Mount St. Nicholas. This area is home to bighorn sheep. The trail continues around Mount Morgan, and rocky pedestals on a spur ridge provide an ideal lunch spot among breathtaking views of Mounts Stimson and Pinchot across the valley, as well as the peaks to the south and north. The trail winds around to Pitamakan Overlook, which affords stunning views to the north and west.

From this point, the trail turns east, following the north slope of Mount Morgan. A connecting trail from the Nyack wilderness rises to meet the Dawson-Pitamakan Trail in the course of its gentle descent to Pitamakan Pass, high above the large lake of the same name to the north. The trail to the north descends to Pitamakan Lake in the Cut Bank Creek Valley. Looking southward, the partial horn of Flinsch Peak soars above Oldman Lake, while pyramid-shaped Rising Wolf Mountain rises farther to the east. The trail descends steeply, switching back frequently through rocky ledges covered with wildflowers and firs, reaching a spur trail to the campground at the foot of Oldman Lake. This lake receives a fair amount of angling pressure, but remains good fishing for Yellowstone cutthroat trout in the 1-to-3-pound class. The campground is set in an open stand of old-growth whitebark pines, about 100 yards east of the lakeshore.

After leaving the campground, the trail descends through parklike stands of fir separated by beargrass-studded fields along the Dry Fork. As the trail continues down the valley, it enters drier meadows of tall grasses reminiscent of high plains habitats. Nearing the foot of the valley, the trail enters a sun-dappled forest of lodgepole pine. Some 2.4 miles before reaching the Two Medicine Campground, a trail forks to the east, leading 2.6 miles through marshy aspen stands to the entrance station on the Two Medicine Road. The main trail swings southward, around the forested base of Rising Wolf, to terminate at the footbridge below Pray Lake.

Key Points

0.0 Trail sign. Trail follows north shore of Two Medicine Lake.

3.3 Junction with trail leading to Twin Falls and the South Shore Trail. Stay right for Dawson Pass.

4.8 Junction with trail to No Name Lake and campground (0.2 mile). Stay right for Dawson Pass. Trail ascends steeply to Dawson Pass.

6.7 Dawson Pass. Trail runs north, following the west face of the Continental Divide.

9.9 Cut Bank Pass. Junction with trail into Nyack Creek. Stay right for Pitamakan Pass.

10.0 Pitamakan Pass. Junction with the trail down Cut Bank Creek. Stay right for Oldman Lake and Two Medicine Campground. Trail descends steeply toward Oldman Lake.

12.0 Oldman Lake.

12.9 Oldman Campground. Trail descends gently, following the Dry Fork Creek.

16.4 Junction with Dry Fork Trail. Stay right for Two Medicine Campground. Trail turns south, traversing the flanks of Rising Wolf Mountain.

18.8 Return to Two Medicine Campground.

30 Cut Bank Creek

A backpack from Cut Bank Ranger Station to Morningstar Lake, 6.6 miles (10.5 km) one way; or from Cut Bank Ranger Station to Pitamakan Pass, 9.8 miles (15.5 km) one way.

Elevation gain to lake: 640 feet
Elevation gain to pass: 2,515 feet
Maximum elevation: 7,557 feet (Pitamakan Pass)

Difficulty: Easy (Morningstar Lake); moderately strenuous (Pitamakan Pass)
Topo map: Cut Bank Pass

Finding the trailhead: Take U.S. Highway 89 to junction with Cut Bank Creek Road, 17 miles north of East Glacier. Drive 4 miles over this improved gravel road past the ranger station to the backcountry parking area. Trail runs west from this parking lot.

The Hike

The Cut Bank Creek Valley is a seldom-visited but beautiful valley, characterized by fir parklands, rushing streams, and towering red mountains from which graceful cascades descend. The valley itself may be the ultimate goal of backpacking trips, and hikers interested in extended trips can connect to the Dawson-Pitamakan and Nyack Creek Trails from junctions at Pitamakan Pass and Cut Bank Pass. Triple Divide Pass provides access to the St. Mary Valley to the north.

Cut Bank Creek Trail begins just beyond the Cut Bank Ranger Station, on a well-maintained gravel road, and crosses low-elevation meadows before entering an open forest of lodgepole pine and Douglas fir. The trail climbs imperceptibly as it follows the north bank of the creek, and openings in the trees reveal a small, rocky canyon as the creek passes below the foot of Bad Marriage Mountain. The process of frost cracking is constantly at work on this mountain. During the winter, water seeps into cracks in the rock. As the water freezes, it expands, creating a wedge that separates large chunks of rock from the parent material. The huge aprons of dislodged boulders below cliff faces, called talus slopes, are a testimony to the powerful impact of this process on local landforms. Game trails can be seen crossing the talus slope at the base of this mountain, which is a good place to look for bighorn sheep.

About 4 miles up the trail, there is a junction with the Triple Divide Pass and Medicine Grizzly Lake Trails, beyond a beaver pond populated with fingerling trout. There is a cache pole at the Atlantic Creek Campground to the east of this junction, so that backpackers can hang their gear and take a day hike to one of these two destinations. From this junction the trail turns south, crossing Atlantic Creek immediately below Atlantic Falls, a small but charming waterfall in a pleasant woodland setting. The trail enters an open, meadowy valley filled with wildflowers, and the red argillite massifs of Eagle Plume and Red Mountains are prominent to the east. As the trail passes in the shadow of Medicine Grizzly Peak, a series of waterfalls cascade from a hidden cirque high above to the valley floor.

After a moderate ascent through subalpine fir forest, the trail winds through tiny meadows created by long-lasting snowbanks. Only small plants that grow rapidly, such as the glacier lily, can take advantage of the short, snow-free growing season found in these tiny spots. The trail then reaches the shore of Morning Star Lake, a shallow, glassy body of water that lies at the base of sheer cliff walls. After crossing the lake's outlet, the trail winds around its eastern shore to a pleasant campground at the head of the lake.

From Morning Star Lake, the trail ascends fairly steeply through stunted trees and grassy meadows to the outlet stream of Katoya Lake, a lovely lake nestled among blocky cliffs, which is reached via a short bushwhack upstream from the trail. After crossing the stream, the trail ascends again for half a mile to the next shelf, which it follows to Pitamakan Lake. This section of the trail often harbors deep snowdrifts into the summer, and the lake often contains twisted icebergs left over from the winter's icepack.

The trail crosses the outlet of Pitamakan Lake and ascends a sparsely wooded spur ridge to the north wall of the cirque, where it switches back repeatedly through gravelly wastes and alpine tundra toward the pass. The trail overlooks Lake of the Seven Winds at the foot of McClintock Peak before emerging on the rounded saddle of Pitamakan Pass, with its spectacular view of rugged Flinsch Peak and Rising Wolf Mountain and the sapphire pool of Oldman Lake below them.

◀ *Oldman Lake and Flinsch Peak*

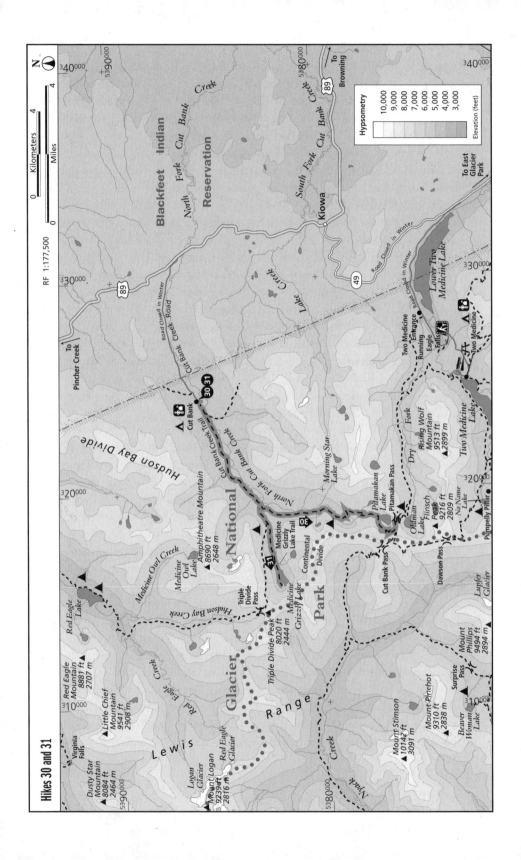

Key Points

0.0 Trail sign. Trail ascends gently, following the North Fork of Cut Bank Creek.

0.1 Junction with old Cut Bank Chalet access road. Stay right for Morningstar Lake.

3.9 Junction with Triple Divide Trail (3.3 miles to Triple Divide Pass, 2.1 miles to Medicine Grizzly Lake). Stay left for Morningstar Lake. Trail turns toward the south and continues ascent of Cut Bank Valley.

4.1 Trail passes Atlantic Falls.

6.6 Morningstar Lake Campground. Trail ascends fairly steeply, then levels off and ascends again before reaching Pitamakan Lake.

8.6 Pitamakan Lake. Trail crosses lake outlet and winds around west side of lake before ascending steeply to the pass.

9.8 Pitamakan Pass.

31 Medicine Grizzly Lake–Triple Divide Pass

A long day hike or short backpack from Cut Bank Ranger Station to Medicine Grizzly Lake, 6.0 miles (9.5 km) one way; or from Cut Bank Ranger Station to Triple Divide Pass, 7.2 miles (11.5 km) one way.

See map on page 112.
Elevation gain to lake: 540 feet
Elevation gain to pass: 2,380 feet
Maximum elevation: 7,397 feet (Triple Divide Pass)

Difficulty: Easy (Medicine Grizzly Lake); moderate (Triple Divide Pass)
Topo maps: Cut Bank Pass, Mount Stimson

Finding the trailhead: Take U.S. Highway 89 to junction with Cut Bank Creek Road, 17 miles north of East Glacier. Drive 4 miles over this improved gravel road past the ranger station to the backcountry parking area. Trail runs west from this parking lot.

The Hike

The Triple Divide Pass Trail begins at the Cut Bank Ranger Station and follows Cut Bank Creek for almost 4 miles before ascending the Atlantic Creek Valley. Both Medicine Grizzly Lake and Triple Divide Pass may be visited on a long day hike, while a campground near the confluence of Atlantic and Cut Bank Creeks provides overnight facilities for backpackers. Triple Divide Pass connects the Cut Bank Creek Trail with the Red Eagle Lake Trail, allowing access for hikers on extended trips into the St. Mary drainage.

The trail begins just beyond the ranger station, on a well-maintained gravel road, and crosses low-elevation meadows before entering an open forest of

lodgepole pine and Douglas fir. The trail climbs imperceptibly as it follows the north bank of the creek, and openings in the trees reveal a small, rocky canyon as the creek passes below the foot of Bad Marriage Mountain. The process of frost cracking is constantly at work on this mountain. During the winter, water seeps into cracks in the rock. As the water freezes, it expands, creating a wedge that separates large chunks of rock from the parent material. The huge aprons of dislodged boulders below cliff faces, called talus slopes, are a testimony to the powerful impact of this process on local landforms. Game trails can be seen crossing the talus slope at the base of this mountain, which is a good place to look for bighorn sheep.

About 4 miles up the trail, at the junction at Atlantic Creek, the Triple Divide Trail climbs gently to the north, passing through the Atlantic Creek Campground. Two-thirds of a mile from the junction, the trail forks, with the left fork following the valley floor for 1.4 miles through beargrass-studded parklands to Medicine Grizzly Lake. The right fork rises steadily along the north wall of the valley, climbing high above Medicine Grizzly Lake. Across the valley, an unnamed lake lies in a hanging cirque embedded in the north face of Medicine Grizzly Peak. The trail continues its pleasant grade upward without a single switchback, passing tiny waterfalls and emerging into a meadowy bowl below the pass.

Triple Divide Pass derives its moniker from the peak of the same name that overlooks the pass to the west. Water flowing from the various sides of this peak will eventually reach the Atlantic, Pacific, and Arctic Oceans. An alpinists' route to the peak's summit crosses the steep talus bowl to the south and climbs the second of two couloirs, which pierces the Atlantic Valley headwall to reach a flat saddle. From this point, it is an easy scramble up the south slope of the peak to the summit.

Wildlife is abundant in the vicinity of the pass. Hoary marmots, chipmunks, and both golden-mantled and Columbia ground squirrels make their homes in the talus surrounding the pass. Bighorn sheep are frequently sighted on the surrounding slopes. Herds of bighorn are segregated by sex—rams and ewes are rarely found in the same herd during the summer months. These animals begin rutting in September, and the thunderous cracks of colliding rams may be heard as early as late August. Looking northward from the pass, Norris Mountain dominates the head of the valley, while Split Mountain rises on its northern perimeter. The south faces of the peaks surrounding Little Chief Mountain can be seen in the background.

◀ *Hiker and marmot below Triple Divide Peak*

Key Points

0.0 Trail sign. Trail climbs gently, following the North Fork of Cut Bank Creek.

0.1 Junction with old chalet road. Stay right for Medicine Grizzly Lake and Triple Divide Pass.

3.9 Junction with Triple Divide Trail. Turn right for the pass and Medicine Grizzly Lake. Trail begins gradual ascent of Atlantic Creek Valley.

4.3 Atlantic Creek Campground.

4.6 Junction with Medicine Grizzly Lake Trail. Turn left for Medicine Grizzly Lake (1.4 miles). Stay right for Triple Divide Pass. Trail climbs north side of Atlantic Creek Valley.

7.2 Triple Divide Pass.

Connecting Hikes

A short spur runs from the Two Medicine South Shore Trail to **Paradise Point,** a total distance of 0.6 mile. The hike is an easy one, over fairly flat ground, that passes through fir forest past several beaver ponds on the way to its destination on the lakeshore.

Another spur trail from the South Shore Trail runs up a ravine to **Aster Falls.** The total distance from the east boat dock to the end of the trail is 1.9 miles. Above the falls is an open meadow known as Aster Park, which affords a pleasant spot for a picnic.

The **Cut Bank Pass Trail** connects Pitamakan Pass to the Nyack Valley, allowing east–west crossings of the Continental Divide in the park's southern areas. This connector is very steep and thus is not recommended for horse parties or the faint-hearted.

A trail running south from Rockwell Falls to **Paradise Park** is still shown on some old maps. This trail is not in existence, however, and it requires a real bushwhack to reach this area.

A short administrative trail runs for a mile from the Cut Bank Ranger Station to **Milk River Ridge** on the park boundary. This trail has little to recommend it in terms of scenery.

The St. Mary Valley

The St. Mary River drainage is bisected by the Going-to-the-Sun Road, which provides easy access for hikers and backpackers. The most dominant feature of the area is St. Mary Lake itself, which reflects a number of stunning vistas of the mountains surrounding it. The front ranges are formed of Grinnell argillite, which imparts a characteristic reddish tint to the peaks. The rain shadow formed by the Continental Divide explains the lack of snow on the eastern peaks during July

Going-to-the-Sun Mountain rises above St. Mary Lake

and August. The peaks along the backbone of the divide are characteristically clad in snow year round, and a few small glaciers remain in the higher cirques that harken back to the time when the entire park was covered in ice.

The grassy flats around Rising Sun provide important winter range for the elk that inhabit this area, and in the autumn the bugling of bulls echoes from the valley walls. The valley is dominated by lodgepole pines at the low elevations, with a few stands of aspen in areas of waterlogged soil. Higher up, spruce and subalpine fir are interspersed with bear grass and other wildflowers. Dry south-facing slopes are covered with the drought-resistant grasses that dominate the high plains to the east.

The town of St. Mary provides all visitor facilities, including a first-rate lodge that serves lake whitefish, a delicacy caught in nearby lakes, on occasion. There is a visitor center just inside the park boundary where information and backcountry permits are available. Half a mile beyond the entrance station is the St. Mary Campground. There is a motel and camp store at Rising Sun, as well as a Park Service–run auto campground. A privately run tour boat operates out of Rising Sun, featuring scenic and interpretive loop cruises on the lake.

32 Red Eagle Lake

A long day hike or backpack from St. Mary Trailhead to Red Eagle Lake foot, 7.5 miles (12 km) one way; or from St. Mary to Triple Divide Pass, 16.2 miles (26 km) one way.

Elevation gain to lake: 300 feet
Elevation gain to pass: 2,980 feet
Maximum elevation: 7,397 feet (Triple Divide Pass)

Difficulty: Easy (Red Eagle); moderately strenuous (Triple Divide Pass)
Topo maps: St. Mary, Rising Sun, Mount Stimson

Finding the trailhead: Take the Going-to-the-Sun Road 0.25 mile east from St. Mary township to a paved road entering on the south before the entrance station. Take this road, bearing right, about 0.5 mile to a parking lot with a trailhead sign. The trail occupies an abandoned roadbed leading to the southwest.

The Hike

Red Eagle Lake lies in a gentle, low-elevation valley that provides surprisingly scenic hiking to the few travelers that venture this way. More adventurous hikers may choose to follow the trail all the way to Triple Divide Pass and beyond into the Cut Bank Creek country. The trail passes through the Red Eagle burn of 2006 and offers a great chance to see how vegetation and wildlife bounce back after fire.

The trail starts as an old dirt road (the original access to St. Mary) below the foot of St. Mary Lake near the old ranger station and leaves the lakeshore quickly to wind through a dense, old stand of windblown Douglas firs. This road winds on through stands of aspen and huge open meadows filled with wildflowers, which offer views of the snowcapped peaks up the St. Mary Valley. At mile 3.9, the trail leaves the dirt track and descends to cross Red Eagle Creek via a suspension bridge. The trail follows the creek for 1.2 miles to a junction with the St. Mary Lake Trail. The trail then recrosses the creek and continues through more intensely burned country to the foot of Red Eagle Lake, which was formed by the damming action of a sill of hard rock at the lake's outlet.

Red Eagle Lake is well-known for its population of huge rainbow-cutthroat hybrid trout, as well as a few smaller brookies. Some sort of boat is needed to reach out beyond the drop-offs where the lunkers lurk in deeper water. From the campground at the foot of the lake, one can view the craggy peaks of Norris Mountain, Split Mountain, and Mount Logan with the Red Eagle and Logan Glaciers on its east face. As the trail winds around the east shore of the lake, Red Eagle Mountain's

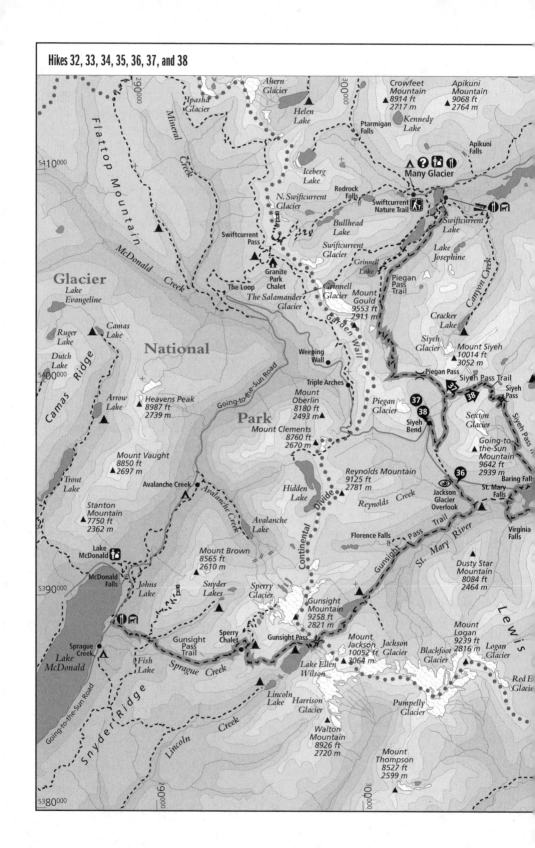

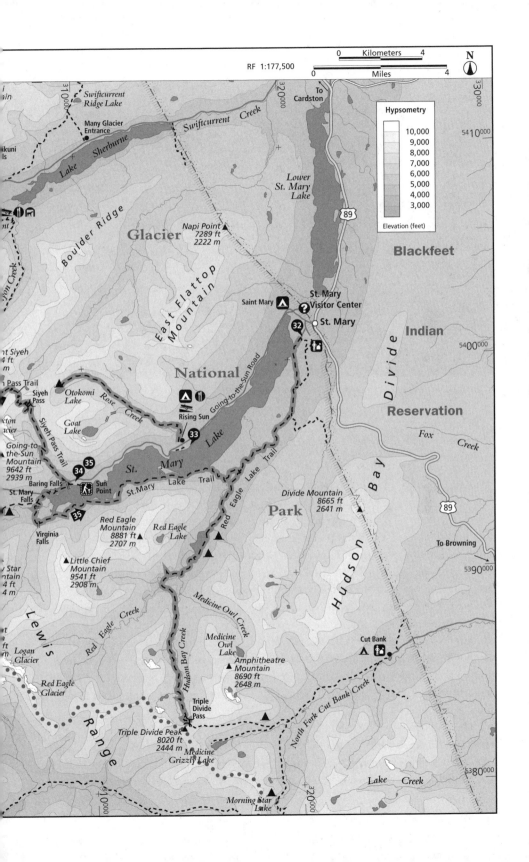

RF 1:177,500

Kilometers

Miles

N

Hypsometry

10,000
9,000
8,000
7,000
6,000
5,000
4,000
3,000

Elevation (feet)

Swiftcurrent
Ridge Lake

Many Glacier
Entrance

Swiftcurrent Creek

To
Cardston

kuni
ls

Lake   Sherburne

Lower
St. Mary
Lake

89

Boulder   Ridge

Glacier

Napi Point
7289 ft
2222 m

Blackfeet

E a s t   F l a t t o p   M o u n t a i n

Saint Mary

St. Mary
Visitor Center

St. Mary

32

Indian

National

Going-to-the-Sun Road

t Siyeh
4 ft
m

n Pass Trail

Siyeh
Pass

Otokomi
Lake

Rose   Creek

Reservation

Rising Sun

Goat
Lake

33

St.   Mary   Lake

Fox   Creek

xton
cier

Going-to-
the-Sun
Mountain
9642 ft
2939 m

35

34

Baring Falls

St. Mary
Falls

Siyeh Pass Trail

Sun
Point

St. Mary   Lake   Trail

Red Eagle Lake Trail

Divide Mountain
8665 ft
2641 m

89

35

Virginia
Falls

Red Eagle
Mountain
8881 ft
2707 m

Red Eagle
Lake

Park

To Browning

Little Chief
Mountain
9541 ft
2908 m

Hudson   Bay

y Star
ntain
4 ft
4 m

Medicine Owl Creek

Medicine
Owl
Lake

Cut Bank

Lewis

Red Eagle Creek

Hudson Bay Creek

Amphitheatre
Mountain
8690 ft
2648 m

Logan
Glacier

Red Eagle
Glacier

North Fork Cut Bank Creek

Triple
Divide
Pass

R a n g e

Triple Divide Peak
8020 ft
2444 m

Medicine
Grizzly Lake

Lake   Creek

Morning Star
Lake

Red Eagle Lake

red argillite mass looms to the west. There is a second campground at the head of the lake.

Triple Divide Pass Option: The trail continues to the south, reaching Triple Divide Pass after almost 8 miles. For the first mile, it follows the east bank of Red Eagle Creek, then crosses a suspension bridge upstream of several substantial waterfalls. The trail dips west, then crosses Red Eagle Creek for the final time and swings to the south to ascend the valley of Hudson Bay Creek. The trail remains fairly level, passing through old-growth forest. After 3 miles the burn gives way to brush fields, and an impressive waterfall can be seen cascading from a cleft high on Split Mountain to the west. The reddish massifs of Medicine Owl Peak, Amphitheater Mountain, and Mount James are visible across the valley.

After crossing the unnamed creek of the aforementioned waterfall, the trail ascends through dense willows (make noise to warn off bears) and emerges into grassy parklands dotted with stands of fir. From these meadows, Norris Mountain is seen at the head of the valley, with Triple Divide Peak protruding as a knobbed ridge from its east face.

The trail climbs gently to the head of the valley, where a series of babbling waterfalls cascades down a low ledge of cretaceous rock. Here the trail begins its assault of Triple Divide Pass in earnest, switching back across parklands and scree slopes to the pass, which lies at the foot of Triple Divide Peak. This peak marks the watershed divide between the Arctic, Atlantic, and Pacific Oceans. An alpinists' route to the peak's summit crosses the steep talus bowl to the south and climbs the second of two couloirs, which pierces the Atlantic Valley headwall to reach a flat saddle. From this point, it is an easy scramble up the south slope of the peak to the summit.

Talus slopes surrounding the pass are home to pikas and marmots, as well as chipmunks and several species of ground squirrel. Bands of bighorn sheep are frequently sighted on the slopes surrounding the pass. Inexperienced climbers with a taste for high places will find an easy ascent along the ridgeline to the northeast, terminating at the summit of 9,375-foot Mount James.

Key Points

0.0 Trail sign. Trail follows abandoned dirt road, leaving the lakeshore within 1 mile.

1.2 Junction with trail returning to 1913 ranger station. Stay right for Red Eagle Lake.

3.9 Trail leaves road, turning south toward Red Eagle Lake. Trail descends to Red Eagle Creek, crosses it, and then follows its north bank.

5.1 Junction with St. Mary Lake Trail. Stay left for Red Eagle Lake. Trail follows Red Eagle Creek, crossing again to the south bank, then leaves the creek and cuts through forested lowlands to Red Eagle Lake.

7.5 Red Eagle Lake (foot) and Campground. Trail follows eastern shore of Red Eagle Lake.

8.4 Red Eagle Lake (head) and Campground. Trail follows Red Eagle Creek, crossing it once.

10.1 Trail turns south, ascending the Hudson Bay Creek Valley.

14.8 Trail begins fairly steep ascent to the pass.

16.2 Triple Divide Pass.

33 Otokomi Lake

A day hike or short backpack from Rising Sun Motor Inn to Otokomi Lake, 5.0 miles (8 km) one way.

See map on pages 122 and 123.
Elevation gain: 1,882 feet
Maximum elevation: 6,125 feet

Difficulty: Moderate
Topo map: Rising Sun

Finding the trailhead: Rising Sun Trailhead is located to the left of the Rising Sun camp store. Park in the large lot located there.

The Hike

This trail passes up Rose Creek along the Lewis thrust fault to a low-elevation cirque lake among blocky, reddish mountains. The trail begins in the wooded St. Mary Valley and climbs around a hillside to the west to enter the Rose Creek drainage. After hiking along the forested creek valley for 2.5 miles past pools and small waterfalls, you climb onto an open rockslide area from which Goat Mountain is clearly visible across the lake. Just before reaching the lake, the trail passes Otokomi Campground to the left. The trail bends around to the southwest before arriving at the outlet to Otokomi Lake. The lake covers the floor of the Rose Basin, named for the ruddy argillite cliffs surrounding the cirque.

Key Points

0.0 Trail sign.
1.5 Trail follows east bank of Rose Creek.
5.0 Otokomi Lake Campground.

34 St. Mary and Virginia Falls

A half-day hike from Going-to-the-Sun Road to St. Mary Falls, 1.2 miles (2 km) one way; or from Going-to-the-Sun Road to Virginia Falls, 1.8 miles (3 km) one way.

See map on pages 122 and 123.
Elevation gain: 285 feet
Elevation loss: 260 feet

Maximum elevation: 4,800 feet
Difficulty: Easy
Topo map: Rising Sun

Finding the trailhead: Trailhead is located on the Going-to-the-Sun Road approximately 0.3 mile west of Baring Creek.

The Hike

This trail is a short and pleasant stroll through sun-dappled forest to several roaring waterfalls in the valley below Going-to-the-Sun Road. From the trailhead, the trail descends to the valley floor, past well-marked trail junctions to cross the river immediately below St. Mary Falls. The trail then opens up, affording views of Little Chief

St. Mary Falls

and Dusty Star Mountains. The path winds around the ends of several hillocks to Virginia Creek, which it follows for half a mile past a narrow gorge to the second falls at the foot of a hanging valley. A small spur trail takes you to the foot of the falls.

Key Points

0.0 Trail sign. Trail descends toward the St. Mary River.

0.3 Junction with the Piegan Pass Trail. Turn right for St. Mary Falls and Virginia Falls.

0.7 Junction with St. Mary Trail. Turn left for falls.

1.2 Trail crosses St. Mary River at St. Mary Falls. Trail continues, ascending the south side of the St. Mary Valley.

1.8 Virginia Falls.

35 St. Mary Lake

A backpack that follows the south shore of St. Mary Lake to Red Eagle Creek, 11.2 miles (18 km) one way.

See map on pages 122 and 123.
Elevation gain: 1,580 feet
Elevation loss: 1,620 feet

Maximum elevation: 4,900 feet
Difficulty: Moderate
Topo maps: St. Mary, Rising Sun

Finding the trailhead: Trailhead is located on the Going-to-the-Sun Road approximately 0.3 mile west of Baring Creek.

The Hike

This trail parallels the south shore of St. Mary Lake, but stays high on the mountain slopes and rarely strays near the shoreline. It is used primarily by backpackers on extended trips along the Continental Divide Trail. There are no campgrounds along its length; backpackers should consider camping at the Reynolds Creek Campground (available for extended trips only) or at Red Eagle Lake.

From the St. Mary Falls Trailhead, a gentle stroll leads down forested slopes to a crossing of the St. Mary River where it pours into St. Mary Lake. The bridge is washed by spray from the thundering cataract of St. Mary Falls, immediately upstream. The trail now continues southward, climbing steadily beside the gorge of Virginia Creek to the base of Virginia Falls. A vigorous climb leads up the slope beside the falls, crossing the creek below an upper cataract.

From this point, the trail traverses high across slopes covered in a shady forest of spruce. Occasional avalanche slopes interrupt the forest to allow views of Going-to-the-Sun Mountain across the valley, as well as the proud cockscomb of Reynolds

St. Mary Lake

Mountain amid a cluster of picturesque summits at the head of the valley. The trail remains high on the mountainsides for a time, passing mossy outcrops of bedrock and wending its way through thickets of thimbleberry and the occasional stinging nettle. The next overlook is a cliff top that commands views of a striking little peninsula in the lake below.

The trail then returns to the forest as the spruces give way to stands of the more drought-tolerant Douglas fir. After crossing a major stream that drains a high basin at the foot of Mahtotopa Mountain, the path glides down through the timber to approach the shore of St. Mary Lake. The actual shoreline remains tantalizingly out of reach, but the shimmering waters can be glimpsed through the trunks of the conifers and cottonwoods.

Rounding a headland, the trail swings across steep slopes of broken shale at the base of Red Eagle Mountain. From here, you can take in fine views of the peaks that rise above the opposite shore of the lake. Silver Dollar Beach can now be seen ahead, but the path ascends onto the slopes once more. It offers only aerial views of this unusual, thin strip of gravel that protects a shallow lagoon against a rocky headland. This beach is a terminal moraine left behind by the toe of the glacier that carved out the St. Mary Valley as it retreated.

The trail now climbs away from the lakeshore into a dense forest, but periodic talus slopes reveal vistas of the aquamarine waters as well as the crags of Red Eagle Mountain overhead. The path eventually glides down toward the lakeshore for a final time, where a side trip to the water's edge is only a short bushwhack away. A cliff-walled headland looms ahead, announcing the path's departure from St. Mary Lake. From here, a workmanlike ascent leads inland through the 2006 Red Eagle burn to the crest of the Red Eagle divide. Here the path descends into the valley of Red Eagle Creek to meet the Red Eagle Lake Trail near its first stream crossing.

Key Points

- **0.0** Trail sign. Trail descends toward the St. Mary River.
- **0.3** Junction with the Piegan Pass Trail. Turn right for St. Mary Falls and Virginia Falls.
- **0.7** Junction with St. Mary Trail. Turn left for falls.
- **1.2** Trail crosses St. Mary River at St. Mary Falls. Trail continues, ascending the south side of the St. Mary Valley.
- **1.9** Virginia Falls.
- **11.2** Junction with Red Eagle Lake Trail.

36 Gunsight Pass

A backpack from Jackson Glacier Overlook to Lake Ellen Wilson, 10.9 miles (17.5 km) one way; from Jackson Glacier Overlook to Sperry Chalet, 13.3 miles (22 km) one way; or from Jackson Glacier Overlook to Lake McDonald, 20.0 miles (32 km) one way.

See map on pages 122 and 123.
Elevation gain: 3,287 feet
Elevation loss: 3,787 feet
Maximum elevation: 7,050 feet (Lincoln Pass)

Difficulty: Moderately strenuous (east to west); strenuous (west to east)
Topo maps: Logan Pass, Mount Jackson, Lake McDonald East

Finding the trailhead: To hike the trail from east to west, take the Going-to-the-Sun Road east of Logan Pass to the Jackson Glacier Overlook. The Gunsight Pass Trail begins at the east end of this overlook. To hike the trail from west to east, start at the Snyder Creek Trailhead, which is located across the Going-to-the-Sun Road from the Lake McDonald Lodge coffee shop.

The Hike

The Gunsight Pass Trail is an extremely popular backpacking route that ascends to the Continental Divide from the St. Mary Valley and crosses rocky ledges and alpine

"Horse and rider" atop the crest of the cliff wall near Lincoln Pass

meadows to Sperry Chalet before descending to Lake McDonald. The high country offers access to active glaciers, excellent fishing in subalpine lakes, and viewing opportunities for many types of wildlife. The trail can be hiked in one grueling day by a dedicated hiker, but one day is insufficient to take advantage of and appreciate the varied opportunities presented by the trail. Gunsight Pass receives heavy snow that may not melt until mid-July and thus is safest in the late summer. Because the backcountry campsites fill up quickly along this trail, backpackers should register for campsites as early as possible.

The trail begins at the Jackson Glacier Overlook, and after a brief descent to the valley floor, the trail follows the meandering course of the St. Mary River. The trail winds through mossy forest and marshy openings, crossing Reynolds Creek below Deadwood Falls. To the south, the St. Mary River winds through open, grassy meadows, and Dusty Star Mountain and Citadel Mountain can be glimpsed to the south. At mile 4.0, a spur trail leads off to the west, rising gently to the base of Florence Falls, a tumbling cascade that issues from the end of the hanging valley containing Twin Lakes. Half a mile farther, the trail begins a moderate ascent up the east slope of Fusillade Mountain. Brushy avalanche slopes allow excellent views of Mounts Jackson and Logan at the head of the valley, with the extensive Jackson and Blackfoot Glaciers, which were once one huge glacier, at their feet. A trail ascends toward these two glaciers, but is no longer brushed out regularly and tends to disappear with disturbing frequency in jungles of cow parsnip. At mile 6.2, the trail reaches the foot of Gunsight Lake, reputed to be good fishing for rainbow trout. There is an extensive campground at the foot of this brushy lake, which is a good place to view ospreys swooping for their fishy prey.

From the foot of Gunsight Lake, the trail crosses the outlet via a suspension bridge and begins a long climb up the open north slope of Mount Jackson to the pass almost 1,600 feet above. As the trail climbs around cliff ledges, there are outstanding views of the folded strata of Gunsight Mountain to the north. As the trail approaches the pass, it enters charming meadow vales with rushing seasonal streams and permanent snowfields gracing the rock walls above on both sides of the valley. At the pass, an old shelter cabin with a nearby stream makes a pleasant rest stop, with views of Lake Ellen Wilson and the cliffs surrounding it. Gunsight Pass is an outstanding place for close-range viewing of mountain goats in their natural environment.

From the pass, the trail descends the steep headwall of the Lincoln Creek Valley, winding around the north wall of the cirque above Lake Ellen Wilson. Approximately 1.5 miles beyond the pass, a spur trail of 0.3 mile descends to the lake and its attendant campground. Overlooking the cooking area of the campground sits a huge glacial erratic, a boulder carried by a glacier and finally deposited when the glacier melted. The lake itself has excellent fishing for large and abundant brook trout.

From the Ellen Wilson spur, the trail begins climbing along the north wall of the cirque. As the trail nears Lincoln Pass (7,050 feet), Lincoln Lake becomes visible in the valley to the south. As the trail swings onto a meadowy bench, the cliff ahead contains the outline of a horse and rider rising from its crest, above and to the east of a hole that pierces the cliff wall. The trail then swings around to the north, crossing a substantial stream that runs beneath rocky talus, before the final ascent to the pass. At this point, it is possible to skirt the cliff base to the west to get a complete view of Lake Ellen Wilson and Lincoln Lake, as well as 1,344-foot Beaver Chief Falls cascading down the rock face between them. Another 0.25 mile on the trail brings you to Lincoln Pass, from which it is a short and easy climb to the summit of Lincoln Peak to the west.

As the trail descends from Lincoln Pass onto a high parkland shelf, it passes a small tarn that provides a refreshing dip to the trail-weary hiker (no soap, please). The trail descends along the shelf, passing the Sperry Campground and entering the Sperry Chalet complex. The trail exits this complex in front of the dining hall and descends 0.2 mile to the junction with the Sperry Glacier Overlook Trail.

From the Sperry Glacier Overlook spur trail, the Gunsight Pass Trail descends steeply past Beaver Medicine Falls to the floor of the Sprague Creek Valley, where it passes through dense stands of Douglas fir inhabited by numerous mule deer. After following Sprague Creek for about 3 miles, the trail rounds the end of a spur ridge and crosses Snyder Creek. After this crossing, known as Crystal Ford, a trail to the east runs for 2.6 miles up a gentle valley to a campground at Snyder Lake, set among towering, snow-clad peaks. The main trail continues its descent down the Snyder Creek Valley for 1.8 miles to the trail's terminus at Lake McDonald Lodge.

Sperry Glacier Overlook Option: The trail to Sperry Glacier is steep and challenging, rising 1,600 feet in 2.5 miles to Comeau Pass and then a little over a mile to the toe of the glacier. Hikers of this trail are rewarded with breathtaking vistas of the desolate Lewis Range peaks. The trail first ascends the headwall of a low cirque to the floor of a higher cirque, where the trail winds among rocky wastes interspersed with miniature meadows. Feather Woman and Akaiyan Lakes form glassy reflecting pools for the cliffs to the south when these alpine lakes become free of ice in July. Beyond these two high tarns, the trail reaches the cirque's low headwall, which it passes through via a narrow stairway blasted into the living rock. Emerging from the top of this stairway, the hiker is greeted by awe-inspiring views of the mountaintops to the north and east, across the rock and snow wastes that stretch away toward Sperry Glacier. By following rock cairns, it is possible to hike a mile farther through this wasteland to the foot of Sperry Glacier, with seasonal lakes at its base. An alpinists' route exists connecting Sperry Glacier to the Hidden Lake Trail. Walking on the glacier is not recommended for hikers inexperienced in glacier travel.

Key Points

0.0 Trail sign downhill from Jackson Glacier Overlook. Trail descends toward Reynolds Creek.

1.3 Junction with Gunsight Pass Trail immediately after Deadwood Falls. Turn right for Gunsight Pass. Trail begins a gentle ascent of the Reynolds Creek Valley.

4.0 Junction with Florence Falls Trail (0.8 mile). Stay left for Gunsight Pass. Trail ascends moderately along the flanks of Fusillade Mountain.

6.2 Gunsight Lake Campground. Trail crosses Gunsight Lake outlet, then climbs steeply up the north face of Mount Jackson.

9.2 Gunsight Pass (6,946 feet). Trail descends steeply toward Lake Ellen Wilson.

10.9 Junction with Lake Ellen Wilson Campground Trail (0.3 mile). Stay right for Sperry Chalet. Trail ascends steeply along the south face of Gunsight Mountain.

12.1 Lincoln Pass. Trail descends into the Glacier Basin.

13.2 Sperry Campground junction.

13.3 Sperry Chalet.

13.8 Junction with Sperry Glacier Overlook Trail (3.7 miles, strenuous, maximum elevation 8,000 feet). Stay left for Lake McDonald. Trail descends steeply, following Sprague Creek, and then turns north around the end of a ridge to Snyder Creek.

18.1 Junction with Snyder Ridge Trail. Stay right for Lake McDonald. Trail crosses to north bank of Snyder Creek.

18.2 Junction with Snyder Lakes Trail. Stay left for Lake McDonald.

18.3 Junction with Mount Brown Lookout Trail. Stay left for Lake McDonald.

20.0 Lake McDonald Lodge.

37 Piegan Pass

A day hike from Siyeh Bend to Piegan Pass, 4.5 miles (7 km) one way; or from Siyeh Bend to Many Glacier Hotel, 12.8 miles (20.5 km) one way.

See map on pages 122 and 123.
Elevation gain: 1,670 feet
Elevation loss: 2,640 feet
Maximum elevation: 7,560 feet

Difficulty: Moderate (south to north); strenuous (north to south)
Topo maps: Logan Pass, Many Glacier

Finding the trailhead: Siyeh Bend parking area, 3 miles east of Logan Pass on the Going-to-the-Sun Road. Trail begins on the east bank of Siyeh Creek.

The Hike

Piegan Pass links the St. Mary drainage with the popular Many Glacier area, through a high, barren col between Cataract Mountain and Pollock Mountain. There are no campgrounds along this route, so it must be attempted as a long day hike. The trail passes through a wide range of elevations, offering a diverse assemblage of ecological communities populated by a variety of wildlife species. Fantastic views are available all along the route, highlighted by a rarely seen view of the eastern face of the Garden Wall. Hikers may opt to detour to Grinnell Lake and continue around the north shore of Lake Josephine. This option increases the length of the trip by approximately 0.5 mile and avoids trail sections heavily used by horse parties. The trail may also be hiked from north to south; this greatly increases its difficulty due to the low starting elevation.

The trail begins at Siyeh Bend on the Going-to-the-Sun Road, at a scenic crossing of Siyeh Creek. The open meadows and tiny fir trees are left behind quickly as the trail climbs onto well-drained slopes covered with tall spruce and fir trees. The trail switchback as it climbs moderately through the trees, reaching a trail junction at mile 1.2. From this junction, the trail turns north, climbing gently through increasingly open forest interrupted by small patches of meadow. Going-to-the-Sun Mountain and Matahpi Peak loom to the east.

At mile 2.7, the trail reaches the Siyeh Pass junction among the open meadows of Preston Park. Looking to the west, the massive hump of Piegan Mountain is crowned by a large glacier bearing the same name, and 10,014-foot Mount Siyeh blocks views to the north. Bearing left, the trail to Piegan Pass crosses a small creek and ascends onto the barren talus slopes of Cataract Mountain. The trail curves around to the head of the basin to reach the high col of Piegan Pass. The dark band of rock near the pass is an igneous intrusion that was laid down long after the older sedimentary strata. Mountain goats are frequently seen capering on rocky slopes and in grassy parklands around the pass, and marmots may be seen ambling along in rockslide areas.

Looking northward, the Bishop's Cap crowns the Garden Wall on the western rim of the valley, while Mount Gould can be seen in the distance. Across the valley, the peak of Mount Grinnell rises above the valley floor. The trail descends steeply to a high bench with subalpine fir parklands and, after crossing the gentle ledge, resumes a precipitous rate of descent. From the bench, the summit of Allen Mountain is easily seen to the northeast, owing its reddish hue to Grinnell argillite. After descending for about a quarter of a mile, the trail draws even with Morning Eagle Falls.

From this point, the trail follows Cataract Creek, crossing it twice on the way to the Feather Plume Cutoff 4.2 miles beyond the pass. Hikers wishing to see Grinnell Lake and avoid the horse trails should bear left at the cutoff trail.

For hikers continuing directly to the hotel, the trail winds around the northwest flank of Allen Mountain, following the contours of the mountain. Below lies aquamarine Lake Josephine, which can be reached via several short cutoff trails along the route. Across the valley, the greenish base of Grinnell Point belies its Appekuny argillite nature. A sharp eye may spot the relatively fresh tailings from an abandoned mine below the tip of the point. Grizzly bears abound in the low-elevation meadows; care must be taken not to disturb these majestic creatures. The trail reaches its terminus at the upper parking lot of the Many Glacier Hotel.—*Candice Hall*

Key Points

0.0 Trail sign.

1.2 Junction with Piegan Pass Trail. Turn left for Piegan Pass.

2.7 Junction with Siyeh Pass Trail. Stay left for Piegan Pass. The trail crosses a small creek and winds around the base of Cataract Mountain.

4.5 Piegan Pass. Trail descends steeply to Morning Eagle Falls.

7.7 Morning Eagle Falls.

8.7 Trail enters Grinnell Complex at junction with Grinnell Lake Trail. Stay right for fastest route to Many Glacier Hotel. Trail follows the foot of Allen Mountain.

10.5 Junction with Josephine Lake Cutoff Trail. Stay right for Many Glacier.

12.8 Many Glacier Hotel upper parking lot.

38 Siyeh Pass

A day hike from Siyeh Bend to Siyeh Pass, 4.7 miles (7.5 km) one way; or from Siyeh Bend to Sunrift Gorge exit, 10.3 miles (16.5 km) one way.

See map on pages 122 and 123
Elevation gain: 2,240 feet
Elevation loss: 3,440 feet

Maximum elevation: 8,080 feet
Difficulty: Moderately strenuous
Topo maps: Logan Pass, Rising Sun

Finding the trailhead: Siyeh Bend, approximately 3 miles east of Logan Pass on the Going-to-the-Sun Road. Trail departs on the east bank of Siyeh Creek.

The Hike

Siyeh Pass is a high-elevation route that traverses two passes on its way around Going-to-the-Sun Mountain. Snow accumulations often persist until late in the season on the south face of Matahpi Peak; rangers should be consulted concerning trail conditions before attempting this route.

The hike begins at Siyeh Bend, a large hairpin turn in the Going-to-the-Sun Road on the east side of the divide. The trail ascends from the east bank of Siyeh Creek onto the forested north flank of Going-to-the-Sun Mountain, through prime elk summer range. As the trail winds upward, it passes through stands of subalpine fir and spruce. At mile 2.7, the trail forks, with the left fork turning west to Piegan Pass and the right fork rising into Preston Park on its way to Siyeh Pass. The trail levels out, among beautiful fields of wildflowers and stands of dwarfed fir and subalpine larch, with unnamed tarns on both sides. At the head of this small bowl, the trail climbs moderately to the barren saddle of Siyeh Pass. To the north lies Mount Siyeh, overlooking Cracker Lake. A popular mountaineers' route ascends the south-facing slope above the pass and follows the spine of the ridge to the summit of Siyeh. Looking to the east, the Boulder Creek Valley frames pleasant vistas of the high plains.

From Siyeh Pass, the trail continues to climb, winding around the northeast slope of Matahpi Peak to a high, unnamed col. Views to the south encompass the ruddy summits across the St. Mary Valley as well as peaks farther south along the Continental Divide. As the trail descends into the Baring Creek Valley, the Sexton Glacier can be clearly observed actively scraping away at the rock face across the valley. Terminal moraines, piles of grayish rock pushed up and deposited at the foot of the glacier, can be clearly seen on the near (north) side of the glacier's toe. The toe of the glacier overhangs a sheer drop-off on its south side, and huge chunks of ice occasionally break off and thunder down the cliff into the valley below.

High saddle above Siyeh Pass

As the trail descends to the extensive, grassy slopes on the valley's west wall, grizzly bears may be encountered, so appropriate caution should be displayed. The trail descends rather rapidly across many short switchbacks and winds through low, tortured stands of Douglas fir toward the valley floor. The trail follows the east bank of Baring Creek as it cuts ever deeper into the rock strata, eventually forming Sunrift Gorge. The trail emerges onto the highway just below the foot of this chasm, at mile 40.

Key Points

0.0   Trail sign. Trail ascends moderately along the west slope of Matahpi Peak.

1.2   Junction with Piegan Pass Trail. Turn left for Siyeh Pass.

2.7   Junction with Siyeh Pass Trail. Turn right for Siyeh Pass. Trail passes through Preston Park, past several glacial tarns, and then ascends moderately to Siyeh Pass.

4.7   Siyeh Pass. Trail ascends through a high saddle on Matahpi Peak.

5.6   Sexton Glacier Overlook. Trail descends steeply, along the east wall of the Baring Creek Valley.

10.0   Sunrift Gorge. Trail passes along the east rim of Sunrift Gorge.

10.3   Baring Creek exit.

Connecting Hikes

An administrative trail crosses from the Red Eagle Trace to **Divide Creek,** over a low spur ridge of Curly Bear Mountain. The trail is poorly maintained and overrun with grizzly bears during the summer, when it should be avoided. However, it provides a popular cross-country ski route in wintertime.

Many Glacier

Many Glacier Hotel was built in 1914 by the Great Northern Railway as a destination resort for its rail tourists. The hotel sits among soaring peaks and jagged arêtes, which give this area the nickname "America's Little Switzerland." Since the park's creation, myriad trails have been built to reach the scenic wonders surrounding the hotel, making the Many Glacier area a hub for day-hiking activities. Lush meadows and tumbling waterfalls below snowy peaks invite the traveler to pause and contemplate the awe-inspiring beauty of the mountains.

Mount Gould and Angel Wing from above Lake Josephine

The lower end of the valley is dominated by Lake Sherburne, which was impounded during the New Deal era. The formation of this reservoir inundated the old mining town of Altyn, which had once served as a center for unsuccessful gold and copper operations in the surrounding mountains.

The Many Glacier area is home to many kinds of wildlife. Most prominent is the majestic grizzly bear, which is frequently seen foraging for bulbs and berries on the open slopes of the surrounding mountains. Mountain goats cavort on the rocky ledges of sheer cliffs, and groups of bighorn sheep ewes with their young are sometimes seen in the lowlands around the hotel. The meadows and forests abound with rodents and songbirds of all kinds.

Visitor services are available in the area around the hotel as well as the nearby town of Babb, on the neighboring Blackfeet Indian Reservation. Trail rides of varying duration depart from the Many Glacier corral above the hotel, and a privately owned tour boat concession runs between the hotel and the upper end of Lake Josephine, providing interpretive tours and transportation to the upper Cataract Creek drainage. The spacious campground at Many Glacier provides sites for all types of vehicles, as well as a few sites reserved free-of-charge to backpackers on extended hikes through the area. The passes in the Many Glacier area access areas to the north, west, and south, providing the best opportunities for backpacking.

39 Cracker Lake

A long day hike or short backpack from Many Glacier Hotel to Cracker Lake Campground, 6.1 miles (10 km) one way.

Elevation gain: 1,120 feet
Maximum elevation: 5,900 feet
Difficulty: Moderate

Topo maps: Many Glacier, Lake Sherburne, Logan Pass

Finding the trailhead: Many Glacier Trailhead, which is located at the south end of the upper parking lot for Many Glacier Hotel.

The Hike

Cracker Lake is a popular day hike destination for travelers in the Many Glacier area. The trail winds from the shore of Swiftcurrent Lake up a forested ridgeline to a wide, meadowy basin filled with wildflowers and butterflies. Cracker Lake is a cold body of water made turquoise by light refraction through its load of suspended glacial silt. At the head of the lake, the old Cracker Mine lies beneath the towering cliff walls of Mount Siyeh. There is also a small campground near the head of the lake for backpackers. This trail receives heavy horse traffic, so you should be prepared to yield to saddle stock when meeting on the trail.

Key Points

0.0 Trail sign. Trail winds around the base of Allen Mountain.
0.8 Trail follows Allen Creek.
1.3 Junction with Cracker Flats Horse Trail. Stay right for Cracker Lake.
1.5 Trail crosses Allen Creek and ascends ridge between Allen and Canyon Creeks.
2.5 Trail follows west bank of Canyon Creek, ascending moderately.
3.8 Trail crosses Canyon Creek.
5.6 Foot of Cracker Lake.
6.1 Cracker Lake Campground.

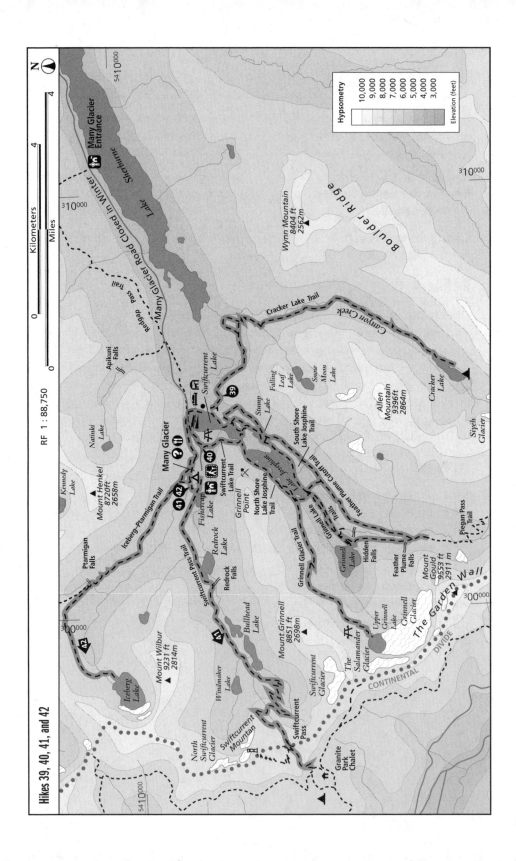

Hikes 39, 40, 41, and 42

RF 1 : 88,750

N

Kilometers
0   4

Miles
0   4

Hypsometry

	Elevation (feet)
10,000	
9,000	
8,000	
7,000	
6,000	
5,000	
4,000	
3,000	

Many Glacier Entrance

Lake Sherburne

Many Glacier Road Closed in Winter

Ridge Pass Trail

Apikuni Falls

Wynn Mountain
8404 ft
2562m

Boulder Ridge

Cracker Lake Trail

Canyon Creek

Swiftcurrent Lake

39

Falling Leaf Lake

Snow Moon Lake

Stump Lake

South Shore Lake Josphine Trail

Allen Mountain
9396ft
2864m

Cracker Lake

Siyeh Glacier

Natinki Lake

Many Glacier

? **?**

40

Swiftcurrent Lake Trail

Feather Plume Cutoff Trail

North Shore Lake Josphine Trail

Lake Josphine

Grinnell Point

41 **42**

Fishercap Lake

Mount Henkel
8720ft
2658m

Kennedy Lake

Iceberg-Ptarmigan Trail

Ptarmigan Falls

Swiftcurrent Pass Trail

Redrock Lake

Redrock Falls

Grinnell Lake Trails

Grinnell Glacier Trail

Grinnell Lake

Hidden Falls

Feather Plume Falls

Piegan Pass Trail

Mount Gould
9553 ft
2911 m

42

Iceberg Lake

Mount Wilbur
9231 ft
2814m

Bullhead Lake

41

Windmaker Lake

Mount Grinnell
8851 ft
2698m

Upper Grinnell Lake

The Salamander Glacier

Grinnell Glacier

The Garden Wall

North Swiftcurrent Glacier

Swiftcurrent Mountain

Swiftcurrent Glacier

Swiftcurrent Pass

Granite Park Chalet

CONTINENTAL DIVIDE

40 The Grinnell Complex

Day hikes from Swiftcurrent Picnic Area to Grinnell Glacier, 5.5 miles (9 km) one way; from Many Glacier Hotel to Grinnell Lake, 3.1 miles (5 km) one way; or from Lake Josephine upper boat dock to Grinnell Lake, 0.9 miles (1.5 km) one way.

See map on page 142.
Difficulty: Moderately strenuous (Grinnell Glacier); easy (Swiftcurrent Lake); moderate (others)

Topo map: Many Glacier

The Hike

An extensive complex of interconnected trails originates near the Many Glacier Hotel and provides a variety of pleasant day hikes in the lower Cataract Creek Valley. For a nominal fee, tour boats provide a guided cruise from the hotel to the upper end of Lake Josephine, also providing easy access to the upper end of the valley. The trails surrounding Lake Josephine provide open views of the high peaks at the head of the valley and provide access to the low-elevation lakes on the valley floor. Trails from upper Lake Josephine pass through relict forests on their way to glittering waterfalls cascading from the valley's headwall. The Grinnell Glacier Trail accesses one of the largest remaining glaciers in the park, and guided naturalist tours into the glacial cirque are offered at regular intervals. The Grinnell Complex is covered in detail by trail number in the following pages. These trails are commonly closed due to the presence of bears; check with rangers before starting your trip. Horses are not permitted on these trails with the exception of #171, 173, 172, 113, 181, and 174 (between the Oastler Shelter and the Piegan Pass Trail).

Swiftcurrent Lake Trail (#167)

The Swiftcurrent Lake Trail is a well-traveled footpath and self-guiding nature trail that makes a complete circuit of this front-country lake, also providing access to hikers bound for points west in the valley. The trail begins at a picnic area 0.5 mile west of the hotel turnoff and immediately enters a stand of smallish lodgepole pines. Emerging from the trees, the trail crosses willow-choked Swiftcurrent Creek via a wooden bridge and reaches the wooded lakeshore shortly thereafter. After 0.7 mile, the trail reaches the upper Swiftcurrent boat dock, where trail #168 takes off to the west, around the north shore of Lake Josephine. Hikers bound for Grinnell Lake and Grinnell Glacier should take this trail.

The Swiftcurrent Lake Trail continues its circuit of the lake, crossing Grinnell Creek. Immediately east of this crossing, a trail (#180) connects to the Lake Josephine South Shore Trail (#171). The main path continues around the lake,

Mount Gould and Swiftcurrent Lake

finally terminating at the hotel. Across the bridge, north of the hotel, another trail section brings you back to the picnic area.

North Shore Lake Josephine Trail (#168)
A paved footpath from the upper Swiftcurrent boat dock runs west to the foot of Lake Josephine, where it continues for 1.4 miles around the north shore of the lake as a dirt trail. The reddish summit of Allen Mountain dominates the skyline to the south. Midway up the lake, trail #170 to Grinnell Glacier climbs to the west. The trail continues to the head of the lake, where a cutoff trail climbs steeply to the Grinnell Glacier Trail, and a connecting trail (#174) crosses the inlet via boardwalks to a trail junction at the Oastler Shelter.

South Shore Lake Josephine Trail (#171)
The first short section of the South Shore Trail is heavily used by guided horse parties and provides a route from the hotel to the head of Lake Josephine. This trail has two origins: the southwest corner of the hotel's upper parking lot and the terminus of the hotel service road. The trail stays inland for 0.5 mile, descending to the valley floor shortly before reaching Stump Lake. At this point, trail #180 enters, connecting the South Shore Trail with the trail around Swiftcurrent Lake.

The trail winds around tiny Stump Lake, emerging at the eastern shore of Lake Josephine. Stunning views across the turquoise waters reveal Mount Gould's blocky profile, with glaciers and snowbanks at its base. As the trail travels the length of the lake, Grinnell Point can be seen in profile above the north shore. Upon reaching the Oastler Shelter near the upper boat dock, this trail meets trails running to Piegan Pass and Grinnell Lake.

Grinnell Glacier Trail (#170)

Hikers accessing Upper Grinnell Lake and Grinnell Glacier start at the picnic area near Swiftcurrent Lake. Skirt the western shore of Swiftcurrent Lake via trail #167 and then continues around Lake Josephine on trail #168.

Halfway up Lake Josephine, trail #170 rises through subalpine firs, above a relict forest spared by severe fires. The trail surmounts several steep switchbacks on the southern flank of Mount Grinnell, emerging in alpine meadows high above the turquoise pool of Grinnell Lake and the waterfall at its head. As the trail gains altitude, panoramic views of the peaks crowding upper Cataract Creek can be seen to the south. The ruddy peak of Allen Mountain dominates the foreground, while Mount Siyeh and Cataract Mountain loom above the head of the valley. The Garden Wall forms the western rim of the vale and rises to a massive peak overlooking the trail to the southwest—Mount Gould.

The trail makes its way around steep cliffs above Grinnell Falls to a picnic area in a wooded glen. The picnic area offers log benches for the weary hiker and a pit toilet for those in search of other forms of relief. Shortly after leaving the picnic area, you will ascend to a recent terminal moraine left by the retreating glacier.

From this point above the milky waters of Upper Grinnell Lake, one can see the fissures and ice caves of Grinnell Glacier. The long, narrow glacier above and to the north, called "the Salamander," was connected with the main glacier until recent times. The tiny glacier high on the north shoulder of Mount Gould is Gem Glacier, which is of great thickness. Upper Grinnell Lake, which lies at the foot of the glacier, derives its milky aquamarine color from the refraction of sunlight through suspended particles of fine dust created by the abrasive action of the glacier. Hikers inexperienced in the arts of glacier travel should not venture onto the ice; it is unstable and shot through with ice caves and fissures that pose a mortal threat to the unprepared.

Grinnell Lake Trails (#173 and #175)

Two trails, one open to horses and the other reserved for foot travel, leave the Oastler Shelter and run parallel for 0.8 mile to Grinnell Lake. The trails follow Cataract Creek through a relict forest for 0.5 mile before reaching a crossing at a suspension bridge. The main trail crosses the creek, while a spur trail (#183) switchbacks up the creek's eastern shore to Hidden Falls. Horses are not permitted on this trail.

The primary trail continues west, reaching Grinnell Lake after another 0.3 mile. The lake sits at the foot of a reddish cliff, down which Grinnell Falls cascades from its source in the glacier above. The graceful promontory that extends from the eastern flank of Mount Gould to overshadow the lake's southern shore is known as Angel Wing. Trail #172 continues south from the lake, passing Feather Plume Falls on its way to meet the Piegan Pass Trail.

Feather Plume Cutoff Trail (#172)

The Feather Plume Cutoff Trail provides a link between the Piegan Pass Trail and the upper Grinnell Complex. From Grinnell Lake, the trail climbs briskly below the eastern wall of Angel Wing, the smallish promontory projecting from the eastern face of Mount Gould. The trail continues south, crossing Cataract Creek to its eastern bank. Shortly after passing below the misty base of Feather Plume Falls, the trail reaches its terminus at the Piegan Pass Trail junction.

Piegan Pass Trail (#113)

The Piegan Pass Trail begins at the upper parking lot at the hotel and follows the contours of Allen Mountain as it skirts above the south shore of Lake Josephine. Connecting trails provide links to Lake Josephine, some 1.2 (trail #181) and 2.3 (trail #174) miles from the hotel. The trail then bends to the south and joins the Feather Plume Cutoff Trail about 4.1 miles from the hotel.

41 Swiftcurrent Pass

A long day hike from Swiftcurrent Inn to Swiftcurrent Pass, 6.6 miles (10.5 km) one way; or a backpack from Swiftcurrent Inn to Granite Park, 7.6 miles (12 km) one way.

See map on page 142.
Elevation gain: 2,225 feet
Elevation loss: 735 feet

Maximum elevation: 6,770 feet
Difficulty: Strenuous
Topo maps: Many Glacier, Ahern Pass

Finding the trailhead: Trail begins at the west end of the Swiftcurrent Inn coffee shop parking lot.

The Hike

The Swiftcurrent Pass Trail follows the Swiftcurrent Valley past a chain of lakes to a steep ascent of the Continental Divide. This ascent to the pass is quite strenuous, but the trail is much easier if taken from other trails in the west toward the east. It may be attempted as a strenuous day hike or plugged into a more extended itinerary by linking up with the Highline Trail.

The trail begins at the Swiftcurrent Motor Inn and winds westward along the valley floor, among groves of tall aspen interspersed with lodgepole pine. The trail passes to the north of Fishercap Lake, which can only be glimpsed briefly through a few gaps in the vegetation. The trail climbs gently, crossing a small stream on its way to Redrock Lake. Notice that harsh growing conditions have stunted the pines and aspens around the lake. The trail continues west, passing Redrock Falls above the head of the lake. Two miles beyond Redrock Lake, the trail reaches Bullhead Lake, from which a northward glance reveals Mount Wilbur, Iceberg Peak, and the North Swiftcurrent Glacier on the east face of Swiftcurrent Mountain.

After Bullhead Lake, the trees fall away entirely, giving way to grassy fields. The trail reaches the towering headwall of the valley and begins a steep ascent beside precipitous waterfalls that issue forth from the Swiftcurrent Glacier high above. The trail crisscrosses cliff faces on its way to the pass, affording spectacular views of the chain of lakes in the valley below. As the trail emerges above the cliff face, it climbs through miniature meadows on its way to the low saddle of Swiftcurrent Pass.

Shortly beyond the pass, a side trail takes off to the north to ascend across steep switchbacks some 1.4 miles to Swiftcurrent Lookout. The view from the lookout is outstanding, with a glacier-carved rockscape sweeping away in all directions. The main trail descends gently for 0.9 mile to Granite Park, where it joins the Highline Trail.

Bullhead Lake

Key Points

0.0   Trail sign.

0.2   Junction with horse trail. Stay left for Swiftcurrent Pass. Trail follows floor of Swiftcurrent Valley, climbing gently.

2.0   Redrock Lake.

3.3   Bullhead Lake.

3.5   Trail begins ascent to Swiftcurrent Pass.

6.6   Swiftcurrent Pass.

6.7   Swiftcurrent Lookout Trail junction. Trail descends gently to Granite Park.

7.6   Granite Park Chalet.

42   Iceberg Lake

A day hike from Swiftcurrent Inn to Iceberg Lake, 4.5 miles (7 km) one way.

See map on page 142.
Elevation gain: 1,194 feet
Maximum elevation: 6,100 feet

Difficulty: Moderate
Topo map: Many Glacier

Finding the trailhead: Iceberg-Ptarmigan Trailhead, which departs from the north end of the Swiftcurrent Motor Inn complex, among the cabins behind the coffee shop. A parking pullout at the trailhead is marked with a trailhead sign.

The Hike

Iceberg Lake is a striking aquamarine tarn surrounded on three sides by towering cliffs. Ice-out may not occur until mid-July, and bergs for which the lake was named may be seen floating about well after that date. This stunning destination, as well as the brilliant wildflowers along the route, makes the Iceberg Lake Trail one of the most popular hikes in the park. It crosses fine grizzly bear habitat, and bears are frequently seen on the open slopes on both sides of the trail.

The hike begins at a short connecting trail that climbs briskly for several hundred yards to join the main trail coming in from the hotel. The trail then turns northwest, climbing gently along the open south slopes high above Wilbur Creek. Look for the magenta spikes of fireweed and the bulblike inflorescences of beargrass (a member of the lily family) early in the season. The trail passes below Altyn Peak, a greenish massif of Appekuny argillite, and Mount Wilbur, known to the Blackfeet as "Heavy Shield Mountain," rises across the valley to the south. The trail passes into open forests on its way to Ptarmigan Falls, a popular rest stop on hot summer days.

Cirque bearing Iceberg Lake

Shortly after passing the falls, the trail reaches the junction with the Ptarmigan Tunnel Trail and then turns southwest along the Ptarmigan Wall through increasingly alpine scenery toward the head of the valley. Looking south, a waterfall on Iceberg Creek can be glimpsed through the trees. The trail climbs gently as it curls around to the south into the glacial cirque that holds the lake.

The 3,000-foot cliffs surrounding the lake provide prime escape habitat for mountain goats, which are frequently seen in this area. Talus slopes along the lake's south shore are home to a variety of small mammals, including pikas and ground squirrels. The permanent snowfields at the head of the lake are remnants of a glacier that until recently occupied the basin beneath the cool shadows of Iceberg Peak.

Key Points

- **0.0** Trail sign.
- **0.1** Junction with trail #167. Turn left for Iceberg Lake.
- **2.4** Trail crosses Ptarmigan Creek at Ptarmigan Falls.
- **2.5** Junction with Ptarmigan Tunnel Trail. Stay left for Iceberg Lake.
- **4.4** Trail crosses Iceberg Creek below an unnamed tarn.
- **4.5** Iceberg Lake.

43 Ptarmigan Tunnel

A day hike from Swiftcurrent Inn to Ptarmigan Tunnel, 5.0 miles (8 km) one way; or a backpack from Swiftcurrent Inn to Elizabeth Lake foot, 9.8 miles (16 km) one way.

See map on page 154.
Elevation gain: 2,480 feet
Elevation loss: 2,518 feet

Maximum elevation: 7,200 feet
Difficulty: Moderately strenuous
Topo maps: Many Glacier, Gable Mountain

Finding the trailhead: Iceberg-Ptarmigan Trailhead, located at the north end of the Swiftcurrent Motor Inn complex, among the cabins behind the coffee shop.

The Hike

The spectacular views and only moderate difficulty of the Ptarmigan Tunnel Trail make it a preferred route among local hikers accessing the Belly River drainage. The trail passes from Swiftcurrent Inn up the Wilbur Creek Valley, turning northward past Ptarmigan Lake. High above the lake, the trail passes through a knife-edge ridge and descends to the foot of Elizabeth Lake, after covering a distance of 9.8 miles. The Ptarmigan Tunnel itself may be a day hike destination from the Many Glacier area as well as an access point to the Belly River country. The tunnel is subject to seasonal closures due to snowdrifts and occasional grizzly bear presence; check at the Many Glacier Ranger Station for trail status.

The route to the Ptarmigan Tunnel begins at Swiftcurrent Inn and follows the Iceberg Lake Trail around the south slopes of Altyn Peak to a trail junction at mile 2.5. At this point, the trail to Ptarmigan Tunnel takes off to the north, ascending through open woodlands to the foot of Ptarmigan Lake, which lies in a gravelly, barren-looking cirque below the tunnel. After a short but challenging ascent, the trail reaches the tunnel, which was blasted through the solid rock of the Ptarmigan Wall in 1931. Looking southward from inside the tunnel, Mount Wilbur is framed by its massive steel doors. After emerging from the north side of the tunnel, you will see Elizabeth Lake in the valley below, with Natoas Peak rising above it.

The best views on the entire trail are only half a mile north of the tunnel, around the east wall of the barren cirque below. From this view point, the twisted spires of Mount Merritt can be seen rising above the Old Sun Glacier, and to the southwest, Helen Lake can be seen nestled at the foot of Ipasha Peak.

The trail continues its descent among stands of twisted whitebark pines to a junction with the Redgap Pass Trail some 2.4 miles beyond the tunnel. From this junction, it's only 2 miles of descent through mixed forests to a suspension bridge that crosses the Belly River into the Elizabeth Lake (foot) Campground. The campground overlooks the fish-laden lake, with views of the cockscomb of the Ptarmigan Wall, through which the hiker has just passed.

Mount Merritt and Natoas Peak, beyond Ptarmigan Tunnel

Key Points

0.0   Trail sign.

0.1   Junction with Iceberg Lake Trail (#167). Turn left for Ptarmigan Tunnel.

2.4   Trail crosses Ptarmigan Creek at Ptarmigan Falls.

2.5   Junction with Ptarmigan Tunnel Trail. Turn right for Ptarmigan Tunnel.

4.1   Ptarmigan Lake. Trail ascends steeply to the tunnel.

5.0   Ptarmigan Tunnel. Trail begins descent into Belly River Valley.

5.4   Best view of Mount Merritt to the north.

7.8   Junction with Redgap Pass Trail. Stay left for Elizabeth Lake.

9.8   Elizabeth Lake.

44 Poia Lake-Redgap Pass

A long day hike or backpack from Many Glacier Road to Poia Lake, 6.4 miles (10.5 km) one way; from Many Glacier Road to Redgap Pass, 12.0 miles (19 km) one way; or from Many Glacier Road to Elizabeth Lake foot, 16.6 miles (26.5 km) one way.

Elevation gain: 3,115 feet
Elevation loss: 3,133 feet
Maximum elevation: 7,520 feet (Redgap Pass)

Difficulty: Moderate (Poia Lake); strenuous (Redgap Pass)
Topo maps: Lake Sherburne, Many Glacier, Gable Mountain

Finding the trailhead: Trailhead parking lot approximately 3 miles west of entrance station and 0.25 mile east of Apikuni Falls Trailhead, on north side of Many Glacier Road.

The Hike

The Redgap Pass Trail offers a long, arduous route through the desolate Kennedy Creek Valley to the Belly River country to the north. Many backpackers opt for Poia Lake as a short-range backpack.

The trail begins at the Many Glacier Road, not far from the Apikuni Falls Trailhead. The trail ascends as it winds eastward beneath the gabled south face of Apikuni Mountain. Lake Sherburne is visible in the valley below. After 3 miles, the trail mounts a wooded ridgeline, where it meets an insanely steep 1-mile cutoff trail from the entrance station coming in from the south. A few hundred yards beyond this junction, the trail passes the west shore of Swiftcurrent Ridge Lake, a marshy mere set in the deep forest of the crest of the ridge.

From this lake, the trail drops into the Kennedy Creek Valley to the north, descending through forests interrupted by small pockets of open marsh. Upon reaching the valley floor, the trail crosses a series of beaver ponds set among large aspens and turns west along the south bank of the creek. The Altyn limestone mass of Yellow Mountain rises to the north, with a pleasant waterfall nestled at its base, as the trail winds its way upward for 1.5 miles through gravelly rock gardens to Poia Lake. The lake was named for a half-mortal in Blackfoot legend named Star Boy who saved the life of Morning Star and thus restored the people to Sun Chief's favor. The campground sits on a wooded knoll at the foot of the lake, looking westward toward the moors above the lake. The lake is deep and cold and is surrounded by blocky cliffs on both sides, but contains no fish.

The trail crosses the outlet of the lake and skirts its north shore on the way to Redgap Pass. From the head of the lake, the trail winds for 3 miles through open muskeg and wooded valley floor before ascending steeply toward the pass. As the trail passes out of whitebark and lodgepole pine forests into open subalpine fir park-

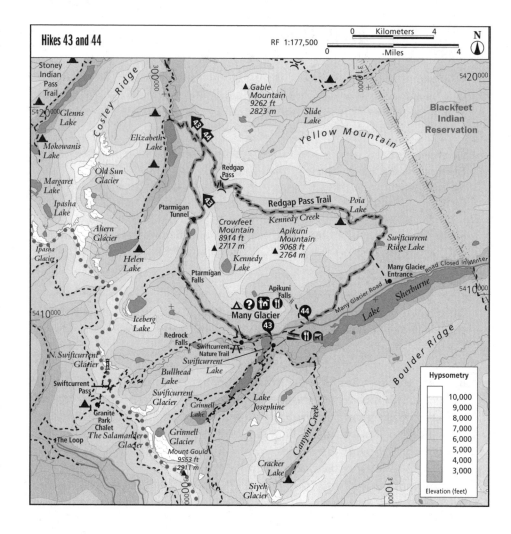

land, beargrass blossoms dot the slopes on all sides. A backward glance reveals the hulking mass of Apikuni Mountain to the south, and Mount Henkel and Crowfeet Mountain crowd the head of the valley, with Kennedy Lake at their feet. As it reaches the windswept pass, the trail passes immediately beneath a towering chimney of reddish Grinnell argillite. Upon cresting the rise, the backpacker is greeted with stunning views of Old Sun Glacier lying at the base of the towering spires of Mount Merritt.

The trail then drops into a high, treeless cirque and winds around the west face of a rocky knob onto a series of high benches. Descending through ragged stands of pine, the trail makes is way to a junction with the Ptarmigan Tunnel Trail. From this point, it is a foot-pounding 2-mile descent to the foot of Elizabeth Lake.

Key Points

0.0   Trail sign.

3.3   Junction with Sherburne Cutoff Trail. Stay left for Poia Lake. Trail winds below Apikuni Mountain and ascends Swiftcurrent Ridge.

3.6   Swiftcurrent Ridge Lake. Trail begins descent into Kennedy Creek Valley.

4.9   Trail reaches Kennedy Creek and begins ascent to Poia Lake.

6.4   Poia Lake Campground. Trail ascends gently along the Kennedy Valley floor.

9.4   Trail begins ascent toward Redgap Pass.

12.0   Redgap Pass. Trail begins steep descent to Elizabeth Lake.

14.6   Junction with Ptarmigan Tunnel Trail. Turn right for Elizabeth Lake.

16.6   Elizabeth Lake (foot) Campground.

Additional Hikes

Cracker Flats. A horse trail runs from the Cracker Lake Trail for 0.5 mile to Cracker Flats along the shore of Lake Sherburne. These flats are the former site of the mining town of Altyn, inundated by the formation of the reservoir. A trail once ran from the flats through forested slopes to the crest of Boulder Ridge, 5 miles to the east, but this trail has disappeared through many years of disuse.

Apikuni Falls. A short, well-maintained trail runs for 1 mile to Apikuni Falls from mile 10.4 of the Many Glacier Road. The high cirque beyond is accessible to climbers via a little scrambling. The enterprising bushwhacker who reaches the head of this tiny bowl is rewarded with views of Natahki Lake and the towering cliff walls surrounding it.

Kennedy Creek. A primitive route once ran up Kennedy Creek from a maze of jeep trails outside the park, linking up with the Poia-Redgap Trail. No trace of this trail remains, and hikers planning to use this route should forget about following the old trail and hike up the creek bed instead.

The Belly River Country

The valley of the Belly River is one of the most untamed and beautiful areas left in North America. It is accessible only by trail, and its remoteness makes it a backpacker's paradise. Chief Mountain, sacred to the Blackfeet, stands as a lone sentinel over the northern plains, an island of ancient limestone spared by the erosive glaciers that once surrounded it. The rugged peaks of the inner ranges are dominated by the massive pinnacles of Mount Merritt, which sports three glaciers on its flanks.

Looking toward Stoney Indian Peaks

Place names reflect the importance of this area to Native Americans: Atsina Lake, Mokowanis Creek, Gros Ventre Falls, and the Belly River itself are named after the Gros Ventre, or "Big Belly," tribe of the northern plains; Kaina Creek was named for a northern band of Blackfeet that reside in Canada; and the Stoney Indians of the Canadian Rockies left their name on the pass and peak at the head of Mokowanis Creek.

The streams and lakes draining toward Hudson Bay abound with fish, including rainbow and brook trout, mountain whitefish, and the arctic grayling. The latter is limited to only a few areas in Montana, including Elizabeth Lake and the Belly River. The grassy meadows of the valley floor provide forage for abundant elk, which share the valley with deer, mountain lions, and many other species of wildlife. The surrounding ridges are covered with a mixture of spruce and lodgepole pines on the well-drained sites, with quaking aspen groves occupying spring and seep areas.

The Belly River Valley can be accessed from the Chief Mountain Highway (Montana Highway 17), or over passes from Goat Haunt Ranger Station on Upper Waterton Lake or the Many Glacier area. Trails tend to take their time in getting places, and thus this area offers few opportunities for day hikers. The closest ranger stations from which permits are available are at Many Glacier and St. Mary. In addition, there is a ranger station near the confluence of the Mokowanis and Belly Rivers, which is manned from May through September. Don't go into the area without a permit.

45 The Belly River Trail

A backpack from Chief Mountain Customs to Belly River Ranger Station, 6.1 miles (10 km) one way; from Chief Mountain Customs to Elizabeth Lake (foot), 9.3 miles (15 km) one way; or from Chief Mountain Customs to Helen Lake, 13.6 miles (22 km) one way.

Elevation loss: 744 feet
Elevation gain: 492 feet
Maximum elevation: 5,329 feet

Difficulty: Moderate
Topo maps: Gable Mountain, Many Glacier

Finding the trailhead: Chief Mountain Customs trailhead, located on Montana Highway 17 (Chief Mountain Highway), within sight of the Border Patrol buildings.

The Hike

The Belly River Trail provides low-elevation access to some of the most beautiful country in Glacier National Park. The valley floor is clear of snow as early as mid-May, making this trail a good choice for early-season access to rugged country.

The trail begins at the Chief Mountain Customs, on a ridge overlooking the Belly River Valley. It immediately enters a dense stand of lodgepole pines on the ridgetop before descending steeply down the ridge face. The trail passes many springs populated by aspen stands, whose white trunks contrast sharply with their bright green foliage. Aspens reproduce most frequently by sending out shoots from existing roots (as opposed to seeds), and thus a thicket of aspen trees most likely represents a collection of clones of the original parent plant.

When the trail reaches the valley floor, it turns south, following the gentle grade of the Belly River through grassy meadows and stands of pine and aspen. At mile 3, the trail climbs up and around the site of a campground that was washed away in the flooding of June 1995. This former campground is a popular lunch spot for both hikers and biting flies. An old trail once crossed the river at the campground, winding around the base of Sentinel Mountain into the North Fork of the Belly River, but this trail is maintained infrequently to provide a primitive route to Miche Wabun Lake. From this area, Bear and Sentinel Mountains can be seen to the west, while the monumental mass of Chief Mountain rises to the east.

The trail continues up the valley floor, passing the Gable Creek Campground in a loose stand of timber that offers views of Bear Mountain. Beyond it lies the Belly River Ranger Station, where trails from Gable Pass and the Mokowanis River Valley converge with the Belly River Trail. The meadow in front of this historic station provides a view up the Mokowanis Valley, and elk can often be seen feeding in the horse paddock at dusk. The ice-cold, clear Belly River contains grayling and rainbow trout but is generally considered poor fishing.

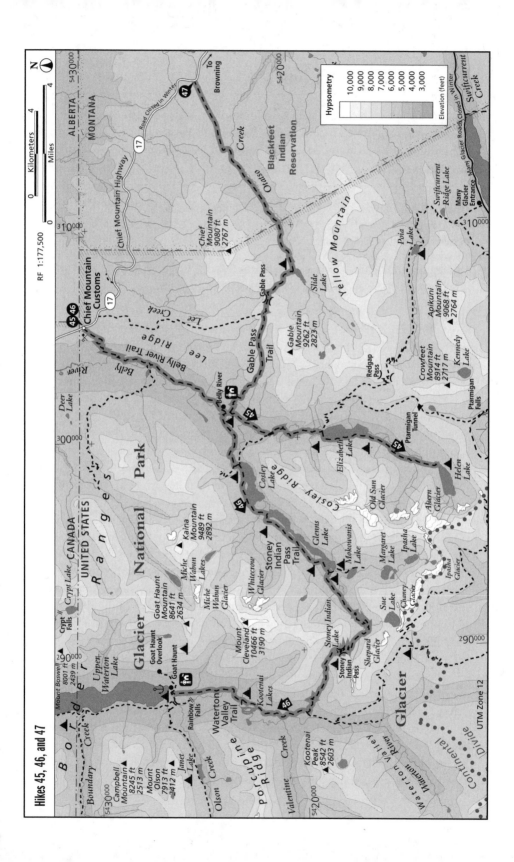

Hikes 45, 46, and 47

RF 1:177,500

Kilometers

Miles

Hypsometry

10,000
9,000
8,000
7,000
6,000
5,000
4,000
3,000

Elevation (feet)

ALBERTA
MONTANA

To Browning

Blackfeet Indian Reservation

Chief Mountain Highway

Chief Mountain
9080 ft
2267 m

Chief Mountain Customs

Yellow Mountain

Gable Pass

Slide Lake

Gable Pass Trail

Gable Mountain
9262 ft
2823 m

Poia Lake

Swiftcurrent Ridge Lake

Many Glacier Entrance

Apikuni Mountain
9068 ft
2764 m

Swiftcurrent Creek

Main Glacier Road Closed in Winter

Redgap Pass

Crowfeet Mountain
8914 ft
2717 m

Kennedy Lake

Ptarmigan Falls

Ptarmigan Tunnel

Helen Lake

Elizabeth Lake

Cosley Ridge

Old Sun Glacier

Margaret Lake

Ipasha Lake

Ahern Glacier

Ipasha Glacier

Belly River Trail

Lee Ridge

Lee Creek

Otatso Creek

Belly River

Deer Lake

Belly River

Cosley Lake

Mokowanis Lake

Glenns Lake

Sue Lake

Chaney Glacier

Chaney Lake

Road Closed in Winter

CANADA
UNITED STATES

Rangers

Glacier National Park

Kaina Mountain
9489 ft
2892 m

Miche Wabun Lakes

Miche Wabun Glacier

Goat Haunt Mountain
8641 ft
2634 m

Whitecrow Glacier

Stoney Indian Pass Trail

Stoney Indian Lakes

Stoney Indian Pass

Shepard Glacier

Goat Haunt Overlook

Mount Cleveland
10456 ft
3190 m

Border

Boundary Creek

Mount Boswell
8001 ft
2439 m

Upper Waterton Lake

Crypt Falls

Crypt Lake

Campbell Mountain
8245 ft
2513 m

Mount Olson
7913 ft
2412 m

Janet Lake

Olson Creek

Valentine Creek

Porcupine Ridge

Kootenai Creek

Goat Haunt

Rainbow Falls

Watperton Valley Trail

Kootenai Lakes

Kootenai Peak
8542 ft
2603 m

Waterton Valley

Waterton River

Continental Divide

Glacier

UTM Zone 12

From the Belly River Ranger Station, the trail ascends through dense lodgepole pine forest and crosses the river via a suspension bridge before arriving at a short spur that leads to Dawn Mist Falls. This torrential waterfall cascades over the hard rock of the Lewis overthrust sill, which extends over several strata of softer rock.

From this point, it is a mile farther to the foot of beautiful Elizabeth Lake, which provides excellent fishing for grayling and rainbow trout in the 1-to-2-pound class. Across the lake, the jagged arête of the Ptarmigan Wall dominates the landscape, and in early spring, frequent avalanches can be seen cascading down its west face. The lake itself is a deep aquamarine color, as a result of glacial flour suspended in the water column.

The trail winds around the western shore of the lake, providing excellent views of the reddish summit of Seward Mountain. At the head of the lake is a smaller, poorly developed campsite. Leaving the lake, the trail continues southward through dense vegetation and past an occasional beaver pond. After crossing a substantial creek, you can see glacier-clad Mount Merritt framed by the steep valley to the west. As the trail continues southward, it crosses several low lateral moraine hills, finally emerging into subalpine fir parkland and crossing the Belly River at the outlet of Helen Lake.

Helen Lake is a desolate, barren body of water situated below the cliffs of Ipasha and Ahern Peaks. The upper part of the Ahern Glacier can be seen in the saddle between these two peaks. The campground at Helen Lake is a dispersed-use area in a meadow next to the lake, with a cooking area farther inland among the trees.

Key Points

0.0   Trail sign. Trail descends steeply into the Belly River Valley.

2.0   Trail reaches the valley floor and turns southwest.

3.0   Site of former Threemile Campground.

5.8   Turnoff for Gable Creek Campground.

6.0   Junction with Stoney Indian Pass Trail. Stay left for Elizabeth Lake.

6.1   Belly River Ranger Station and junction with trail to Gable Pass. Keep right as Belly River Trail ascends wooded valley and then crosses to north bank of the river.

7.6   Junction with Cosley Lake Cutoff Trail. Stay left for Elizabeth Lake.

8.1   Dawn Mist Falls.

9.3   Elizabeth Lake (foot) Campground. Ptarmigan-Redgap Trail enters behind horse hitching post. Bear right to lake head and Helen Lake. Trail follows west shore of Elizabeth Lake.

10.9   Elizabeth Lake (head) Campground. Trail continues south, climbing gradually. Trail crosses outlet of Helen Lake before reaching campground on the eastern shore.

13.6   Helen Lake Campground.

46 Mokowanis River–Stoney Indian Pass

A backpack from Chief Mountain Customs to Cosley Lake Campground, 8.8 miles (14 km) one way; from Chief Mountain Customs to Stoney Indian Pass, 17.9 miles (29 km) one way; or from Chief Mountain Customs to Goat Haunt Ranger Station, 26.4 miles (42.5 km) one way.

See map on page 160.
Elevation gain: 2,725 feet
Elevation loss: 3,869 feet
Maximum elevation: 6,908 feet

Difficulty: Moderate (Upper Glenns Lake); moderately strenuous (Goat Haunt)
Topo maps: Gable Mountain, Mount Cleveland, Ahern Pass, Porcupine Ridge

Finding the trailhead: Chief Mountain Customs Trailhead, on Montana Highway 17 (Chief Mountain Highway) within sight of the border facilities, or Goat Haunt Ranger Station, reached by ferry or trail from Waterton (Alberta) township.

The Hike

The trail to Stoney Indian Pass begins in common with the Belly River Trail, which it follows for 6 miles before splitting off to the north at the Belly River Ranger Station.

Start off from the Chief Mountain Customs, on a ridge overlooking the Belly River Valley. It immediately enters a dense stand of lodgepole pines before descending steeply down the ridge face. When the trail reaches the valley floor, it turns south, following the gentle grade of the Belly River through grassy meadows and stands of pine and aspen. At mile 3, the trail climbs up and around the site of a former campground. From this area, Bear and Sentinel Mountains can be seen to the west, while the monumental mass of Chief Mountain rises to the east.

The trail continues up the valley floor, passing the Gable Creek Campground with views of Bear Mountain. Beyond it lies the Belly River Ranger Station, where trails from Gable Pass and the Mokowanis River Valley converge with the Belly River Trail. The meadow in front of this historic station provides a view up the Mokowanis Valley, and elk can often be seen at dusk.

From the Belly River Ranger Station, the trail turns west, descending gently to the river, which is crossed via a suspension bridge. The trail then ascends onto a thin ridgetop covered in lodgepole pines and bear grass, where numerous butterflies may be seen on sunny days. As the trail traverses the slopes above the Mokowanis River, a short spur to the left passes above Gros Ventre Falls, a roaring cataract that plunges over 100 feet.

Shortly before reaching Cosley Lake, the trail reaches a junction with the Bear Mountain Overlook Trail. This trail winds steeply 1.7 miles to an old lookout site,

Mokowanis Lake

high on the southwest flank of Bear Mountain. From various points on the trail, the Whitecrow Glacier can be seen at the base of Mount Cleveland, the tallest peak in the park. A spur peak projects from the eastern side of this mountain, appearing isolated from the rest of the range by a trick of perspective.

Just beyond the Overlook Trail junction, the main trail reaches the foot of Cosley Lake. Following the northern shore, the trail reaches a cutoff trail to a campground about one-third of the way up the lake. After this junction, the trail continues along the lakeshore, among stands of large conifers. Above the head of the lake, the trail crosses rushing Whitecrow Creek. The delta formed by silt deposited by this creek completely dammed the Mokowanis River, forming Glenns Lake above it. The trail continues up the western shore of Glenns Lake, which is 2.8 miles long. There are two campgrounds along the shore of the lake, at the foot and the head. Across this lake, the tall summit of Mount Merritt rises at the western end of Cosley Ridge. The symmetrical form of Pyramid Peak graces the head of the valley.

At the head of Glenns Lake, a trail to Mokowanis Lake enters from the south. This trail is only about 1 mile long, and the extra detour is well worth the effort. The trail crosses the inlet to Glenns Lake below White Quiver Falls, a delicate skein of lacy water that flows down the surface of a tilted stratum of rock. The trail then climbs briefly through pine forest and across naked rock to the foot of Mokowanis Lake. This lake lies at the base of a natural amphitheater surrounded by soaring pinnacles. A large waterfall that descends from Margaret Lake is visible above the head of the lake. There is a campground located at the head of this lake, on the eastern shore.

Immediately after the Mokowanis Lake Trail junction, the trail arrives at a campground on the main river. The trail ascends the forested valley floor, then climbs rather steeply past several falls on its way to Atsina Lake. The trail crosses the inlet stream and surmounts the headwall above the lake, passing near a pair of twin cascades: Paiota Falls is the closer, Atsina Falls the more distant. As the trail gains altitude, fantastic views open up on all sides. To the south, Mount Kipp rises above Raven Quiver Falls. The Shepard Glacier enrobes the eastern flank of Cathedral Peak, which rises ahead.

The trail climbs quickly into a small basin occupied by a small tarn, among charming alpine parklands. Above the tarn, the trail climbs steeply to the high, bare col of Stoney Indian Pass. The Stoney Indians were a small band related to the Assiniboine that inhabited the Belly River country. From the pass, the Stoney Indian Peaks dominate the skyline to the north, and Wahcheechee Mountain overlooks the pass to the west.

The trail descends steeply across many switchbacks to the treeless valley below, occupied by Stoney Indian Lake. There is a campground at the outlet of this high alpine tarn. Below the lake, the trail continues a fairly steep descent past some falls to the floor of the Waterton Valley. Here, the Stoney Indian Pass Trail joins the Waterton Valley Trail, which descends gently for 4.9 miles to Goat Haunt Ranger Station.

Key Points

0.0 Trail sign. Trail descends steeply to the Belly River Valley.

2.0 Trail reaches the valley floor and turns southwest.

3.0 Site of former Threemile Campground.

6.0 Junction with Stoney Indian Pass Trail, just before Belly River Ranger Station. Turn right for Stoney Indian Pass. Trail crosses Belly River and ascends a finger ridge westward.

7.9 Gros Ventre Falls.

8.0 Junction with Bear Mountain Overlook Trail (1.7 miles, strenuous). Stay left for Stoney Indian Pass.

8.2 Junction with Belly River Cutoff Trail at foot of Cosley Lake. Stay right for Stoney Indian Pass.

8.7 Spur trail to Cosley Lake Campground. Trail follows north shore of Cosley Lake, then crosses Whitecrow Creek.

10.2 Glenns Lake (foot) Campground. Trail follows northwest shore of Glenns Lake.

12.8 Glenns Lake (head) Campground.

13.1 Junction with Mokowanis Lake Trail (about 1 mile, easy). Stay right for Stoney Indian Pass.

13.2 Mokowanis Junction Campground. Trail climbs moderately, following Mokowanis River.

15.9	Atsina Lake. Trail climbs steeply, flattens out, then begins steep ascent of pass.
17.9	Stoney Indian Pass. Trail descends steeply.
18.9	Stoney Indian Lake Campground. Trail descends fairly steeply.
21.5	Junction with Waterton Valley Trail. Turn right for Goat Haunt.
23.9	Junction with Kootenai Lake Spur Trail. Stay right for Goat Haunt.
26.4	Goat Haunt Ranger Station.

47 Slide Lake–Gable Pass

A backpack from Montana Highway 17 to Slide Lake, 8.6 miles (14 km) one way; from Montana Highway 17 to Gable Pass, 10.6 miles (17 km) one way; or from Montana Highway 17 to Belly River Ranger Station, 13.2 miles (21 km) one way.

See map on page 160.
Elevation gain: 2,100 feet
Elevation loss: 3,300 feet

Maximum elevation: 7,220 feet
Difficulty: Moderate
Topo maps: Chief Mountain, Gable Mountain

Finding the trailhead: Otatso Creek Road, an unmarked, primitive road with a cattle guard and barbed-wire fence gate across it, approximately 0.3 mile southeast of the Chief Mountain Overlook on Montana Highway 17 (Chief Mountain Highway). For a skilled driver, the road is passable to high-clearance vehicles for 2 miles, to the second cattle guard. After this point, the road was badly damaged in the flooding of June 1995 and is in poor condition. Some hikers are mountain biking to the boundary, but beware of the sticky mud when it is wet out.

The Hike

Slide Lake occupies a forgotten but rugged corner of Glacier National Park. The lake was once known for its bull trout fishery, but in recent years this species of trout has been designated an endangered species, and now it is illegal to fish for them. Slide Lake is situated in a glacial valley, surrounded by desolate peaks and windblown parkland. Visitors who wish to follow this route across reservation lands must get a tribal permit in addition to a national park backcountry permit for overnight trips.

Access is provided by an unimproved jeep trail that crosses the last rolling ridges of the high plains, among meadows and aspen stands, before descending into the Otatso Creek Valley. This track passes immediately to the south of Chief Mountain, sacred to the Blackfoot tribe, providing seldom-seen views of the mountain's south face. The blocklike form of this solitary monument has long provided a landmark for travelers of the northern plains. To the west, along the same ridge, rise the twisted spires of Ninaki (Squaw) and Papoose Peaks.

Papoose from Gable Pass

As the dirt track enters the park and becomes a trail, it passes a small complex of dilapidated patrol cabins. The trail then winds up through parklike benches, following the rushing rivulet of Otatso Creek. As the trail ascends into a clearing, it passes along the north shore of a small, unnamed tarn at the base of Yellow Mountain. This tarn and the larger body of Slide Lake above it were formed when landslides from the flanks of Yellow Mountain blocked the flow of Otatso Creek, forming natural dams. The Slide Lake Campground is situated above the trail along the lower lake.

Shortly after leaving the campground, the trail tops a rise and offers a panoramic view of Slide Lake and the barren peaks beyond. Yellow and Gable Mountains flank the lake to the south and north, and the rounded summit of Seward Mountain can be seen to the south of a more jagged, unnamed peak which lies at the head of the valley. A trail once ran up the valley above Slide Lake to an old mine site, but the trail has been long abandoned and can no longer be followed.

Gable Pass Option: From the lower end of Slide Lake, the Gable Pass Trail ascends to the north, climbing up forested benches and along boulder-filled ravines to the summit of Gable Pass. A short bushwhack up the ridgeline to the east is rewarded by panoramic views of the Belly River country to the north, as well as the tortured forms of the mountains flanking the pass.

From Gable Pass, the trail passes around the base of Gable Mountain, through alpine parkland inhabited by numerous rodents and songbirds. The trail is difficult to follow in places, but rock cairns have been built to guide hikers across the rocky area.

The trail passes the junction with the Lee Ridge Trail, a poorly maintained trail that runs northward along a gentle ridge to its intersection with the Chief Mountain Highway. From this point, the trail descends into lodgepole pine forest and continues downward fairly steeply until it emerges behind the Belly River Ranger Station.

Key Points

0.0 Barbed-wire gate at Montana Highway 17. Please remember to close gate. Primitive road follows top of Sandy Ridge.

2.0 Cattle guard. Road begins moderate descent to Otatso Creek Valley.

6.0 Road washout.

7.0 Park boundary.

7.2 Old Otatso Creek patrol cabins.

8.4 Slide Lake Campground.

8.6 Slide Lake. Junction with Gable Pass Trail. Turn right for Gable Pass. Trail ascends, crossing benches.

10.2 Trail crosses boulder field and continues moderate climb to Gable Pass.

10.6 Gable Pass. Trail winds westward, descending along the flanks of Gable Mountain.

10.9 Junction with Lee Ridge trail. Stay left for Belly River Ranger Station.

13.2 Belly River Ranger Station.

Connecting Hikes

A secondary trail runs up the wooded crest of **Lee Ridge** from mile 17.8 of the Chief Mountain Highway (Montana Highway 17). The trail is not a primary one but can be followed fairly easily as it winds through pine and spruce forests below the west face of Chief Mountain to connect with the Gable Pass Trail 0.3 mile west of the pass.

The **North Fork Trail** is a primitive trail that runs north from the former Three-mile Campground for 4.8 miles to reach the North Fork of the Belly River. It climbs across a wooded hillside before winding around the east flank of Sentinel Mountain and descending into the North Fork Valley. An old trail used to run up this valley to its head at Miche Wabun Lake but receives no maintenance and provides a more primitive experience than the main trails.

The **Belly–Mokowanis Cutoff Trail** runs from the foot of Cosley Lake to a point on the Belly River just below Dawn Mist Falls. For hikers traveling from Goat Haunt to the upper Belly River Valley, this trail eliminated unnecessary distance by "cutting the corner" over the shoulder of Natoas Peak instead of following the drainage patterns. You must wade the outlet of Cosley Lake; a wire is strung across the creek for stability.

Waterton Lakes National Park

L ong before being protected as part of an international peace park, the mountains and valleys of the Waterton area were frequently visited by Indians, particularly the Kootenai and Blackfoot tribes, who hunted bison and gathered other resources there. For a relatively small park, the land supports a diverse array of plants, wildlife, and landscapes, leading to varied opportunities for hikers.

A June snowstorm in the upper reaches of Galwey Brook (Hike 59)

The first white men to take in these breathtaking landscapes were undoubtedly fur traders and missionaries, who came in the late 1850s. In the late 1800s, the discovery of oil in the Cameron Valley drew speculators to establish a drilling operation, which flourished only a short time and is remembered today at the First Oil Well in Western Canada National Historic Site—or, more colloquially, Discovery Well historic site.

A portion of the present-day national park was protected in 1895 as Waterton Lakes Forest Park and later called Kootenai Lakes Forest Reserve. Protection of this natural treasure was increased in response to the urgings of such conservation-minded local residents as Frederick Godsal and John "Kootenai" Brown. The park was much larger in 1914 and reduced to its present size in 1921. In 1932 an international accord with the United States established the Waterton-Glacier complex as the world's first international peace park. The ensuing years have seen extensive development, highlighted by a complex network of trails, roads, and campgrounds. However, the land beyond the roads retains its wild character.

Waterton townsite provides most services found in large towns, including a variety of hotel accommodations, restaurants, and stores. There are automobile campgrounds at the townsite and along the Red Rock Parkway, developed picnic facilities exist along all major roads, motorized boats are allowed on Upper and Middle Waterton Lakes, and all lakes have facilities for launching unpowered boats. In addition, a water taxi on Upper Waterton Lake provides daily service to Crypt Landing and Goat Haunt Ranger Station across the border.

No registration is required for day trips, but overnight expeditions into the backcountry require a special permit, which can be purchased at the visitor center outside Waterton townsite. Backpackers must stay in the established campgrounds, although minimum-impact camping in some remote areas may be allowed by special permit. Fishing in the park requires a special license, available for a small fee at the visitor center.

48 The Carthew-Alderson Trail

A long day hike or backpack from Cameron Lake to Waterton townsite, 11.8 miles (19.0 km) one way.

Elevation gain: 1,440 feet
Elevation loss: 3,150 feet
Maximum elevation: 7,720 feet

Difficulty: Moderate (west to east); moderately strenuous (east to west)

Finding the trailhead: Trail departs from the day-use facility at Cameron Lake.

The Hike

For travelers seeking the high country, the Carthew-Alderson Trail will prove one of the most rewarding hikes in the Waterton area. While it is possible for hardy hikers to complete the trail from Cameron Lake to the townsite of Waterton in a single day, it is much more pleasant to split the trip into two days with a stay at the Alderson Lake Campground. The slower pace of the two-day trek will allow more time to relax and enjoy the spectacular mountain scenery that abounds throughout the length of this popular trail.

The trail begins as a paved walkway that heads southeast from the Cameron Lake boat launching ramp. It soon turns into a wide dirt path skirting the eastern shore of the lake, accompanied by picturesque views of the aquamarine lake and the snow-encrusted headwall that towers above its head. After following the lake for about a quarter of a mile, the trail turns inland in a series of long, gradual switchbacks. As the trail ascends the eastern wall of the valley, it passes through stands of towering old-growth subalpine fir, some of the largest trees to be found in the park. As the trail nears the top of the rise, the dark forest gives way to sunsplashed parklands, where scattered clumps of diminutive firs stand as islands in a sea of beargrass.

The trail continues its gentle ascent for another half mile to reach Summit Lake, a fragile alpine jewel that is nestled in the folds of a high plateau. The lake straddles the divide between Cameron and Boundary Creeks and offers outstanding views of Mount Custer and Chapman Peak across the international border. On the north shore of the lake, the trail reaches a junction with the Boundary Creek Trail, which descends eastward to run for 8 miles through a brushy valley before reaching the shore of Waterton Lake. A ten-minute detour down this trail yields a nice view of azure Lake Wurdeman nestled among the sheer cliffs of Chapman Peak.

From the Summit Lake junction, the Carthew-Alderson Trail turns uphill, climbing steadily as it finds its way into the arid cirque that makes up the southern

face of Mount Carthew. As the scrubby fir forest gives way to open talus, the trail ahead can be seen zigzagging up the slope to the east. Views of the snowy crags to the south open up as the trail ascends across the loose scree. As the trail approaches the windblown crest of the pass known as Carthew Summit, Thunderbird Mountain can be seen behind the rocky mass of Chapman Peak, while Kintla and Kinnerly Peaks rise farther west of Mount Custer.

Upon reaching the barren summit, a southward glance reveals the hidden pool of Lake Nooney in its cliff-walled niche, while Mount Cleveland dominates the eastern skyline. This peak is the loftiest summit in the international peace park and lies just inside the northern border of Glacier. The summit of Mount Carthew lies to the north, decked out in green and red shales. Looking ahead, barren slopes descend toward the Carthew Lakes in their windswept basin. The arid slopes around Carthew Summit support some of the most fragile plant communities in the park. Plants growing here must face constant wind, which chill and desiccate the plants as they struggle to flower and set seed in the brief span of the alpine growing season. Tread lightly here.

As the trail makes its way down from the pass, it curves away to the north, passing among copses of subalpine fir that winter blasts have tortured into a dwarfed growth form. It switchbacks a number of times as it descends across loose talus to reach the head of the uppermost lake. The trail follows the north shore of the lake, where persistent snowdrifts often linger into July. After climbing over a low rise, it continues its descent via a series of switchbacks to reach the lower lake. After skirting its western shore, the trail curls to the left and descends into a sparsely wooded valley overlooked by the tawny rock of Buchanan Mountain. The trail runs eastward as it descends past a waterfall toward Alderson Lake. The lake swings into view, heralding a steady half-mile descent to a trail junction above its northern shore.

The Carthew-Alderson Trail stays left, while a short spur trail runs to the right to reach the lakeshore campground. This pleasant tenting spot faces the towering cliffs of Mount Alderson, which looms above the head of the lake. During late spring, chunks of ice and snow periodically break away from the cliffs, announcing their departure with a shotlike report before tumbling thousands of feet into the lake below. Alderson Lake is home to a population of cutthroat trout, which provides fairly good fishing for those with a taste for angling.

As the main trail continues down the Carthew Valley, openings in the trees provide good views of the multifaceted mass of Buchanan Mountain to the northwest. The broad valley soon narrows into a steep-sided canyon, as open stands of subalpine fir give way to a lowland forest of Douglas fir. The trail runs level for a time, passing across an opening torn from the forest by frequent avalanches roaring down the slopes of Bertha Peak. As the trail approaches the Cameron Valley, lady's slipper orchids and trailing purple clematis appear amid the mossy forest undergrowth. As

◄ *Cliffs of Alderson Peak*

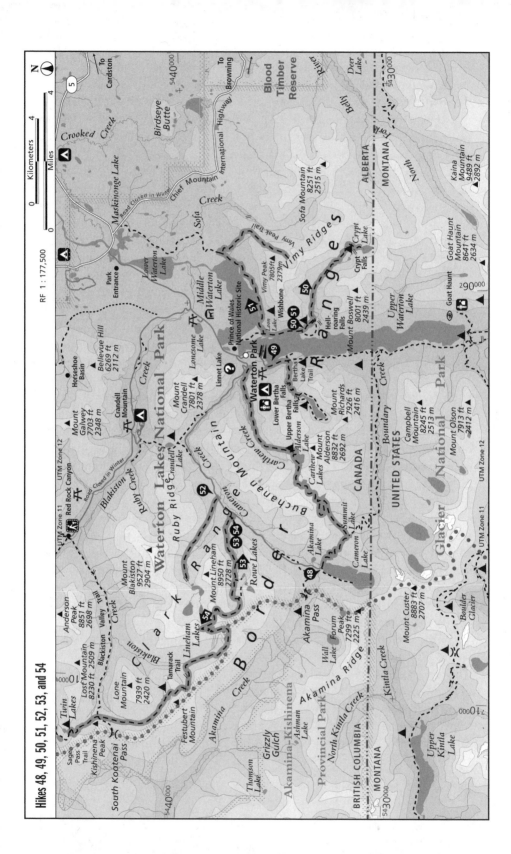

Hikes 48, 49, 50, 51, 52, 53, and 54

RF 1 : 177,500

the trail bends eastward into the Cameron Valley, holes in the forest canopy reveal views of Waterton Lake, with Vimy Peak rising on its far side. The trail descends past the concrete remains that once provided the water supply for Waterton, then wanders down an open slope. A final left turn lands you at the trail's end, at a bridge below the stately torrent of Cameron Falls.

Key Points

0.0 Cameron Lake day-use facility.

2.5 Summit Lake.

4.5 Carthew Summit.

6.1 Lower Carthew Lake.

7.6 Junction with Alderson Lake Spur Trail. Stay left for Waterton.

11.8 End of trail at Cameron Falls.

49 Bertha Lake

A day hike or short backpack from Waterton townsite to Bertha Lake, 3.5 miles (5.5 km) one way.

See map on page 174.
Elevation gain: 1,480 feet
Elevation loss: 170 feet

Maximum elevation: 5,850 feet
Difficulty: Moderate (Lower Bertha Falls); moderately strenuous (Bertha Lake)

Finding the trailhead: The trail begins in the southwestern corner of Waterton townsite, across from the automobile campground. The trailhead is marked by a sign and has its own parking lot.

The Hike

This popular day hike from Waterton townsite follows the shore of Upper Waterton Lake, then climbs a side valley past waterfalls to reach an alpine lake. For travelers that make the climb to the lake, a campground offers opportunities for a short overnighter. The trail begins in a stand of aspens, climbing gradually as it follows the western shore of Upper Waterton Lake. As the trail rises above the lakeshore, there is a mixed forest of lodgepole pine, fir, and mountain maple. Rocky outcroppings are home to the limber pine, which thrives in extreme environments. An overlook about a mile down the trail offers sweeping views of the ranges to the east of the lake, as far south as Mount Cleveland.

Just beyond this overlook, the Bertha Lake Trail splits off from the trail running along the shores of Upper Waterton Lake. A left turn here yields a steep half-mile

Prince of Wales Hotel, Waterton Park PHOTO BY MONICA BAER

descent to the Bertha Bay Campground; the Waterton Lakeshore Trail continues south another 7.7 miles to reach Goat Haunt Ranger Station at the head of the lake. The Bertha Lake Trail bends to the west, entering the beargrass-studded Bertha Creek Valley. After a distance of 1 mile, the trail reaches the foot of Lower Bertha Falls. Here, Bertha Creek cascades across layers of resistant rock, tumbling into a rushing flume created by a joint in the bedrock. This spot is a nice place for a picnic.

The trail crosses a bridge below the falls and begins the long, fairly steep climb to Bertha Lake. The trail switchbacks frequently as it ascends into a subalpine forest dominated by firs of short stature. Three-quarters of a mile beyond the Lower Falls, the trail climbs the hillside beside Upper Bertha Falls. This larger cascade drops down a steep, rocky headwall. Beyond the falls, the trail crests a rise that overlooks Bertha Lake, a sinuous tarn crowded around by rugged, gray walls. Mount Richards dominates the cliffs to the south, while the summit of Mount Alderson lies hidden in an alcove to the west of the lake's head.

After descending to the lakeshore, travelers bound for the campground should turn right, crossing a footbridge over the outlet stream to reach the tent sites. A few hundred yards beyond, a cooking shelter and picnic area are nestled in the forest at the edge of the lake. A footpath completes a circuit around the lake, but is not maintained by the park.

Key Points

0.0   Trail sign.

0.9   Junction with Waterton Lakeshore Trail. Stay right for Bertha Lake.

1.9   Lower Bertha Falls. End of self-guiding nature trail.

2.7   Upper Bertha Falls.

3.4   Bertha Lake.

3.5   Bertha Lake Campground.

50 Crypt Lake

A day hike from Crypt Landing to Crypt Lake, 5.3 miles (8.5 km) one way.

See map on page 174.
Elevation gain: 2,100 feet
Elevation loss: 630 feet

Maximum elevation: 6,680 feet
Difficulty: Moderately strenuous

Finding the trailhead: The trail begins at Crypt Landing, from a signpost in the southwestern part of the camping area.

The Hike

This popular trail can be reached by taking the water taxi that runs from Waterton townsite to Goat Haunt. As backcountry campgrounds on the eastern shore of Waterton Lake have been closed, the only option to hike this trail is via a day hike by taking the morning boat to Crypt Landing and catching the afternoon boat back to Waterton. However, this itinerary requires a pace that adheres to a timetable. The trail can also be accessed via a long journey down the Wishbone Trail, which follows the eastern shore of Upper Waterton Lake.

The trail begins in a lowland forest of Douglas fir and birch and immediately begins a series of uphill switchbacks. Shortly beyond the trailhead, the Hellroaring Canyon Trail takes off to the right. This trail will be discussed below. The Crypt Lake Trail continues upward, winding north onto the flanks of Vimy Ridge, where openings afford views of Mounts Alderson and Richards across Upper Waterton Lake. Further on, views open up to the south, and the Citadel Spires and Kootenai Peak become visible.

As the trail climbs around into the Hellroaring Creek Valley, the grade becomes much gentler. The forests of lodgepole pine high above the creek are home to bears;

Crypt Falls

remember to make some noise in spots where the trail ahead is obscured by the trees. Openings in the canopy allow views of Mount Boswell across the narrow valley. At mile 1.4, the Hellroaring Canyon Trail rejoins the trail to Crypt Lake. The path slowly makes its way to the valley floor, passing Twin Falls as the valley bends around to the south. The forest gives way to wide openings, yielding views of the rugged Wilson Range. The trail then climbs gently for a brief passage through a forest of spruce, with a dense canopy that shuts out the sky.

Once clear of the trees, the trail begins a steep ascent up a rocky face, switching back frequently as it climbs. The impressive Burnt Rock Falls shoots out from an overhanging ledge of resistant rock to fall free to the valley floor. The trail continues to climb past the top of the falls, rising high above the valley floor and proceeding southward through meadowy patches inhabited by colonies of playful ground squirrels. Copses of aspen, fir, limber pine, and subalpine larch dot the hillside, and the yellow blossoms of glacier lilies light up the swales. Crypt Falls drapes its shimmering veil across the 500-foot headwall to the south, and the gabled summits of the Wilson Range rise all around.

As the trail crosses the hillsides high above the valley, it passes above a shallow tarn that lies on the valley floor. This tarn is slowly being filled in with silt brought down by the erosive force of the creek, and the encroaching wet meadows crowd its shores on all sides. A copse of conifers even grows within the faint outline that marks the former lakeshore. In this way, all of these mountain lakes are slowly filling in, just as the mountains are constantly being torn down by the forces of erosion. Over the course of eons, these lakes will be slowly transformed into meadow and forest.

The trail bends around to the east, into a small side valley that shelters a grove of stout subalpine firs. The trail ultimately crosses the creek and heads southward once more into an expanse of jumbled boulders. Look for pikas among the rocks above, and listen for their nasal warning whistle. The trail climbs gently to the edge of the boulder field, where an iron ladder leads into a tunnel blasted into the living rock of the cliff face. The tunnel is no more than 4 feet high throughout most of its length, so you will have to crawl or duck-walk to squeeze through. The tunnel emerges high on the cliff face, and a steel cable has been installed as a handrail for the short but harrowing ascent to reach safer footing.

The trail finally winds onto a ledge above the cliff and passes through alpine parklands on its way to the lake. As the trail approaches the outlet stream, a side trail runs to the point where the creek emerges from an underground passage into a still pool, then rushes toward its plunge over the edge of the cliff. The main trail bends to the left, climbing over one final rise to reach the shore of the lake. Crypt Lake is walled in tightly by sheer cliffs on three sides and drains through an underground channel somewhere beneath the lake bed. The international border lies at the south end of the lake, and the peaks looming to the south lie within Glacier National Park. Camping is not allowed at the lake, as this is a fragile alpine area that is quite susceptible to damage from overuse.

Hellroaring Canyon Option: The Hellroaring Canyon Trail (1.3 miles, strenuous) travels the length of Hellroaring Canyon before climbing to return to the Crypt Lake Trail. The trail begins in a stand of old-growth Douglas fir, meandering around a wooded hillside and onto a wooded bench that overlooks Upper Waterton Lake. After half a mile, the trail climbs briefly and descends to the rim of Hellroaring Canyon, where tumbling spouts of water shoot down a steep slickrock bed. As the trail follows the stream upward, the falls become gentler as the creek wanders among moss-covered walls. The trail begins to climb steeply as the canyon opens out again. Far below, the gravel bed of the creek bears the foaming waters beneath tilted slabs of bedrock. The trail then turns almost straight uphill in the final half-mile grunt to reach its junction with the Crypt Lake Trail. All in all, this trail is well worth the hike, but it is best saved for the return trip from Crypt Lake.

Key Points

0.0 Trail sign at Crypt Landing. Trail runs southeast.

0.2 Junction with the trail to Hellroaring Canyon. Stay left for Crypt Lake.

1.4 Junction with the trail coming up from Hellroaring Canyon. Stay left for Crypt Lake.

5.3 Crypt Lake.

51 Vimy Peak

A backpack from Crypt Landing to the summit of Vimy Peak, 8.3 miles (13.3 km) one way.

See map on page 174.
Elevation gain: 4,050 feet
Elevation loss: 410 feet

Maximum elevation: 7,805 feet
Difficulty: Strenuous

Finding the trailhead: Trail starts from Crypt Landing, at a trail sign at the north end of the campground.

The Hike

This remote and rather strenuous trail climbs from the shores of Upper and Middle Waterton Lakes to the top of 7,805-foot Vimy Peak. Because Crypt Landing provides the most scenic access point for the trail, our description of the hike starts here. However, Vimy Peak may also be accessed via a rather dull 4-mile trek along the Wishbone Trail from the Chief Mountain Highway.

From Crypt Landing, the trail climbs gradually northward, following the eastern shore of Upper Waterton Lake. Douglas firs block out the view, but the forest is lit by the yellow blossoms of columbines and other wildflowers. The trail levels out as the forest gives way to a series of dry, open meadows interspersed with aspen stands and a smattering of conifers. The trail dips toward the lakeshore at a small cove, then climbs through a veritable rock garden on its way to Loon Lake. This shallow pond sits at the base of Vimy Peak and is a good spot to look for waterfowl. Just beyond the lake, a rock cairn marks the junction with the Bosporus Trail (0.8 mile, easy), which runs to the tip of a rocky headland overlooking the town of Upper Waterton.

After the junction, the trail curves around to the east, ascending a steep hill as it passes behind an outcropping of white bedrock. The trail then winds downhill toward the Middle Waterton lakeshore. The unmarked path taking off toward the lake runs 0.2 mile to the Wishbone dock, which is situated on the south shore of Middle Waterton Lake. Beyond this point, the trail rises to an elevation several hundred feet above the water, where it runs level through forests and across meadowy benches. The trail descends once again as it approaches a tiny tributary and enters a damp aspen forest underlain by a jungle of cow parsnip and stinging nettles. Just after passing the end of Middle Waterton Lake, the trail arrives at the junction with the trail running east toward Vimy Peak.

This trail runs southeast through rolling grassy hills before beginning a sharp ascent into the coniferous forest. Nearing a low saddle in the ridgeline, openings offer views of a pleasant waterfall cascading downward beside Lions Head Rock.

Looking through the aspens at Sofa Mountain

Vimy Peak towers in the background, aloof in its lofty remoteness. The trail passes through the saddle and onto the back side of the ridge, providing a brief but captivating glimpse of the rugged spires of Sofa Mountain and the more distant peaks farther south. The trail then enters a deep forest, broken only by the small meadows behind Lions Head.

As the trail gains elevation, it emerges from the forest into the subalpine parkland of a narrow valley descending from the north slope of Vimy Peak. When the valley forks, the trail crosses the eastern branch of the stream and ascends the low ridge between the two ravines. The trail then descends to the eastern fork and continues to climb to the southwest, as subalpine firs give way to larches. After passing the spring that is the headwaters of the creek, the trail enters a barren bowl and turns west, passing among stunted firs, larches, and old snags. Vimy Peak is straight ahead.

Official trail maintenance ceases here, but a well-used path can be discerned, meandering westward across the basin and climbing the east slope of Vimy in a series of steep switchbacks. Looking into the basin below, a curious blind depression sits at the head of the valley, while ragged crags rise beyond a headwall to the south. From the summit of Vimy, there are sweeping views of the Waterton Lakes and the mountains that ring them on all sides.

Key Points

0.0 Trail sign.

1.7 Loon Lake. Junction with the Bosporus Trail. Stay right for Vimy Peak.

2.0 Junction with the Wishbone Dock Spur Trail. Stay right for Vimy Peak.

4.5 Junction with the Vimy Peak Trail. Turn right for Vimy Peak.

7.5 Maintained trail ends in basin below Vimy Peak.

8.3 Vimy Peak.

52 Lineham Falls

A day hike from the Cameron Lake Road to Lineham Falls, 2.6 miles (4.2 km) one way.

See map on page 174.
Elevation gain: 1,290 feet
Elevation loss: 130 feet

Maximum elevation: 6,300 feet
Difficulty: Moderate

Finding the trailhead: The trail begins at a marked pullout on the north side of the Cameron Lake Road, just beyond the historic oil well site.

The Hike

This brief but pleasant jaunt runs up Lineham Creek to a headwall that rises below a high lake basin. A trail once climbed the headwall with the assistance of cable handrails but has been long since abandoned. The rock of the headwall is loose and crumbly and is considered hazardous even by experienced climbers; travelers should not attempt to reach the Lineham Lakes via this route.

From the trailhead, the trail takes you across wooded flats, populated by lodge-pole pines and aspens. A short distance from the road, a steady ascent through the forest takes you onto the shoulders of Ruby Ridge as the trail runs westward, high above Lineham Creek. The forest gives way to grassy slopes, and the trail continues to climb as Mount Lineham rises like a lone sentinel across the valley. A backward glance reveals the massive peaks of Buchanan Mountain, which blocks out the skyline to the east. A mile farther on, the trail enters a forest of tall fir trees and begins to level out. Views are limited to brief glimpses through openings in the forest canopy as the trail tracks west across the soft duff of the forest floor.

Upon entering a broad avalanche path that descends from the rocky face of Mount Blakiston, the trail switchbacks downward about 100 feet to reach the level of the creek. As the path meanders beside the water, the stream tumbles down a

Mount Lineham

series of cheerful cascades within a narrow canyon. When the trail runs out onto the alpine meadows to reach its official terminus, a spur trail runs down to the creek for a clear view of the 410-foot falls, while a higher path runs uphill for a loftier perspective.

Key Points

0.0 Trail begins as an old dirt road.

2.6 Lineham Falls.

53 Rowe Lakes

A day hike from the Cameron Lake Road to Upper Rowe Lake, 3.9 miles (6.3 km) one way.

See map on page 174.
Elevation gain: 2,040 feet
Elevation loss: 230 feet

Maximum elevation: 7,100 feet
Difficulty: Moderate (Lower Rowe Lake); moderately strenuous (Upper Rowe Lake)

Finding the trailhead: The trail begins on the east bank of Rowe Creek on the Cameron Lake Road.

The Hike

This trail provides pleasant day-hiking opportunities for hikers with a range of abilities. Lower Rowe Lake and Rowe Meadows can be reached without strenuous exertion, while Upper Rowe Lake requires a stiff climb.

The trail begins on the north bank of Rowe Creek, which it follows briefly before climbing through the lodgepole pines to the arid hillside above. After a short ascent, the trail turns west, passing through the forest high above the stream. To the southwest, the top of Mount Rowe can be glimpsed through openings in the trees. Eventually, the forest comes to an abrupt end at an open avalanche slope that affords views in all directions. Mount Lineham is the tallest peak in view, hulking above the trail to the north. The trail passes briefly through a stand of subalpine firs before reaching a second opening, where a pleasant waterfall pours forth the foaming waters of Rowe Creek. Shortly thereafter, a spur trail (0.3 mile, easy) runs south to the shore of Lower Rowe Lake. Here, blue waters rest at the foot of rugged cliffs, while the outlet to the upper lake courses down the headwall.

The main trail continues in a westerly direction, passing through a mossy alpine forest on its way to Rowe Meadows. This grassy bowl is rimmed by steep slopes that rise skyward toward the lofty peaks above the head of the valley. The meadow is home to a busy colony of ground squirrels, which frolic playfully in the sunny grass to the delight of passersby. After turning south to cross the meadow, the trail reaches a junction with the Tamarack Trail. Take the left fork, which climbs strenuously up the valley wall for half a mile, then crests a rise and climbs onto a high shelf filled with subalpine larch. The trail continues to ascend gently as it passes above the middle lake, then crests a rise and descends to the north shore of Upper Rowe Lake. This tarn sits in a high, windswept basin, with the blunt summit of Mount Rowe rising above its south shore.

Brown-eyed Susan, Waterton Lakes PHOTO BY MONICA BAER

Key Points

- **0.0** Trail sign.
- **2.4** Junction with trail to Lower Rowe Lake. Stay right for Upper Rowe Lake.
- **3.2** Junction with the Tamarack Trail. Turn left for Upper Rowe Lake.
- **3.9** Upper Rowe Lake.

54 The Tamarack Trail

An extended backpack accessed via the Rowe Lakes Trail. Rowe Meadows to Twin Lakes, 12.6 miles (20.5 km) one way plus 3.2 miles (5.1 km) to reach the trailhead.

See map on page 174.
Elevation gain: 3,810 feet
Elevation loss: 3,920 feet

Maximum elevation: 8,450 feet
Difficulty: Strenuous

Finding the trailhead: The trail begins at a marked trail junction on the south side of Rowe Meadows, reached via a 3.2-mile hike along the Rowe Lakes Trail.

The Hike

The Tamarack Trail provides access to the most remote corner of Waterton Lakes National Park—the high valleys that lie below the Continental Divide. It is possible to make a long day hike via the Tamarack and Blakiston Creek Trails, but this option is only for the hardcore hiker. The trail is named for the tamarack, or alpine larch, which grows on the north-facing slopes of the high passes traversed by the trail. This unusual conifer turns bright yellow and loses all of its needles in autumn, providing an amazing display of colors. Snow lingers late in the high bowls along the Continental Divide, making this trail impassible until the middle part of summer.

From Rowe Meadows, the Tamarack Trail climbs steadily around the head of the Rowe Creek Valley. As the trail winds around to the north, it is marked by metal diamonds and circles that have been driven into the rock. The trail continues eastward across the north wall of the valley, approaching the saddle behind Mount Lineham. As the trail switchbacks to the west, a short spur trail runs to the saddle, which overlooks the Lineham Lake Basin and Mount Hawkins rising above it. The main trail climbs steadily west on its way to the rocky summit that divides the Rowe, Lineham, and Blakiston drainages. To the west, the lofty crags of the Akamina-Kishinena Provincial Park in British Columbia rise in regal splendor. After reaching the summit, the trail turns north, passing below several other saddles that offer good views into the Lineham Basin. A hazardous route runs north along the ridgeline before descending across steep scree slopes to the Lineham Lakes.

After a northward leg of a third of a mile, the trail doglegs back to the south and begins to descend toward the headwaters of Blakiston Creek. The loose scree of the ridge slope gives way to grassy meadows as the trail reaches the bottom of the grade, and the trail becomes faint and overgrown. The route becomes distinct again as it moves into glades of dwarfed subalpine fir and follows a tiny rivulet to the valley

Mount Lineham towers above the Lineham Lakes ▶

floor. Here, the trail levels out and begins a cruise through grassy glades surrounded by towering conifers. After a time, the forest closes in around the trail, which runs along the hillside past a tiny woodland pond.

The trail makes several fords of the outlet stream before climbing steadily up the western wall of the valley. The ascent comes in steep spurts interspersed with brief downhill grades. As the ridge begins to peter out, the trail makes a long, steep descent back to the valley floor. After fording a substantial tributary stream, the trail climbs eagerly up the far bank to reach a flat, wooded bench high above Blakiston Creek. After traveling north for a short distance, the route meets a tiny rivulet and runs west along its course as it passes into the cirque at the foot of Festubert Mountain. Here, the trail turns north once again, ascending a series of brutally steep switchbacks on its way to the windblown saddle that overlooks Lone Lake.

Once over the hump, the trail descends through a pure stand of mature alpine larch. Most of these trees have a "snow knee," which is a downslope bend at the base of the trunk. This growth aberration occurs early in the tree's development, when the heavy, wet snows of winter slump downhill and bend the saplings to the ground. The sapling naturally compensates by growing upward and finally becomes stout enough to remain in a vertical position in spite of the weight of the snow.

As the trail nears the valley floor, it crosses a series of small meadows that flank the southern shore of Lone Lake. The lake itself sits atop a drainage divide and drains not into Lone Creek but rather into the valley that runs east to Blakiston Creek. The trail crosses the outlet stream and follows the crest of a terminal moraine left by a retreating glacier. This wall of debris formed a natural dam that created the lake and has been long since covered over in forest. The campground is located at the northeast corner of the lake and has a cache pole for hanging food out of the reach of hungry bears. The lake is populated with pan-sized cutthroat trout, which provide excellent fishing possibilities.

From Lone Lake, the trail crosses the low depression between Festubert and Lone Mountains and begins a steady descent through wet meadows spangled with glacier and corn lilies. Glades of subalpine fir, spruce, and the occasional alpine larch provide shady contrasts to the bright green of the alpine glades. The trail swings past a series of tiny, shallow ponds that sit beneath the sheer cliffs towering to the west. Farther on, the trail passes through a wasteland of broken trees caused by a devastating avalanche that thundered down from the overhanging cliffs some years ago. Young saplings are becoming established where once the tall trees grew, demonstrating the power of the forest to heal itself over the course of time.

Shortly after leaving the slide site, the trail begins to meander gently uphill. As the valley bottom falls away to the east, the trail follows along through the dry, open forest at a level clip. The trail passes the path running uphill to South Kootenai Pass and then reaches the Blakiston Creek Trail junction. Beyond this point, the trail climbs gently, curving into a beautiful alpine cirque overlooked by Kishinena Peak. At the floor of the cirque lies a tiny gem of a lake, surrounded by luxuriant meadows and copses of shapely firs. The trail crosses the outlet of the lake and continues north-ward, rising into a high saddle crowned with alpine larch.

The trail winds around to the west as it descends on the far side, following the cirque wall above Lower Twin Lake. The trail passes above the head of this lake on its way to the low ridge separating the two cold bodies of water. Upon reaching this ridge, a spur trail breaks off to the right, toward the lower lake. The main trail con-tinues straight ahead, descending gradually to a campground at the foot of Upper Twin Lake. To continue see The Snowshoe Trail–Twin Lakes.

Key Points

0.0	Trail junction at Rowe Meadows. Turn right for the Tamarack Trail.
1.9	Trail crosses the top of an unnamed peak to drop into the Blakiston Creek Valley.
3.2	Junction with trail to Upper Rowe Lake. Stay right for Tamarack Trail.
5.4	Trail crosses a tributary stream and begins an uphill climb to an unnamed pass.
7.9	Lone Lake.
10.4	Junction with trail to South Kootenai Pass. Stay right for Twin Lakes.
10.5	Junction with the Blakiston Creek Trail. Stay left for Twin Lakes.
12.6	Twin Lakes. Junction with the Snowshoe Trail.

55 Blakiston Valley

A long day hike or backpack from Red Rock Canyon to a junction with the Tama-rack Trail, 6.3 miles (10.1 km) one way; Red Rock Canyon to South Kootenai Pass, 7.3 miles (11.8 km) one way.

Elevation gain to junction: 2,170 feet
Elevation loss to junction: 120 feet

Maximum elevation: 7,000 feet (South Kootenai Pass)
Difficulty: Moderate

Finding the trailhead: Trail begins from the Red Rock Canyon parking lot. Cross Red Rock Creek and take a left to descend to the bridge over Bauerman Creek, which is the starting point for the Blakiston Trail.

The Hike

This trail provides an access corridor to reach the Tamarack Trail and then climbs to reach South Kootenai Pass on the Continental Divide. From the parking lot at Red Rock Canyon, cross Red Rock Creek and turn left, following its northwest bank to reach a stout bridge above Bauerman Creek. Once across this bridge, take the rightmost trail, which is for hikers. The trail climbs gently through coniferous forest-land, with views of Mount Blakiston through numerous openings. At Blakiston Falls,

Kishinena Peak as seen from the meadows of Lone Creek

the trail passes a wooden observation platform that leans out over the water to provide excellent views of the thundering cascade.

Beyond the falls, the trail narrows and continues to climb gently beside Blakiston Creek's own red shale gorge. Crossing the gravel fan from an intermittent stream, the trail becomes faint. Look for the trail to pick up again just inside the edge of the woods. The trail then climbs high above the stream, which passes through a series of gravel bars. The trail passes through relatively open country dotted with aspen groves, then enters a tiny burn. Leaving the burn behind, the trail descends back to the level of the creek to wander among sun-dappled aspen stands. When the trail reaches a small feeder stream, look across the valley to view a graceful waterfall tumbling across the wall of the valley.

The trail then enters a dense forest that blocks out the surrounding landscape. As the valley forks, the trail wanders toward the creek once more before turning west to ascend the Lone Creek Valley. A small cascade passes by before the silent woods close around the trail. Eventually, the trail emerges into a wide expanse of open meadow, densely populated by clumps of beargrass. To the west, the sheer face of Kishinena Peak rises along the backbone of the Great Divide, while the avalanche slopes of Lost Mountain rise skyward to the south. After crossing a second meadow,

Hikes 55, 56, 57, 58, and 59

RF 1 : 177,500

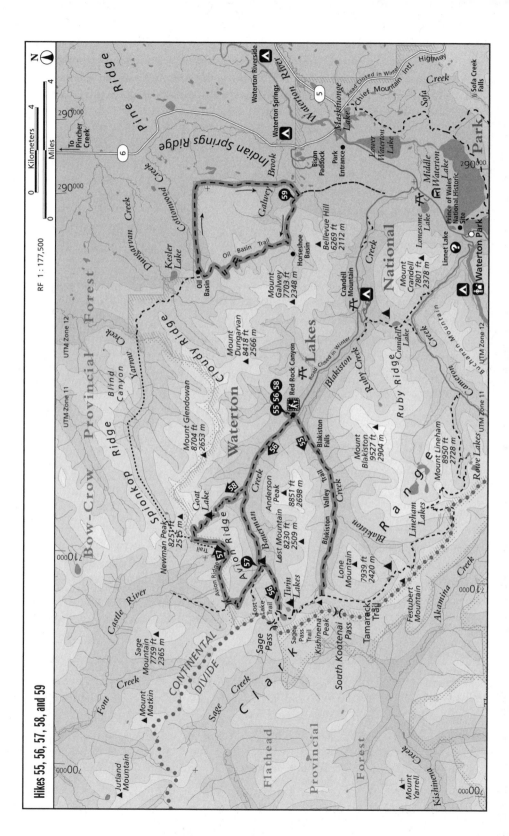

the trail reenters the forest, crosses a substantial tributary, and begins to climb the north wall of the valley. The ascent becomes quite steep, with numerous switchbacks, as the trail makes the final push through subalpine firs and snags to reach its junction with the Tamarack Trail.

South Kootenai Pass Option: From the Tamarack Trail junction, a short jog to the south brings you to a spur trail to South Kootenai Pass (1 mile, moderately strenuous). This trail resumes the switchbacking climb to the west, then skirts far to the south through an old burn to reach South Kootenai Pass. It was through this pass that Lieutenant Thomas Blakiston, for whom the valley was named, traveled to become the first European visitor to the Waterton area. Through the snags, the pass offers views of Kishinena Ridge and Kenow Mountain to the southwest.

Key Points

0.0 Trail sign. Take the paved trail across Red Rock Creek, then turn left.

0.2 Bridge over Bauerman Creek.

0.8 Blakiston Falls.

3.6 Confluence of Lone and Blakiston Creeks.

6.3 Junction with the Tamarack Trail. Turn left and then right for South Kootenai Pass.

7.3 South Kootenai Pass.

56 The Snowshoe Trail–Twin Lakes

A long day hike or backpack from Red Rock Canyon to Twin Lakes, 7.2 miles (11.6 km) one way.

See map on page 191.
Elevation gain: 1,640 feet
Elevation loss: 70 feet

Maximum elevation: 6,470 feet
Difficulty: Moderate to Snowshoe Campground; moderately strenuous beyond

Finding the trailhead: The trail begins at a marked trailhead at the Red Rock Canyon parking lot. Cross the bridge and follow an old fire road northwest for the Snowshoe Trail.

The Hike

This trail runs from Red Rock Canyon to a high alpine lake below the Continental Divide. The trail follows an old fire-access road as far as the Snowshoe Campground, and this part of the trail is open to cyclists as well as hikers and horse parties. Bicycles are strictly prohibited beyond the campground.

From the Red Rock Canyon parking lot, the Snowshoe Trail crosses Red Rock Creek via a paved path that heads northwest. The pavement soon gives way to a

Red Rock Canyon PHOTO BY MONICA BAER

network of trails running along the old roadbed. The route climbs moderately through aspens and lodgepole pines, reaching a high point several hundred feet above Bauerman Creek. To the west, the gabled spires of Anderson Peak dominate the skyline, while ahead and to the right are the rocky bones of Mount Glendowan. As the trail descends back toward the creek, it enters a grassy meadow that boasts a burgeoning population of Columbia ground squirrels. Straight ahead, the reddish pimple crowning the ridgeline is Newman Peak. A backward glance yields a stunning view of Mount Blakiston.

The trail then enters an open forest of aspen, spruce, and fir interspersed with tall grasses. The trail crosses two small tributaries that descend from the flanks of Mount Glendowan, then follows the curve of the valley around to the west. As the trail nears the Goat Lake Trail junction, the north face of Anderson Peak looms across the valley, while the barren spurs of Avion Ridge loom above the northern side of the trail. After passing the Goat Lake Trail, the Snowshoe Trail crosses the gravelly bed of Goat Creek. Half a mile farther is a spectacular cascade descending from the cliffs of Avion Ridge toward the trail. The ascent becomes more insistent as the trail passes among scattered groves of aspen, and Lone Mountain swings into view to the southwest.

The open glades give way to an old-growth forest of Douglas fir that accompanies the trail on its final leg into the Snowshoe Campground. This campground is adjacent to a patrol cabin on the north bank of a large tributary stream and is the site of a junction with the Avion Ridge Trail. The main trail leaves the campground by crossing a bridge over the creek, then climbs around the tail end of a ridge to enter the upper valley of Bauerman Creek. The trail leaves the forest to follow the willow-choked stream course, and a look back reveals the tawny crags of Newman Peak, Mount Glendowan, and Anderson Peak surrounding the valley. The trail enters a meadowy basin just before it begins to ascend the wooded headwall below Upper Twin Lake.

After a steep climb, the trail levels out and runs west, passing the Sage Pass Trail on its way to the foot of Upper Twin Lake. The trail crosses the outlet via a log on its way to the campground that marks the terminus of the trail. The blue waters of the lake reflect the rugged east face of Kishinena Peak, and alpine wildflowers dot the glades between stands of stately firs. The Tamarack Trail departs the campground to the south, offering access to Lower Twin Lake on its way to the Cameron Lake Road.

Sage Pass Option: The Sage Pass Trail begins at a junction just below Upper Twin Lake. It climbs steadily for half a mile, through open forests that allow excellent views of Mount Bauerman and Kishinena Peak. After reaching a false summit, the trail turns north, climbing across a high bench before reaching an outcrop of red mudstone. Here the trail bends right, following a shallow cleft to the low saddle of Sage Pass. There is little to see from the pass itself, but a short bushwhack onto the rocky knoll to the west yields an excellent view of La Coulotte Ridge and Sunkist Mountain to the north.

Key Points

0.0 Trail sign. Trail crosses bridge over Red Rock Creek.

2.4 Junction with the Goat Lake Trail. Proceed straight ahead for the Snowshoe Trail.

5.1 Snowshoe Campground and junction with the Avion Ridge/Lone Lake Trail. Turn left and cross bridge for Twin Lakes.

6.8 Junction with Sage Pass Trail. Stay left for Twin Lakes.

7.1 Upper Twin Lake.

7.2 Junction with the Tamarack Trail and a spur trail to Lower Twin Lake.

57 Lost Lake–Avion Ridge

An extended trip on an unmaintained trail from the Snowshoe Campground (a 5.1-mile [8.2 km] hike from parking) to Goat Lake, 5.0 more miles (8.0 km) one way; or Snowshoe Campground to Lost Lake, 1.5 more miles (1.9 km) one way.

See map on page 191.
Elevation gain: 2,400 feet
Elevation loss: 1,520 feet

Maximum elevation: 7,950 feet
Difficulty: Moderately strenuous

Finding the trail: This trail departs from the north side of the Snowshoe Campground, a 5.1-mile hike from Red Rock Canyon. Trail is unmaintained and difficult to find in places. Not recommended for beginning hikers.

The Hike

The Avion Ridge Trail provides one of the most spectacular, and primitive, routes in the park. It shares its first section with the trail to Lost Lake, a popular side trip from the Snowshoe Campground. Avion Ridge can be hiked through from Snowshoe Campground to Goat Lake, or an alternate trail can be taken into the Yarrow Creek Valley to descend to an oil drilling road north of the park boundary. The trail to Lost Lake is well beaten and easy to follow, but the Avion Ridge Trail is often faint and provides a challenge in some places. This is a hike for experienced off-trail hikers with strong map-and-compass skills. Lingering snowdrifts on Avion Ridge may make this hike a difficult one through late June.

From the Snowshoe backcountry campground, the trail begins with a brisk uphill climb, crossing several small streams on its way through timbered country. The trail soon levels out and follows the course of one of these woodland brooks. After half a mile, the trail forks. To the left, the more distinct path runs another half mile to the west on its way to Lost Lake. This trail crosses another stream and climbs steadily across wooded benches to reach the foot of the lake. Lost Lake is a kidney-shaped affair that sits below the cliffs of an unnamed hogback.

Meanwhile, the fainter right fork of the trail runs northwest toward Avion Ridge. It crosses a babbling rivulet and climbs gradually to reach the Castle Divide, a wooded pass between the Castle River and Bauerman Creek watersheds. At an unmarked junction, a route descends into the valley beyond, while the Avion Ridge Trail mounts the ridgeline to the east. The trail begins as a well-defined path, climbing steeply just to the south of the ridgeline. Nearing the first wooded summit, the trail veers right to pass below it and into the saddle beyond. Looking southwest, Lost Lake lies cupped in the verdant forest far below. Mount Bauerman and Lost Peak rise prominently on the far side of the Bauerman Valley.

Black bear PHOTO BY MONICA BAER

As the trail climbs the next hill, it passes through groves of subalpine larch; larches are the only conifers that lose needles every fall. Autumn displays in late September can be spectacular, as these trees burn with a golden orange flame. However, capricious weather keeps most sane backpackers out of the high country during this time of year. The route becomes much fainter in this area, so keep an eye out for patches of earth worn bare by the passage of feet and the yellow park boundary markers that mark the route here. As the trail approaches a second point, it again dips to the right, missing the summit and working its way into the barren saddle at the foot of Avion Ridge's high point.

At first, the trail follows the crest of the ridge, then veers to the right when the going gets steep, and passes around the southwestern slope toward the summit. Upon gaining the top, the trail reveals fantastic views into British Columbia, featuring the massive facades and jagged spires that crowd the western skyline. As the trail bends northward, it descends steeply down the ridgeline into the next saddle and approaches the next summit. Instead of climbing it, however, the route skirts to the west, passing over a bed of loose scree. To the west, the cliffs of Avion Ridge overshadow the heavily clearcut valley of the Castle River. After rounding the rocky nub, the trail reaches a saddle that boasts a stunning view of the deep blue waters of Goat Lake resting at the foot of a rocky pinnacle.

Straight ahead, the route to the Yarrow Creek Valley can be made out as it traverses across the western slope of Newman Peak. Meanwhile, the Avion Ridge Trail switchbacks downward across a steep scree slope on its way to the alpine meadows in the basin below. Upon reaching the valley floor, the trail runs southeast toward the lake, descending to the east of the seasonal stream at the center of the valley. After passing two small headwalls, the trail swings westward to reach the creek bed. After crossing the stream, the trail sticks to the western side of the valley, passing through subalpine parkland below a sheer rock face of Avion Ridge.

The trail reaches Goat Lake at the eastern edge of the large meadow that dominates the western corner of the lake. Hikers accessing the Avion Ridge Trail from the Goat Lake end will find it necessary to cast about for the trail as it exits the meadow; the path does not become distinct until it is about 100 yards away from the lakeshore. To reach the trail to the Bauerman Creek Valley, follow a network of well-worn trails around the eastern shore of the lake to pick up the main trail at the outlet stream.

Key Points

0.0 Trail sign at north end of Snowshoe Campground.

0.6 Junction with Lost Lake Spur Trail (0.9 mile, moderate). Take the right fork for Avion Ridge.

1.8 Castle River Divide. Turn right to ascend onto Avion Ridge.

3.0 Summit of Avion Ridge.

3.8 Junction with route to Yarrow Creek. Turn right and descend from saddle toward Goat Lake.

5.0 Goat Lake.

58 Goat Lake

A day hike or short backpack from Red Rock Canyon to Goat Lake, 3.9 miles (6.3 km) one way.

See map on page 191.
Elevation gain: 1,750 feet
Elevation loss: 70 feet

Maximum elevation: 6,580
Difficulty: Moderately strenuous

Finding the trailhead: Trail begins as the Snowshoe Trail, which heads west from the Red Rock Canyon Trailhead, across a bridge over Red Rock Creek.

The Hike

The Goat Lake Trail provides a popular and heavily used day hike or short overnight trip. From the Red Rock Canyon parking lot, the Snowshoe Trail follows an old fire-access road for 2.4 miles to reach Goat Lake Trail at Snowshoe Campground. This part of the trail is open to cyclists as well as hikers and horse parties. Bicycles are strictly prohibited beyond the campground.

Snowshoe Trail crosses Red Rock Creek via a paved path that heads northwest. Soon a network of trails takes over, running along the old roadbed. The route climbs moderately through aspens and lodgepole pines before descending back toward the creek through a grassy meadow. Straight ahead, the reddish pimple crowning the ridgeline is Newman Peak. A backward glance yields a stunning view of Mount Blakiston.

The trail then enters an open forest of aspen, spruce, and fir interspersed with tall grasses. Crossing two small tributaries, which descend from the flanks of Mount Glendowan, the trail follows the curve of the valley around to the west. Here it leaves the Bauerman Creek Valley with a steep and steady climb through dense forest. The trail quickly emerges onto open slopes carpeted with wildflowers, highlighted by white bulbs of beargrass. Across the valley, Anderson Peak and Lost Mountain rear their vertical masses of rock. Farther on, the peaks surrounding the head of the Bauerman Creek Valley become plainly visible.

Looking ahead, the outlet stream of the lake plummets through a series of scenic falls beneath the towering cliffs of Avion Ridge. Continuing its unrelenting ascent, the trail switchbacks upward, passing across a barren, cliffy area on its way toward the falls. Before the trail reaches the stream, however, it passes up another series of switchbacks through stunted firs and flowery glades. Turning west again, the trail finally reaches the streamside at the uppermost of the waterfalls and follows the stream through a narrow, wooded gulch. Leaving the stream behind, the trail climbs upward through the silent forest to reach the lake at its outlet.

Cliffs of Avion Ridge above still waters of Goat Lake ▶

Several streamlets must be crossed to reach the lakeshore, which is crowded with trees along its southern and eastern shores. Talus slopes from Avion Ridge grade into grassy meadows on the western shoreline. To reach the campground, follow the trail around the eastern side of the lake. The camping area is located inland in a series of flowery meadows interspersed with copses of fir near the north shore of the lake. The campground is populated by a multitude of ground squirrels and almost-tame mule deer. It is wise to secure your food and sweaty clothing out of reach of these critters, who will gladly chew them in search of salt. The cliffs above the lake serve as a nursery area for mountain goats, and the lake offers excellent fishing for cutthroat trout. A trail takes off from the northwest corner of the lake toward Avion Ridge.

Key Points

0.0 Trail sign and bridge over Red Rock Creek. Stay straight for Goat Lake.

2.4 Goat Lake Trail junction. Turn right for Goat Lake.

3.9 Goat Lake.

59 The Oil Basin Loop

A long day hike or backpack. Bison paddock to Oil Basin, 7.8 miles (12.6 km) one way; complete loop, 12.8 miles (20.6 km).

See map on page 191.
Elevation gain: 2,240 feet
Elevation loss: 2,240 feet

Maximum elevation: 5,850 feet
Difficulty: Moderately strenuous

Finding the trailhead: The trail begins as a gravel road running along the northern edge of the bison paddock.

The Hike

This trail is a popular one for horse parties and follows a series of grassy valleys along the edge of the open prairie, dipping in and out of the front range of the Rockies. The unmaintained Park Line Trail running from the Oil Basin southward along the park boundary allows a complete loop of 12.8 miles from the bison paddock. Alternately, a hard-to-find route runs north from the Oil Basin through the Dungarvan Creek country to reach a patrol cabin on the Yarrow Creek oil field road. There is also a trail marked on some park maps linking the loop to the Red Rock Canyon Road. This "trail" does not exist, but the route is easy to follow as it crosses the level grasslands at the foot of Bellevue Hill. There are no designated

Fresh snow on Dungarvan Peak

camping areas along the Oil Basin Trail, and overnight stays are officially discouraged in this area; backpackers will need to secure a special permit for minimum-impact camping in this area.

The trail departs from the end of the gravel road that runs along the northern edge of the bison enclosure. It climbs through grassy meadows and dense stands of aspens as it runs westward toward the mountains. After climbing for half a mile, the trail swings north to pass around the tip of Bellevue Hill and into a small depression. The trail then resumes its westward course, passing below the forested slopes of Bellevue's eastern face on its way into the Horseshoe Basin.

Upon reaching the banks of Galwey Brook, the trail descends quickly to ford the knee-deep stream. The trail then swings west as it climbs the far bank before turning northward through a meadowy valley. The rocky crest of Mount Galwey rises to the southwest, while Lakeview Ridge guards the northeastern approaches to the Horseshoe Basin. The trail follows a tributary stream on its way north, fording it three times on its way to the base of a high pass. The trail climbs rather steeply as it switchbacks among dead snags to reach the saddle behind Lakeview Ridge. This high pass commands a view of the Oil Basin to the immediate north and endless rolling prairie stretching to the horizon. The trail continues to climb as it crosses the rocky shoulder of the ridge to the west, then bends westward as it descends into the steep ravine that holds the headwaters of Cottonwood Creek. Once across this tiny stream, the trail turns northeast to descend out onto the high plains of the Oil Basin.

The trail becomes a bit challenging to follow as it traces the north bank of Cottonwood Creek toward the park boundary. The route northward to Yarrow Creek meets the Oil Basin Loop somewhere in the tall grass of the basin; it will be discussed separately below. Upon reaching the park boundary, the trail follows the fence east for 1.3 miles, climbing over a rise on its way to a corner in the fence. Here the trail turns south, climbing over the eastern flank of Lakeview Ridge. The trail dips westward as it fords Galwey Brook again, then returns to the park boundary for the final southward leg of 0.4 mile to Indian Springs, where the trail returns to the gravel road to complete the loop.

Dungarvan Creek Option: From the Oil Basin, this route runs north across the prairie. It does not exist as a discernible path until it climbs onto the slopes above Kesler Lake, and even here it is easy to confuse it with game trails. Elk abound on the meadowy slopes interspersed with aspen groves during early summer, providing opportunities for viewing to hikers that have binoculars and a good measure of patience. The trail is discernible as it passes through the aspens, but quite faint as it crosses the grassy swales between them.

Hikers who haven't found the path at this point can pick it up where it descends to cross Dungarvan Creek just above the confluence of its two forks. The trail is easy to find as it crosses the gravel outwash of the creek. Looking up the valley to the southwest, the rugged crest of Dungarvan Mountain rises beyond the gnarled cottonwoods that crowd the stream banks. As the trail leaves the valley floor and climbs onto the eastern marches of Cloudy Ridge, note the intermixture of prairie and montane plant communities. Grasses and cinquefoil mix freely with aspens and subalpine firs in a bizarre hodgepodge of vegetation. The trail crosses meadowy slopes interspersed with coppices of aspen, then drops into a forest of lodgepole pines as the hillside falls away toward Yarrow Creek.

As the trail descends through the trees, it wanders westward for two-thirds of a mile to reach an opening in the fence at the southeast corner of the Yarrow patrol cabin compound. Follow the dirt jeep trail leaving the cabin to the north. This track runs a short distance to a barbed-wire fence gate along the Yarrow Creek oil field road, between the bridge over the creek and a sharp bend in the road.

Key Points

0.0 Trail sign at Horseshoe Basin Trailhead.

2.0 Trail fords Galwey Brook.

5.2 Summit of pass behind Lakeview Ridge.

6.8 Route northward to Dungarvan Creek and the Yarrow Creek Road departs to the north. Bear east to complete the loop.

7.8 Trail reaches park boundary.

12.0 Trail recrosses Galwey Brook.

12.8 Trail arrives back at the bison paddock.

Additional Hikes

A trail begins at the Belly River Campground and wanders upstream for 1.8 miles beside the banks of the **Belly River,** featuring flowery meadows and views of Chief Mountain and the other glacier-carved spires that rim the valley.

The **Wishbone Trail** runs from the Chief Mountain Highway across the aspen-clad flats for 4 miles to reach the Vimy Peak Trail junction. The trail running from Loon Lake to the **Bosporus** is no longer being maintained and exists only as a primitive route.

There is a trail that follows the **Cameron Creek Valley,** parallel to the road. The trail is open to mountain bikes. A short trail runs 0.7 mile from the Cameron Lake Road to reach a campground beside **Crandell Lake.** The lake is situated in a low saddle between Mount Crandell and Ruby Ridge and can also be reached via a 1.3-mile trail from the Red Rock Campground. These trails are also open to mountain bikes.

An old roadbed climbs gradually from the Cameron Lake Road to **Akamina Pass.** The pass offers little in the way of scenery, but does provide access to trails running to Forum and Wall Lakes in the Akamina-Kishinena Provincial Park (British Columbia) beyond.

A trail starts from the southeast side of the Cameron Lake parking lot and runs for 0.3 mile through swampy forest to reach **Little Akamina Lake.** A 1-mile trail runs along the western shore of **Cameron Lake,** offering fine views of Mounts Custer and Forum. The trail ends at an avalanche chute near the head of the lake. This chute provides ideal habitat for grizzly bears, and an interpretive sign at the viewing platform explains the presence of the bears in this area.

Extended Trips

The trail system in Glacier National Park is composed of miles of interlinked trails that allow the adventurous backpacker an almost infinite array of choices. Outlined in the following pages are a few recommended routes for travelers wishing to escape for longer than a couple of days. Travelers are reminded that backcountry permits are issued for a maximum of six nights. For extended trips, it is especially important to ascertain trail conditions before leaving and also to prepare for all types of weather conditions. The mountains reward those who come prepared, but are frequently unforgiving to those who tempt the fates. By playing it safe, wise hikers ensure that they will have an enjoyable trip.

The Continental Divide National Scenic Trail

Marias Pass to Canadian Border
Allow 10 days

The Hike

The Continental Divide National Scenic Trail, authorized by Congress in 1968, follows a 3,100-mile route along the spine of the continent from Mexico to the Canadian border. The segment of the trail running through Glacier National Park was designated in 1988 and originates at Marias Pass and runs through the heart of the park, following well-maintained trails that feature spectacular views of Glacier's diverse wildlands.

The Continental Divide Trail enters the park at a trailhead located at the summit of Marias Pass on U.S. Highway 2. The route follows this spur trail to a junction with the Autumn Creek Trail, which it follows eastward all the way to the town of East Glacier. From East Glacier, the route hooks up with the trail to Scenic Point, which exits town behind the golf course. You'll need a tribal permit for this segment. This trail ascends steadily to a summit at Scenic Point, from which sweeping views of the high plains can be taken in on a clear day. The trail descends steeply to a trailhead on the Two Medicine Road, at which point the hiker should turn left, following the road for a quarter mile to the Two Medicine Campground.

From the campground, the route crosses a footbridge and heads up the Dry Fork Valley to Pitamakan Pass (see Dawson-Pitamakan hike). From this high point, the trail descends steadily into the Cut Bank Creek Valley, past Pitamakan and Morning Star Lakes to a junction with the trail to Triple Divide Pass. Turning west here, the Continental Divide Trail ascends steadily to the aforementioned pass, then descends quickly to the head of the Hudson Bay Creek drainage, which it follows to Red Eagle Lake. Several miles beyond the foot of the lake, the route turns west again at a trail junction that leads the hiker to the south shore of St. Mary Lake.

The trail runs westward above the lakeshore for about 10 miles, passing Virginia Falls and reaching St. Mary Falls. Upon crossing the St. Mary River, turn west for the Piegan Pass Trail, which follows the valley floor for 1.4 miles and then ascends steadily up the north wall of the valley, eventually crossing the Going-to-the-Sun Road. After crossing the highway, follow the signs to Piegan Pass as the trail passes beneath the western flanks of Going-to-the-Sun Mountain. After reaching the pass, the trail descends, and the hiker should keep right to follow the quickest route to the Many Glacier Hotel.

From this point, an alternate route runs over Redgap Pass and descends into the Belly River Valley, ending up at Chief Mountain Customs on Montana Highway 17. The primary route resumes at the Swiftcurrent Motor Inn and heads westward, ascending steeply to Swiftcurrent Pass. Once over the pass, the route reaches the

Highline Trail at Granite Park Chalet. From here, it is comparatively easy going along the Continental Divide to Fifty Mountain Campground, where the trail drops steeply into the Waterton Valley. This trail terminates at Goat Haunt Ranger Station, from which hikers can either take a ferry to Waterton townsite in Canada or continue the trek around the western shore of Upper Waterton Lake, reaching the town by trail. Either way, hikers entering Canada will have to pass through customs.

The Great Northern Traverse

Kintla Lake to Chief Mountain Customs
Allow 6 days

The Hike

This route encompasses some of the wildest and most scenic terrain in the park and affords a strenuous challenge to the serious backpacker. The trail begins at Kintla Lake, on the trail to Boulder Pass. The first 12 miles are an easy stroll along the shores of Kintla and Upper Kintla Lakes, where views are limited by the density of the forest. Beyond Upper Kintla Lake, the trail begins a grueling ascent to Boulder Pass as the views begin to open up, exposing the majestic peaks on all sides. After passing through Boulder Pass, the trail descends around the Hole in the Wall cirque and then drops farther to Brown Pass. A relatively easy descent lands the hiker in the Olson Creek Valley, which the trail follows through the trees to the junction with the Waterton Lake Trail.

From this junction, the hiker should follow the trail signs to Goat Haunt Ranger Station, on the south shore of Upper Waterton Lake. From the ranger station, the route heads south, following the Waterton Valley beneath the boles of old-growth conifers. After topping a brief rise, the route meets a junction with the Stoney Indian Pass Trail, which it follows eastward again, rising into open meadows and rocky fields. The summit of this pass rewards the hiker with more fantastic vistas of glacier-carved pinnacles before descending past numerous waterfalls into the Mokowanis River Valley. A gentle descent past a chain of lakes takes you to a junction with the Belly River Trail. Just to the north is a seasonally manned ranger station, while the primary route takes you northward, following the meanders of the Belly River through meadows and copses toward the Chief Mountain Customs. The last several miles are a surprisingly steep and strenuous ascent up a hillside to the trail's terminus; save some energy for this final push.

The Highline Trail

Logan Pass to Goat Haunt Ranger Station
Allow 3 days

The Hike

This trail is popular because it allows easy access to the high country without requiring pass-climbing heroics or special wilderness skills. The easiest routing is to hike the trail from south to north, as this avoids a grueling ascent up the southern wall of the Waterton Valley. The trail begins at Logan Pass and runs below the crest of the Garden Wall to Granite Park Chalet, which offers beds and hot meals to travelers with reservations. For those who prefer to camp, a nearby campground is reserved especially for hikers on extended trips during most of the season.

From Granite Park, the route continues north, following the Northern Highline as it descends and then rises again on its way to Fifty Mountain Campground. The route then descends steeply down an open hillside to the shaded depths of the Waterton Valley, which it follows to its terminus at Goat Haunt Ranger Station. A nearby boat dock provides shuttle service to Waterton townsite for a modest fee. The adventurous traveler may also decide to follow the trail around the western shore of Upper Waterton Lake, which provides a longer route to this Canadian destination.

The North Circle

Loop begins and terminates at Swiftcurrent Motor Inn
Allow 5 days

The Hike

The North Circle is a traditional route for backpackers who wish to sample the charms of the Belly River country. Although three major passes are crossed, this route is suitable for intermediate-level backpackers, and a wealth of campgrounds along the way make more extended visits possible. The route follows the Ptarmigan Tunnel Trail northward from Swiftcurrent to a junction with the Iceberg Lake Trail; a side trip to Iceberg Lake is well worth the effort. From this junction, the primary route runs northward past the barren tarn of Ptarmigan Lake to the Ptarmigan Tunnel, which cuts through a sheer rock wall and allows passage into the Belly River country beyond.

After the tunnel, spectacular views open up on the long descent to Elizabeth Lake. From the shore of this favored fishing spot, the trail follows the Belly River northward to Dawn Mist Falls. Shortly after this milestone, a connecting trail that cuts off to the west brings you across a ford below Cosley Lake to the Stoney Indian Pass Trail. Here the trail turns southwest, passing a chain of lakes that offer fine opportunities for the angler. After reaching the head of Glenns Lake, the trail ascends past tumbling waterfalls to the heights of Stoney Indian Pass. A foot-pounding descent brings you to the foot of the Waterton Valley, where the route turns southward and begins a toilsome ascent up open slopes to the meadowy expanses of the Fifty Mountain area.

From Fifty Mountain Campground, the route continues southward on the Northern Highline, descending slightly and then ascending again before reaching Granite Park. At this juncture, hikers completing the loop should turn east, taking the easy route over Swiftcurrent Pass. After the pass is reached, views of the Swiftcurrent Valley are revealed along the steep descent to the valley floor. The last few miles are an almost imperceptible descent past dwarfed aspens and shallow lakes to the original starting point.

Appendix A: Further Reading

Available from the Glacier Natural History Association:

Along the Trail, Summer and On, 114 pp. (Glacier Natural History Association Publication)

Bear Attacks: Their Causes and Avoidance, Herrero, 286 pp. (Lyons and Burford)

Birds of the Northern Rockies, Ulrich, 160 pp. (Mountain Press)

Climber's Guide to Glacier National Park, Edwards, 347 pp. (Glacier Natural History Association Publication)

Fishing Glacier National Park, Hintzen (Glacier Natural History Association Publication)

Jewel Basin Hiking Map: Flathead National Forest, 18" x 18" (Glacier Natural History Association Publication)

Mammals of the Northern Rockies, Ulrich, 160 pp. (Mountain Press)

Many Storied Mountains, Beaumont, 138 pp. (National Park Service)

Place Names of Waterton-Glacier National Parks, Holterman, 170 pp. (Glacier Natural History Association Publication)

Plants of Waterton-Glacier National Parks and the Northern Rockies, Shaw and On, 160 pp. (Mountain Press)

Three Forks of the Flathead, 36 pp. (Glacier Natural History Association Publication)

Topographic Quadrangle Maps for Glacier National Park, Scale 1:24,000 (U.S. Geological Survey)

USGS Topographic Map of Glacier National Park, 41" x 38" (U.S. Geological Survey)

Appendix B: For More Information

Superintendent
Glacier National Park
P.O. Box 128
West Glacier, MT 59936
(406) 888–7800
www.nps.gov/glac

Waterton Lakes National Park
Waterton Park
Alberta, Canada T0K 2M0
(403) 859–2224
www.parkscanada.gc.ca/waterton

Appendix C: Fishing Opportunities

Fish Species
BKT – Brook Trout
BTR – Bull Trout★
GRY – Grayling
LKT – Lake Trout
RBT – Rainbow Trout
WCT – Westslope Cutthroat Trout
WTF – Whitefish
YCT – Yellowstone Cutthroat Trout
KOK – Kokanee (landlocked sockeye salmon)

Fishing Quality
VG – Very Good
G – Good
F – Fair
P – Poor

★Bull trout fishing is closed parkwide, and any bull trout caught by anglers must be immediately released.

Lakes	Fish Species	Quality	Comments
Avalanche	WCT	F	
Cosley	RBT	G	
Elizabeth	RBT, GRY	VG	
Ellen Wilson	BKT	VG	
Francis	RBT	G	
Glenns	RBT, WTF, BKT	F	
Grace	WCT	VG	
Gunsight	RBT	VG	
Hidden	WCT	F	
Isabel	WCT, BTR	VG	
Josephine	BKT, KOK	F	
Lincoln	WCT, BKT	F	
Logging	WCT	F	
McDonald	LKT, WCT, WTF, BTR	P	
Mokowanis	BKT	G	
Oldman	YCT	G	
Quartz	RBT, WCT	F	
Red Eagle	RBT, WCT, BKT	G	
Slide	BTR	F	
St. Mary	RBT, WTF	F	
Swiftcurrent	BKT, KOK	F	
Trout	WCT, RBT	F	Fly Fishing Only
Two Medicine	BKT, RBT	F	

Streams	Fish Species	Quality	Comments
Belly River	GRY, RBT	P	
Lower McDonald Creek	WCT	F	Catch & Release
Middle Fork Flathead	BTR, WCT	P	
Midvale Creek	RBT, BKT	G	
North Fork Flathead	BTR, WCT	F	
Red Eagle Creek	RBT	F	
Two Medicine Creek	BKT, RBT	F	

Appendix D: Backcountry Campground Table

Ratings

5 - Campground is a scenic attraction in itself.

4 - Campground is in an area of high scenic value.

3 - Campground is in an area of moderate scenic value.

2 - Campground is in an area with low scenic value.

Comments

1 - One-night stay limit July and August.

2 - Extended trips only in July and August.

3 - Open June 1 to September 11, when launch is running.

4 - May not be scheduled for first night of trip.

5 - Special approval required.

6 - Two-night stay limit.

Campground Name	Rating	Sites	Fires	Horses	Comments
Glacier Campgrounds					
Adair Lake	3	4	yes	6	
Akokala Lake	3	3	no	6	
Arrow Lake	4	2	no	5	
Atlantic Creek	2	4	yes	6	
Beaver Woman Lake	2	2	yes		
Boulder Pass	5	3	no	no	
Bowman Lake, Head	3	6	yes	10	
Brown Pass	3	3	no	no	
Camas Lake	3	2	no	no	
Coal Creek	2	2	yes	10	
Cobalt Lake	3	2	no	no	
Cosley Lake	3	4	yes	6	
Cracker Lake	5	3	no	no	
Elizabeth Lake, Foot	4	6	no	8	1
Elizabeth Lake, Head	2	3	yes	6	6
Fifty Mountain	4	5	no	6	
Flattop	3	3	no	6	
Gable Creek	4	4	yes	yes	
Glenns Lake, Foot	3	4	yes	8	
Glenns Lake, Head	4	3	yes	no	
Goat Haunt Shelters	3	7	yes	no	1, 3
Grace Lake	4	3	yes	no	
Granite Park	5	4	no	no	1, 2

Campground Name	Rating	Sites	Fires	Horses	Comments
Gunsight Lake	4	8	no	6	
Harrison Lake	3	3	yes	6	
Hawksbill	3	2	no	no	
Helen Lake	3	2	no	no	
Hole in the Wall	5	5	no	no	
Kintla Lake, Head	2	6	yes	10	
Kootenai Lake	3	4	no	6	
Lake Ellen Wilson	4	4	no	6	1
Lake Frances	4	2	no	no	1
Lake Isabel	4	2	yes	no	
Lake Janet	1	2	yes	6	
Lincoln Lake	5	3	no	8	
Logging Lake, Foot	4	3	yes	no	
Lower Nyack	2	2	yes	10	
Lower Quartz Lake	3	4	yes	6	
Many Glacier	4	2	yes	no	1, 2, 4
Mokowanis Junction	2	5	yes	8	
Mokowanis Lake	4	2	no	no	1
Morning Star	4	3	no	no	
No Name Lake	4	3	no	no	1
Oldman Lake	4	4	no	5	1
Ole Creek	2	3	yes	8	
Ole Lake	3	2	yes	5	
Otokomi Lake	3	3	no	no	
Park Creek	2	3	yes	6	
Poia Lake	3	4	no	10	
Quartz Lake	4	3	no	no	
Red Eagle Lake, Foot	4	4	yes	no	
Red Eagle Lake, Head	3	4	yes	10	
Reynolds Creek	3	2	yes	6	5
Slide Lake	2	2	yes	5	
Snyder Lake	4	3	no	5	
Sperry	3	4	no	no	1
Stoney Indian Lake	5	3	no	no	
Upper Kintla Lake	4	4	yes	10	
Upper Nyack	4	2	yes	10	
Upper Park Creek	3	3	yes	6	
Upper Two Medicine	5	4	no	no	1
Waterton River	2	5	yes	6	

Campground Name	Rating	Sites	Fires	Horses	Comments
Waterton Campgrounds					
Alderson Lake	4	4	no	yes	
Bertha Bay	2	4	yes	no	
Bertha Lake	4	4	no	no	
Boundary Bay	3	3	yes	no	
Crandell Lake	3	4	yes	no	
Goat Lake	5	4	no	no	
Lone Lake	4	4	yes	yes	
Snowshoe	2	4	yes	yes	
Upper Twin Lake	4	4	no	no	

Index

A

Akamina Pass, 204
Akokala Creek trail, 41
Akokala Lake, 34
Apgar Lookout, 50
Apikuni Falls, 18, 156
Appistoki Falls, 16
Aster Falls, 117
Aster Park, 17
Autumn Creek Trail, 96
Avalanche Lake, 59
Avion Ridge–Lost Lake, 195

B

Bears Hump, 19
Beaver Pond Trail, 15
Belly River Trail, 159, 204
Belly-Mokowanis Cutoff Trail, 168
Bertha Lake, 175
Blakiston Falls, 21
Blakiston Valley, 189
Bosporus route, 204
Boulder Pass, 27
Bowman Lake–Brown Pass, 33
Brown Pass–Bowman Lake, 33
Bullhead Lake, 19

C

Camas Creek Trail, 61
Cameron Creek Valley trail, 204
Cameron Lake, 20, 204
Carthew-Alderson Trail, 171
Coal Creek–Fielding Trail, 96
Coal Creek–Nyack Loop, 84
Cobalt Lake–Two Medicine Pass, 103
Continental Divide National Scenic
    Trail, 206
Cracker Flats trail, 156
Cracker Lake, 141
Crandell Lake trail, 204
Crypt Lake, 177
Cut Bank Access Trail, 96
Cut Bank Creek, 109
Cut Bank Pass Trail, 117

D

Dawson-Pitamakan, 106
Divide Creek, 138
Dutch Creek complex, 41

F

Fern Creek trail, 61
Fielding–Coal Creek Trail, 96
Firebrand Pass–Ole Lake, 94
Fish Lake, 55
Flattop Mountain Trail, 76

G

Gable Pass–Slide Lake, 165
Garden Wall, 67
Goat Haunt Overlook, 76
Goat Haunt Shelters, 76
Goat Lake, 198
Great Northern Traverse, 207
Grinnell Complex, 143
Gunsight Pass, 130

H

Harrison Lake, 81
Hidden Lake, 65
Highline Trail, 208
Howe Lake Trail, 61
Huckleberry Mountain Lookout, 49
Huckleberry Mountain Trail, 61

I

Iceberg Lake, 149

J

Johns Lake Loop, 11

K

Kennedy Creek trail, 156
Kishenehn Creek trails, 41
Kootenai Creek Trail, 76

L

Lake Isabel, 88
Lake McDonald, 52
Lee Ridge trail, 168
Lincoln Creek trail, 61
Lincoln Lake, 53
Lineham Falls, 182
Little Akamina Lake trail, 204
Logging Lake, 38
Loneman Lookout, 83
Lost Lake–Avion Ridge, 195
Lower Bertha Falls, 20

M

McDonald Creek, 12, 61
Medicine Grizzly Lake–Triple Divide Pass, 113
Milk River Ridge, 117
Mineral Creek Trail, 76
Mokowanis Cutoff Trail, Belly-, 168
Mokowanis River–Stoney Indian Pass, 162
Mount Brown Lookout, 57

N

North Boundary Trail, 76
North Circle, 208
North Fork Trail, 168
Northern Highline, 70
Numa Ridge Lookout, 36
Nyack–Coal Creek Loop, 84

O

Oil Basin Loop, 200
Old Creek Trail, 96
Ole Lake–Firebrand Pass, 94
Otokomi Lake, 126

P

Paradise Park, 117
Paradise Point, 117
Piegan Pass, 134
Pinchot Creek trails, 96
Poia Lake–Redgap Pass, 153
Porcupine Lookout trail, 76
Ptarmigan Tunnel, 151

Q

Quartz Creek trail, 41
Quartz Lakes Loop, 37

R

Rainbow Falls, 19, 76
Red Eagle Lake, 121

Redgap Pass–Poia Lake, 153
Rowe Lakes, 184
Running Eagle Falls, 16

S

Scalplock Lookout, 92
Scenic Point, 101
Siyeh Pass, 136
Slide Lake–Gable Pass, 165
Snowshoe Trail–Twin Lakes, 192
Snyder Lakes, 58
Snyder Ridge Trail, 61
South Boundary Trail, 96
St. Mary and Virginia Falls, 127
St. Mary Lake, 128
Sun Point Nature Trail, 14
Swiftcurrent Nature Trail (Loop), 18
Swiftcurrent Pass, 147

T

Tamarack Trail, 186
Trail of the Cedars, 12
Triple Divide Pass–Medicine Grizzly Lake, 113
Trout Lake, 45
Twin Lakes–Snowshoe Trail, 192
Two Medicine Pass–Cobalt Lake, 103

U

Upper Two Medicine Lake, 105

V

Vimy Peak, 180

W

Waterton Lake trail, 76
Waterton Valley, 72
Wishbone Trail, 204

About the Authors

Erik Molvar discovered backpacking while working on a volunteer trail crew in the North Cascades of Washington. A newfound taste for the wilderness experience inspired him to choose a career in the outdoors, and he soon found himself at the University of Montana pursuing a bachelor's degree in wildlife biology. Montana's craggy ranges were to be his weekend playground for the next five years, and two summers of bartending at Lake McDonald Lodge gave Erik the perfect opportunity to fully explore Glacier National Park's backcountry. An adventurous spirit has led Erik to embark upon backpacking expeditions throughout the Rocky Mountains, the Great Basin, western Canada, and Alaska. After studying moose behavior in Alaska on the way to a master's degree, Erik is now

Author Erik Molvar atop Scalplock Mountain PHOTO BY SHANNON SMITH

executive director of Biodiversity Conservation Alliance, one of the most effective nonprofit conservation organizations in the West. Erik is also the author of *Hiking Montana's Bob Marshall Country, Hiking Olympic National Park, Hiking Arizona's Cactus Country, Hiking Zion and Bryce Canyon National Parks, Hiking the North Cascades, Hiking Wyoming's Cloud Peak Wilderness, Hiking Colorado's Maroon Bells–Snowmass Wilderness, Wild Wyoming, The Insider's Guide to Scenic Driving Alaska and the Yukon,* and *Alaska on Foot: Wilderness Techniques for the Far North.*

Matthew Cutler grew up pursuing trout and elk in the high country of his native Utah. An inborn taste for the outdoors and the call of unspoiled wilderness lured Matt to Glacier as a seasonal concessions worker. Matt's peak-bagging talents and innate good humor have added immeasurably to the experiences of his backcountry companions through the years.

Candice Hall is a naturalized Montanan who has dedicated herself to a rigorous life of physical fitness. Originally from the Dakotas, Candy forsook the flatlands to become a ranger in Glacier National Park, where she served for several seasons. Candy is now a fitness instructor in Whitefish, Montana.

The authors feel honored to share their firsthand knowledge and insights with those less familiar with Glacier's delights. Between these three, thousands of miles have passed underfoot, including all of the major trails of Glacier country. It is their hope that this book will serve as a window into Glacier's many-faceted beauty, enticing those who read it to leave the cares of the world behind and lose themselves in the majesty of the mountains.

The Glacier Natural History Association (GNHA) is a cooperating association of the National Park Service incorporated in the State of Montana in 1946 and recognized by the Internal Revenue Service as a nonprofit 501(c)3 organization.

GNHA supports educational and interpretive programming at several land management sites located across western Montana including Glacier National Park, Big Hole National Battlefield, Grant Kohrs Historic Ranch, the National Bison Range, and the Flathead National Forest. Support is generated through bookstore sales of educational and interpretive materials at these locations.

Proceeds from bookstore sales are returned to further the support of research, educational and interpretive activities, cultural preservation, and specialized equipment and project needs.

Anyone wishing to support the goals and activities of the association may become a member. Members receive a 15 percent discount on purchases from the association and similar discounts from many cooperating associations in other national park areas. For membership and product information, please contact: Glacier Natural History Association, Box 310, West Glacier, MT 59936; visit GNHA's Web site at www.glacierassociation.org or call (406) 888–5756.